# MIGRANT WOMEN TRANSFORMING CITIZENSHIP

# Studies in Migration and Diaspora

*Series Editor:*
Anne J. Kershen, Queen Mary College, University of London, UK

*Studies in Migration and Diaspora* is a series designed to showcase the interdisciplinary and multidisciplinary nature of research in this important field. Volumes in the series cover local, national and global issues and engage with both historical and contemporary events. The books will appeal to scholars, students and all those engaged in the study of migration and diaspora. Amongst the topics covered are minority ethnic relations, transnational movements and the cultural, social and political implications of moving from 'over there', to 'over here'.

*Also in the series:*

*Polish Migration to the UK in the 'New' European Union*
*After 2004*
*Edited by Kathy Burrell*
ISBN 978-0-7546-7387-3

*Gendering Migration*
*Masculinity, Femininity and Ethnicity in Post-War Britain*
*Edited by Louise Ryan and Wendy Webster*
ISBN 978-0-7546-7178-7

*Contemporary British Identity*
*English Language, Migrants and Public Discourse*
*Christina Julios*
ISBN 978-0-7546-7158-9

*Migration and Domestic Work*
*A European Perspective on a Global Theme*
*Edited by Helma Lutz*
ISBN 978-0-7546-4790-4

*Negotiating Boundaries in the City*
*Migration, Ethnicity and Gender in Britain*
*Joanna Herbert*
ISBN 978-0-7546-4677-8

# Migrant Women Transforming Citizenship

## Life-stories From Britain and Germany

UMUT EREL
*The Open University, UK*

ASHGATE

Published by
Ashgate Publishing Limited
Wey Court East
Union Road
Farnham
Surrey, GU9 7PT
England

Ashgate Publishing Company
Suite 420
101 Cherry Street
Burlington
VT 05401-4405
USA

www.ashgate.com

**British Library Cataloguing in Publication Data**
Erel, Umut
 Migrant women transforming citizenship : life-stories from
 Britain and Germany. - (Studies in migration and diaspora)
 1. Women immigrants - Great Britain 2. Women immigrants -
 Germany 3. Women immigrants - Turkey 4. Turks - Great
 Britain 5. Turks - Germany 6. Citizenship - Great Britain
 7. Citizenship - Germany 8. Great Britain - Ethnic
 relations 9. Germany - Ethnic relations
 I. Title
 304.8'41'0561

**Library of Congress Cataloging-in-Publication Data**
Erel, Umut.
 Migrant women transforming citizenship : life-stories from Britain and Germany
/ by Umut Erel.
   p. cm. -- (Studies in migration and diaspora)
 Includes bibliographical references and index.
 ISBN 978-0-7546-7494-8
 1. Women immigrants--Great Britain--Case studies. 2. Women
immigrants--Germany--Case studies. 3. Citizenship--Great Britain--Case studies.
4. Citizenship--Germany--Case studies. I. Title.

 JV7684.E74 2009
 305.48'969120941--dc22

                                                                    2008053688
ISBN 978-0-7546-7494-8

**Mixed Sources**
Product group from well-managed
forests and other controlled sources
www.fsc.org Cert no. SGS-COC-2482
© 1996 Forest Stewardship Council

Printed and bound in Great Britain by
TJ International Ltd, Padstow, Cornwall

# Contents

# Series Editor's Preface

On 15 March 1885, in an address to the Royal Statistical Society, Ernst Georg Ravenstein put forward his 'Laws of Migration'. It was a watershed lecture, the first time that someone had sought to define the movement of people – regionally or nationally – as a phenomenon in its own right. Ravenstein intended his laws to provide a means by which the significance of recent migratory patterns, as reflected in the England and Wales Decennial Censuses for 1871 and 1881, could be deconstructed and accounted for. One of his Twelve Laws noted that the migratory patterns of women followed a rural to urban direction and that women moved far shorter distances than their male counterparts. There, for almost one hundred years, the study of gendered migration remained. Women became the hidden others of migration; secondary migrants who, with rare exceptions, left point A to travel to point B, only as wives, daughters, mothers or prospective brides, to be reunited with men who had travelled away from 'home' and, as the 'myth of return' became an integral part of their migrant experience, needed female support and care. It took until the 1980s for feminist studies to propel women to centre stage. Amongst the cast of *new* actors appeared a growing number of independent female migrants travelling increasingly long distances in order to achieve economic mobility and security.

Yet, as the author of this book points out, even within this new regime there was a bias, this time one which focused on the unskilled females who were finding work as cleaners, domestics and carers in the burgeoning global care chain. Little or no recognition was given to the smaller number of skilled females who sought to use their education and professional status to advance themselves in Western Europe and North America. In this volume, Umut Erel has sought to redress this inadequacy and, at the same time, take the study of female migration further. By focusing on women that she categorizes as the 'other, other', she has demonstrated the way in which skilled female immigrants have developed strategies which enable them not only to achieve economic security and professional status but, at the same time, combine this with transforming the rights and duties of citizenship within the landscape of the working female immigrant.

In this ground breaking work Erel juxtaposes the experience of skilled female migrants from Turkey in Britain and Germany. The choice of the two nation study is highly pertinent, locating as it does the struggle for recognition as 'full citizens' within contrasting frameworks, ones where the pathways to citizenship follow different routes. Using a micro binary approach she describes the various ways in which female agency has been operated by first, and in the case of Germany second, generation migrants on their journey. Through this we discover the ability of females from the same sending society to fashion their economic, cultural, social and political behaviour in order to traverse the structures and needs of the society in which they have settled and within which they wish to be 'received' on equal terms. Not only does this volume provide us with lessons from the recent past it also provides guidance and hope for female migrants in the future.

Anne J Kershen
Queen Mary, University of London

# Acknowledgements

This book is an intervention into citizenship debates, but it is also a tribute to the women whose life stories are presented here, so I thank them first and foremost for generously sharing with me. It is based on my PhD thesis, supervised by Richard Johnson, Eleonore Kofman and Tracey Skelton at Nottingham Trent University who have been wonderful teachers. Their commitment, support and encouragement were invaluable. I am thankful for a PhD bursary from Nottingham Trent University. Yet, the book has moved on from the PhD thesis and many others have been vital. I thank my parents Ümit and Hüseyin Ozer, Aysel Adıgüzel, Tatiana La Mura Flores, Emma Myatt, Gamal Ibrahim, Kirsten Ullmann, Mandy Walker, Can Yıldız, Necla Acık, and Vicki Squire for social and emotional support. I had great intellectual company, stimulation and feedback from Christian Klesse, Susanne Schwalgin, Tijen Uğuriş, Chin-Ju Li, Barbara Henkes and the Gender Ethnicity and Social Research Discussion Group. Nira Yuval-Davis, Elaine Unterhalter and Helma Lutz have been essential in encouraging me to become an academic; I don't think I would have written this book without their encouragement. Tim Strangleman was a great mentor in difficult times and gave me the confidence to start thinking about this book. Special thanks to Engin Isin, who has nurtured the writing process of this book as my mentor with enthusiasm, intellectual and practical support, thoughtful and extremely helpful feedback. Vron Ware and John Clarke have also generously provided feedback on versions of chapters, Jin Haritaworn and Christian Klesse have untiringly read and commented on multiple drafts, I cannot thank them enough. Jackee Holden and the Supporting the Process group have been uniquely helpful in the writing process, lots of thanks to them all. Finally, thank you to Janroj for sustaining me, and to Arjen for sharing her joy of life!

*To Nazife, Ümit and Arjen*

# Chapter 1
# Constructing Meaningful Lives[1]

Migrant women are laying claim to citizenship practices. Though marginalized from the nation as legal or cultural outsiders, they create new meanings of belonging. This book explores how. While there has been considerable debate on the changing meaning of belonging to a national society with accelerating transnational relations, migrations and the experience of 'new ethnicities' there has been little, if any, attention paid to how migrant women themselves re-define the concepts of postnational, multicultural or transnational citizenship. Through the life-stories of migrant women this books provides a missing link between theories and realities of transnational lives. The book closely reads life-stories of migrant women from Turkey in Europe to theorize how these emerging subjects create new, counter-hegemonic citizenship practices across boundaries of class, gender, ethnicity and nation. Just consider the following examples: Birgül, a Turkish medical doctor in Germany successfully takes legal action to be allowed to open a surgery. She argues that the law foresees provision of medical services to the 'population' that is inclusive of women from Turkey, rather than the nationally bounded citizens (see Chapter 4). Pınar, a single mother carefully builds a cross-ethnic family of choice. While she wants her daughter to learn the Turkish language and cultural practices, cultural pluralism is the core value she wants to transmit to her daughter (see Chapter 5). Selin challenges community representatives' and leaders' lack of democratic accountability. She incisively critiques that the British multicultural system's reliance on community organizations reproduces intra-community power relations of gender, class and ethnicity (see Chapter 6). These women's lives, both through their actions and as life-stories, help us to theorize the meaning of citizenship. The life-stories engage critically with the changing realities of growing up, work, family and social activism, providing a situated account of how the big issues of migration, culture and citizenship play out in actual social relations.

How do different national contexts lead to distinct forms of transnational citizenship? The two contexts of Britain and Germany provide diverging concepts and policies of citizenship that allow for a differentiated examination of ethnicity, gender, multiculturalism and citizenship in Europe. Starting from the life-stories of migrant women from Turkey, the book explores notions of gendered and

1   I thank Sociological Research Online for permission to publish parts of Chapter 1, which have been previously published as 'Constructing Meaningful Lives: Biological Methods in Research on Migrant Women' http://www.socresonline.org.uk/12/4/5.html in Volume 12, Issue 4, published 31 July 2007.

ethnicized subjectivity. Subjectivity here is understood as the narrative construction of a liveable notion of self. This process of 'making the self' is not simply a free choice of different national, ethnic, or gendered 'ingredients'. As migrant women from a so-called Muslim country, they are faced with Orientalist representations of themselves as passive, oppressed by men and backward traditions (see Chapter 2). The migrant population from Turkey is the biggest national minority group in the old Europe, where it plays an important role as Europe's 'Other'. Indeed, representations of gender relations have been at the heart of constructing these Others and research in European countries has often contributed to stereotypical representations of migrant women from Turkey.

By focusing on the experiences of highly educated and skilled migrant women, a group that has until now been neglected, this book looks at part of the story of gendered and ethnicized citizenship that has not yet been told. The life-stories provide rich insights into the agency of migrant women in 'making themselves' through engaging with social divisions and power relations of gender, ethnicity, class and sexuality. Governments in both Germany and Britain argue that the countries need to be allowed to choose the 'right sort' of migrants, i.e. skilled migrants. It is implied that 'skill' is a personal attribute of the migrant which helps avoid any problems of integration that previous waves of migrants or refugees experience. This book instead focuses on a group of migrant women who are skilled, yet, had great difficulty in having these skills recognized and being able to realize them in their working lives. Instead of viewing skill as a personal attribute, as human capital approaches do, this book explores the social construction of skill, asking how migration regulation, gendered and ethnicized power relations across a range of social sites contribute to the validation or devaluation of skill in the process of gaining employment and in the workplace itself. The social construction of skill furthermore sheds light on the processes by which the migrant women are recognized, or not, as competent citizens who can actively shape the societies they live in.

The two contexts of Britain and Germany are often presented as paradigmatically different cases of multiculturalist versus 'volk'-based models of citizenship and integration for migrants. Diverging histories and policies of migration, nationality and citizenship have led to differential processes of gendered ethnicization. However, the book explores where both countries employ common modes of (partial) inclusion and exclusion, challenging the notion of two paradigmatically opposed cases. Indeed, the book critiques the failure of dominant modes of incorporation in Britain to fully theorize and engage with experiences of ethnic minorities other than the post-colonial Black and Asian groups. On the other hand, the dominant modes of incorporation in Germany reproduce ethnic hierarchies and exclusions, in particular by continuously disavowing migrant women's active contributions to citizenship (Chapter 2).

The book uses an intersectional perspective – that is it views gender, ethnicity and class as intermeshing social divisions. These social relations and discourses on gendered ethnicization and class form the conditions of women's lives, but also inform the ways they make sense of their experience. In particular, the book examines the different ways in which the interviewees reject, incorporate or otherwise negotiate discourses and practices of gendered ethnicization as forms of belonging and participation. The distinctive aim and emphasis is to explore the ways in which the migrant women exercise agency, narratively in the stories they tell, subjectively in the self-identities they produce, and materially in the ways they act upon their circumstances. I am especially interested in how they construct their subjectivities through producing commonalties and differences with others.

## The Context: Britain and Germany

The specific conditions that the women find in Germany and Britain differ and give them differential scope for constructing their subjectivity, as well as regulating their agency. This cross-national perspective throws into relief the relation between different migration and citizenship regimes and processes of differential ethnicization and racialization. While this research design may raise expectations that the book will explore the differential positioning of *ethnic communities* in Britain and Germany, this is not the scope of this book. Instead, I explore how the *individual migrant women* relate to notions of community and construct their own notions and practices of community. Indeed, the position taken in this book differs from that often adopted in studies on ethnic minority communities. One problem of community studies is that they tend to assume the membership and boundaries of ethnic minority communities as given. Instead, this book explores the boundaries and criteria for group membership that the women elaborate. These can change over the life-course and shift situationally. In order not to foreclose an exploration of these dynamic processes of identification the longwinded term 'migrant women from Turkey' or 'of Turkish background' is used to describe the sample. This is intended to take account of the ethnic diversity of the population of Turkey and avoid reifying nationalist and Turkish supremacist discourses and practices of the Turkish state, often reproduced in the Diaspora. Though some critique this notion of 'migrants from Turkey' for obscuring Kurdish identities, as it falls short of explicitly naming and recognizing them, it is argued that the non-recognition of Kurdish ethnic identity cannot be resolved simply by using a 'correct' linguistic term. While it is important to scandalize the racism and ethnocidal policies directed at Kurds, the migrant women in this study had a variety of ethnic allegiances and identifications: Azeri, Kurdish, Zaza, Cherkess, Macedonian, Yörük and Turkish. Thus, an ethnic label of 'Turkish and Kurdish' would be reductionist. Second, the term 'migrant women from Turkey' is intended to encompass the multiple forms of identification of migrant women with their countries of residence such as 'British', 'German-Turkish', 'bi-cultural' or 'migrant'.

## Structure of the Book

Before turning to the methodological underpinnings in the remainder of this chapter, this section will outline the structure of the book. An exploration of issues of citizenship and agency as articulating 'subjugated knowledges' runs like a red thread right through the book. The remainder of this chapter explores the value of life-story methods for the study of citizenship to understand migrant women's agency and knowledge of the world in which they live. Chapter 2 discusses theories of citizenship, the ways in which the migrant women are positioned discursively, legally and socially in Britain and Germany. From Chapter 3 onwards, the book examines the different sites of citizenship the migrant women elaborate in their life-stories. Their experiences in concrete situations guide me to explore what the abstract concepts of agency, citizenship and culture mean in everyday life. In this sense, Chapters 3 to 6 can be read as illustrating, questioning and developing further our theoretical understanding. Yet, the life-stories are also important interventions into the representation of migrant women in their own right, using the words, concepts and ideas of migrant women, the book portrays important aspects of their lives. Chapter 3 traces the ways in which they developed themselves as subjects with agency in the site of schooling and family. Both family and schooling are central sites of producing gendered, ethnicized and class identities. For young migrant women, these are often viewed as pulling them in different directions. Chapters 4 to 6 look at how the migrant women substantiate their agentic capacities. In Chapter 4, the occupational trajectories and self-presentations of the interviewees are examined. The book looks at the ways in which gender, ethnicity, class, migration status and specific forms of transnational social and cultural capital influence their access to skilled work. Chapter 5 explores migrant women's negotiations of sexual identities and personal status and looks in detail at their practices of transnational mothering and intergenerational transformation of ethnic identities. It argues that prevalent views of migrant women as 'traditional' fall short of the complex social positioning and do not take their agency in challenging racialized boundaries of modernity and tradition into account. Chapter 6 examines the migrant women's political activism and active dimensions of citizenship and articulations of a politics of belonging. Chapter 7 draws these strands together and discusses how this in-depth engagement with migrant women's everyday lives can help us refine our understanding of citizenship by linking the three moments of becoming subjects with agency, substantiating agentic capacities and becoming rights-claiming subjects. Furthermore it evaluates life-story methods as useful epistemological starting points for intersectional analyses of citizenship. But first I will discuss why life-story methods can help us understand migrant women's self-presentations and how their subjugated knowledges can contribute to transforming our thinking about citizenship.

## Constructing Meaningful Lives

Despite all disciplinary differences in the use of life-story methods there have been some shared assumptions about life-story methods.[2] The first is that of authenticity and giving a voice to marginalized views and voices. This has been an important emancipatory step in recognizing that history and society are also lived and constructed 'from below'. Yet, the underlying notions of authenticity and 'giving a voice' have been criticized from different vantage points. One of the criticisms is that the power relation between researcher and researched involves a setting of the agenda by the researcher, most importantly in the process of analysing and interpreting (cf. Gluck and Patai 1991) as well as presenting (Lejeune 1980) the life-story. Therefore, Stanley (1992) suggests the notion of auto/biographies to take account of different moments of ambiguity: narrativizing a life involves degrees of fictionalizing through selecting and interpreting the events told and shaped into narrative genres. However pronounced the narrator(s)' desire to be true to fact, these fictionalizing moments are irreducible, since life itself is ambiguous and always bound up with our making sense of it. The relation between author and subject of a biography constitutes the second moment of ambiguity. Stanley (1992) concedes that the understanding of the subject is mediated through the researcher's own biographical experiences. So that the 'I' that speaks or writes is inflected by both the researcher's and the subject's biographies. The distinction between autobiography, biography and fiction is thus more usefully viewed as a continuum.

Life-story methods elicit not only what happened, but also how people experienced events, and how they make sense of them. Thus, life-stories are an important vantage point for exploring the links between subjectivity and social structures. Memory and narrative are used for constructing a liveable, meaningful life-story, aiming for a narrative wholeness of the self, notwithstanding the fact that these biographies are revisable. In this sense, life-stories are an important element in constructing personal identity and its relation to collective identities (cf. Antze and Lambek 1996, Giddens 1991, Plummer 2001).[3]

*Migrant Women as Subjects of Life-stories:*
*Uniqueness versus Collective Identities*

Life-story methods raise complex epistemological and ontological questions on the constitution of subjects as individual and collective, the role of self knowledge

---

2   In the following the terms life-story method, and auto/biographical method are used interchangeably to denote this wide field of study and its varying aspects.

3   Identity here is understood as a dynamic process of becoming that negotiates ascriptions and social positioning, when referring to the 'self' I refer more to the meanings elaborated by the interviewees rather than ascriptive aspects.

and presentation in the constitution of the 'Self' as well as the 'life'. This chapter will unpick some of the gendered and ethnicized aspects of these.

The canonization of the autobiographical genre projects its origins to practices of introspection and memory developed in the Christian confessional. The canonization of 'great' biographies and elevation of some autobiographies into the status of seminal texts thus contains specific gendered, racialized and classed evaluations about the form and subject of biography (Marcus 1994). This is particularly significant in the context of Orientalist power/knowledge structures that deny the quality of introspection and rationality to those from so-called Muslim cultures, instead viewing them as over determined by 'Oriental fatalism' and therefore lacking true originality and agency (cf. Said 1978).

Tracing the development of philosophy and criticism of the autobiographical genre from the nineteenth century onwards, Marcus (1994) argues that in the twentieth century, 'creative' persons' autobiographies have come to be seen as the ideal type of the genre: 'seminal' autobiographies therefore are seen to express uniqueness. Auto/biographies of marginalized people challenge the gender, class, ethnic and culturally specific assumptions of an ideal subject of auto/biography. While this importantly aims at democratizing practices of auto/biography, often there is an underlying dichotomization that views these new voices 'from below' (Plummer 2001: 90) a priori as 'collective stories' (ibid.). As Plummer argues, 'more marginal voices (…) speak not just of themselves but of and for "others" in the world. The autobiographies "from below" hence work to create a different sense of autobiographical form, one where consciousness of self becomes more of a collective exploration than just a private one' (ibid.).

As Plummer rightly points out, these new voices often self-consciously aim at articulating collective identities and experiences of marginalization. However, there is a danger that this disregards the complexities of subjected people's experiences and their representation.[4] I agree with the importance of de-constructing de-socialized notions of 'individuality' as hegemonizing particular forms of white, European, male, bourgeois subjectivity. However, approaching life-stories as either expressive of individuality or collectivity, does not challenge the dominance of subject positions viewed as 'individual' or 'unique'. Instead, it simplifies the constitution of subjected subjectivities by ascribing them a collective voice only. The capacity of marginalized people to express uniqueness and individuality is denied: Lewis argues that class and race have become the binary divide along which the notion of self-knowledge as individual or collective is organized, assuming 'white people having psyches while black people have community' (1996: 25), however instead of dichotomizing the notions of individuality and collectivity they should be seen as aspects worth exploring in every life-story. In this sense,

---

4   Thus, with regard to Italian working class oral cultures Luisa Passerini argues that often people prefer employing stereotypical story telling personas to an introspective tone. However she cautions against confusing the choice of narrative style with the life as it was lived (1987).

dichotomizations of individual versus collective modes of biography do not take account of the complexity of life-stories, both those told with an individual or collective inflection.

The methodological approach of this book bridges the tension between an emphasis on the uniqueness of a life-story, often associated with the humanities, and social science approaches to life-story methods. While life-stories in literary/ cultural studies are often studied as expressive of individuality, social sciences approaches to life-stories tend to look at life-stories as expressive of collective experiences, illustrating the social structures these collectivities experience. This dichotomy is problematic, in particular where it pertains to marginalized groups, who have little access to self-presentations in publicly validated forms. If life-stories that are structurally similar are presented one after the other, this produces an effect of seriality, suggesting to the reader that the subjects are devoid of individuality and simply represent one variation in the collective modes of being. Dominant representations of migrant women from Turkey reify them as the 'Other Other' (Chapter 2), essentializing gendered and ethnicized cultural assumptions in the image of the oppressed woman of Muslim background. One of the effects of such representations is to portray them as a homogeneous group, downplaying individuality and scope for agency. Women who do not conform to such representations are bracketed out as 'exceptional' (cf. Chapter 3), too individual to really matter for any endeavour of understanding the social positioning of migrant women of Turkish background. Thus, the notion of individuality (too much or too little of it) is not a simple descriptor but indeed a tool for constructing the very category of migrant women of Turkish background. When presenting material from this book at conferences, I have often been told that the women whose life-stories are presented here are not 'typical'; could I please talk about the majority of migrant women from Turkey whose lives are mired in integration problems? Against this backdrop this chapter tries to balance an attempt to do justice to the idiosyncrasies and expressions of individuality in order to avoid casting them into ideal- or stereo-types, while maintaining that they do illuminate wider social structures. While the life-stories presented here produce and reflect both individuality and collectivity, they cannot be neatly typologized.

Instead, I would like to question the desire for typologizing. Typologies are reductionist representations of migrant women's lives that tend to reproduce Orientalist power/knowledge structures: excesses of meaning, contradictions and dynamic processes of self-production in dialogue with a range of others disappear in favour of static, entirely knowable objects of social science. Therefore, instead of categorizing the migrant women's experiences, narratives and the selves produced through these, this book aims to uncover different themes in their life-stories and how these are constituted by fixing or destabilizing subject positions which the interviewees claim, negotiate or reject. Thus, particular types of stories and sense making are shown. This sense making is not only individual, even if the experiences of the story tellers are, but relates to various collectivities within and across gendered and ethnicized subjectivities. By avoiding a typologization of the interviewees and their life-stories, the book aims to de-construct the dichotomization of individual and collective/mass, an issue with which the interviewees themselves struggle (cf. Chapter 7). The subject positions and the discursive repertoires with which they are constructed and interpreted are fluid and open to be used by different social actors. Individuality and collectivity form different strategies of legitimizing authenticity; instead of ranking such claims for authenticity, this book questions their bases and dynamics.

Authenticity is always a purposeful construction. Migrant women are minoritized and marginalized in the societies of residence. They are constituted in official and everyday discourses as objects of knowledge and their legitimacy is surveyed, rendering their speaking position unstable and in question. The demands of others or their own desire for authenticity then may become a specifically gendered and ethnicized incitement for fixing particular notions of self. Constructions of authenticity can become means of access or exclusion to ethnically and gender specific subject positions, belonging to communities and entitlements. Rather than taking them at face value, one should interrogate constructions of authentic 'Turkish femininity' as to the political and social projects they articulate, bearing in mind that biographical representations often elide with models of the ideal life (cf. Marcus 1994).

Thus, the choice of in-depth study of a small number (10) of life-story interviews reflects the author's concern with engaging in-depth with the complexities in each of the self-representations. The focus of this study is precisely to uncover moments of agency in the migrant women's life-stories. These forms of agency are revealed in the narrative self-representations. In this context, the argument of this book pertains to the meaning making processes in the life-stories rather than the frequency with which particular experiences occur in the group of skilled migrant women. This group of skilled migrant women from Turkey is numerically small and we know little about it, therefore any form of statistical representativity is not meaningful as a sampling tool. The interviewees were chosen because of the ways in which their life-stories and experiences illuminate on one hand the structural positioning of skilled migrant women, and on the other hand because they have made choices which are particularly relevant in shedding light on the processes that can transform our understanding of citizenship practices.

*Structural Readings*

Life-stories can be read in various ways. They may be used to provide factual data on events that are not, or only partially, recorded otherwise. They also provide data on the impact of social structures on people, which is not obvious from looking at structural data itself. These ways of reading life-stories have been termed by the Popular Memory Group (1982) 'structural readings'. Those aspects of a life-story that pertain to the ways in which meaning is constructed, they term 'cultural readings'. A cultural reading focuses on the way the interviewees give meaning to their experiences. These two aspects mutually constitute each other.

Structural readings of the migrant women's life-stories reveal effects of immigration legislation on personal lives, where one cannot simply read off the legal or policy texts. They reveal structures of exclusion and resistance that quantitative or larger scale studies render invisible. Moreover they can call into question the categories of legislation and theorization based on these as for example the discreteness of statuses of refugees, labour migrants, au pair, marriage migration, student migration, professional or undocumented migration. The life-stories also offer critical insights into constructions of identity and belonging constitutive of citizenship. Some contemporary research still assumes that the migration into a Western country and the living conditions female migrants find there constitute their first encounter with modernity. It is assumed that European societies provide an entirely new avenue to emancipation. Instead, I would argue that migrant women are faced with multiple formations of modernity with contradicting effects of gendered control in both countries (cf. Pessar and Mahler 2003, Piper 2008). The structures of incorporation into the receiving society may, at least initially, indeed enhance their gendered vulnerabilities. Since life-stories do not narrow down lived experience to one single category or event, they offer a privileged vantage point for understanding and theorizing the processual dynamics of migration and the intersectionality of gendered, ethnicized and class structures of power as the following example shows.

Nilüfer entered England as an au pair, the only legal entry category open to her at the time. She wanted to learn English to prepare for joining her father in Canada, when he fulfilled the residence requirements that would enable him to sponsor his daughter on the basis of family reunification. Soon after arriving in England however, she quit the au pair job because she felt she was treated 'like a slave'. Technically, she had become an illegal resident. However, she managed to get an au pair contract from a friend to maintain legal residence. In spite of this legal residence, she did not have the right to take up other employment, having thus become semi-compliant (Anderson and Ruhs 2006), i.e. while aspects of her life in the UK were deemed legal, others (i.e. working) were not. She found an undocumented job as a waitress, which did not however pay enough for her to realize her aspirations of higher education because of the excessive overseas student fees. Nor could she afford to pay the fees to attend vocational colleges and English language schools, which she perceived as an alternative route to education. The irregularity of her residence and work permit status as well as the lack of social networks on whose financial, social and emotional support she could rely put her in a very vulnerable position. Despite this, she took the initiative to gain access to education, she entered a sexual relationship with her employer, who in turn paid her higher wages and guaranteed her employment:

> N: But when I was working in that restaurant there, and I was very desperate as well. I had a relationship with the owner of the restaurant. He was thirty years older than me (laughs).

U: (laughing) Most of your boyfriends were much older, hah?

N: But this one was not boyfriend, this one was mostly[to] secure my job, secure my place and get more money. So this one was that. ... Was terrible, it was disgusting.

U: Yeah.

N: It wasn't anything that I wanted to do because I love to do.

This extract shows how power relations of gender, class, and migration status rendered Nilüfer vulnerable to sexual and economic exploitation. However, she used the limited resources to gain education which she hoped would enable her to 'get out' of this situation. As it turned out, she found the situation of sexual exploitation so unbearable that she quit this job, lost her income and access to education. Agency and victimization in this instance were closely intertwined, the limitation of her choices through immigration legislation put her in a 'desperate' situation where the course of action she chose, i.e. bartering or selling sex, was one that she strongly disliked. Thus, her victimization propelled her into a form of agency that in turn victimized her. At another waitressing job, she worked for some months without getting paid. Her semi-compliant residence status and the undocumented nature of the work made it practically impossible for her to take any legal steps to receive her wages as she feared it might lead to the discovery of her semi-compliance (cf. Bosniak 2008). At this workplace, Nilüfer met a man whom she eventually married. While they were initially happy, her husband's suspicion that she had married him mainly to obtain a secure residence status became a strain on their relationship. When her husband turned violent the considerations of leaving him or getting divorced for Nilüfer also included the fact that she had not yet got an independent right of residence. In spite of these structural constraints Nilüfer entered higher education and separated from her husband. At the time of interview, she was finishing her degree. Already this brief reading of Nilüfer's life-story gives us factual information on the factors impacting on migrant women's life chances and choices. Moreover, it shows ways in which structural positioning constrained and channelled her agency but did not preclude it. In fact, Nilüfer's life-story reveals counter structures to those of immigration control. These structures of undocumented residence arrangements and employment within an ethnic community are highly contradictory: while circumventing the restrictions of the British migration regime, they exploit other power relations such as gender and class (cf. Erdemir and Vasta 2007, Romhild 2007). In a climate of changing and ever more differentiated civic stratification, i.e. a stratification of rights of migration, residence, work and access to social services (Morris 2004), it is important to investigate the emergence of new hierarchies and power relations within the migrant group, too (cf. Lutz and Koser 1998, Vertovec 2007). I suggest that by employing both structural and cultural readings to the migrant women's life-stories, we can explore these hierarchical structures and dynamics, calling attention to inadequate conceptualizations of gendered migration experiences. The migrant women's situated knowledges provide a good entry point for researching the increasing diversification and the contradictions of gendered migration experiences and dynamics, a critical task for studies of gender and migration (cf. Carling 2005, Pessar and Mahler 2003, Piper 2008).

As discussed in the next chapter, a dominant paradigm in the research on migrant women to Europe has viewed them as passive victims of processes of dislocation and modernization. They have been seen as victimized at once through the process of migration and through the particularly strict patriarchal control by the men of their ethnic group. Life-story methods that take the subjectivity of the migrant women as their starting point have a powerful potential to redress such representations since 'biography provides the link between the migrant agent and the structure of society' (Lutz 1995: 314). Pessar and Mahler suggest in their framework for studying gendered transnational practices that we need to include 'cognitive agency' (2003: 817), i.e. how people imagine, plan, strategize and think about their migration, in our study of migrants' agency. Such aspects of imagining and planning a migration can affect people's life-course. As Dilek points out, an important reason why she entered an academic career rather than work in industry, was bound up with her hope that the particular university she worked for would allow her to go abroad. For her, migration had thus been a 'fantastic dream' long before she finally did migrate to the UK. Bound up with this fantastic dream was her desire to realize alternative gendered lifestyle as a single woman with no intention of getting married or partnered. This, however, she had found difficult to realize in Turkey, both because she could not afford to live on her own and because she encountered subtle and open pressures to conform to expectations of colleagues, some family members and friends. In this sense, her dream of migration had structured her life, through choice of jobs, before migration and the fantasy of what life in Europe might be like intertwined with her adamant resistance to conform to sanctioned gendered lifestyles within Turkey. Thus, it is important to pay attention to how the migrant women give meaning to their experiences, i.e. apply 'cultural readings' (Popular Memory Group 1982) to their life-stories.

*Cultural Readings*

Cultural readings involve different aspects: on the one hand, there are more or less idiosyncratic meanings created from particular personal experiences, yet, these are never independent of social meanings, be it on a smaller scale of family, friends, work place, social or political groups or on a wider scale, mediated through generalized others (Plummer 2001: 44). Media, legal and institutional as well as transnational movements' discourses provide frameworks for the telling and interpreting of life-stories. Nowadays, the life-story has proliferated within media and has become a major mode of transmission of information of all kinds on a large scale. Be it in the fields of politics, publicity, literature or sport, 'as soon as one switches the button [of the tv or radio] one baths in the intimate, the direct, from man to man (sic!)' (Lejeune 1980: 316, my translation from French). This public proliferation of life-stories calls into question the assumptions primarily of classic literary biographies and autobiographies representing an authentic 'I' in the mode of sincere and painful confessional which can only find truthful expression as the outcome of introspection and reflection (cf. Marcus 1994).

'Story telling communities' (Plummer 1995) are important in producing social identities, through claiming a space to tell stories hitherto unspeakable and through forming a public that is prepared to listen and validate to stories about formerly marginalized or taboo experiences. Through the interplay of audience and speakers, such experiences and new validations of identities can be spoken. As they become established, these story telling communities create certain scripts for 'self-stories' (Denzin 1989) of how to tell and think about identities. In Plummer's example, stories about what it meant to be gay can be enabling and inclusive for building a community. Yet, these scripts also set limits and rules e.g. on the ability to speak of continuing heterosexual desire or relationships (cf. Stein 1997), or on how ethnic minority gay and lesbian identities could be (mis-)recognized and consequently became themselves disciplining and normalizing.

In the interviews with migrant women from Turkey I have found that some stories were told, discussed and re-told and contributed to the establishment of collective identities. For example, in Germany, this took place on a large scale in the constitution of a social movement based on the political subject position of 'migrant' in the late 1980s and early 1990s, which elaborated a political identity of 'migrant' as the privileged subject of anti-racist politics. This movement and identity developed in opposition to the dominant notion of 'foreigner' ('*Ausländer*') which was embedded in discourses which posited them as culturally incompetent strangers to German society, who could only be seen as either problems for, or victims of, German society. The migrants' movement elaborated a subject position in which 'migrant' came to signify a politically resistant identity against nationalist and racist discourses. As such it afforded a degree of autonomous political agency that the subject position of '*Ausländer*' did not. Many of the second generation migrant women in this study posited themselves in this discourse in their life-stories (cf. Chapters 3 and 6).

One story that played an important part in the identity constructions of second generation migrant women was that of leaving the parental home. For most of my interviewees their leaving home took place against the wishes of their parents, in some cases the parents put up massive resistance to the young women's project of leaving home. Leaving home to live independently from parents or husband was ethnicized as 'leaving Turkishness' and parents tried to sanction their daughters' behaviour with threats of exclusion from the family and/or wider ethnic community. Most young women had to deal with this traumatic process of leaving the parental home on their own, as Suzan recounts:

S: ... earlier for me it was either you're a Turkish [female], then you've got to get married, you've got to do what your parents say, you've got to stay respectable, blah blah blah. Or, you are thus like virgin – whore, but in this case like Turkish-German. You're German, you've got a boyfriend, you can [have a] profession, blah blah blah. It was all extremes, it was divided, either-or, there was no being in-between. ... in order to be with Germans, you had to reject everything that was Turkish absolutely, there was no way of keeping anything. (...) And I could not imagine having Turkish friends, I did not know any others who were like me.

U: Yes.

S: And for me it was (...) I ran away from home when I was 18, didn't have any contact with my parents, didn't speak any Turkish – I nearly forgot all my Turkish and didn't want anything to do with it. And I moved out – ran away with the idea (...) that my parents would reject me. I never thought that instead they would lament me. [I thought] that my leaving home would mean giving up my Turkish identity, giving it up completely.

Thus when later in their life they met migrant women from Turkey who did not reject the gender roles they embodied, this became a turning point in their life-stories.

S: [When a male German friend told her about his female Turkish flatmate and her friends], you would really like them, they are like you. I was like, 'I don't think so'. I was so certain that they'd be totally different. When I went to see him [the Turkish flat mate] was out (...) but her dissertation [about second generation migrant women] was lying around. My friend had done a drawing for her so I started leafing through it and when I started reading I could not believe it. This was my story and it was a hundred per cent. I sat there and cried because for the first time I found ourselves in this – oh my god ... you know that was incredible, this feeling of being torn between the family and the boyfriend, having to adjust to both sides. It was incredible, a wonderful experience. (...) [When she met other women in this group] well for the first time I [realized] you can be Turkish and leave home and still do belly dancing, despite this you can still joke around in Turkish or in German if you feel like it, and yet none of them is a virgin! Oh that was so cool, for the first time I had found women who were like me – yet the fantastic thing about the group was that each one was different.

They talked about their different experiences of leaving the parental home and in these discussions elaborated a new identity for themselves that refused both 'German' and 'Turkish' hegemonic gender regulations. They could only begin to articulate these identities when an audience of young migrant women developed who were open for this and offered its support by listening. Of course, it is important to note that the space for a feminist migrants' audience was partly and importantly constituted through the emergence of political movements and the social spaces they initiated. In this sense the young migrant women played an important role for each other by collectively constructing new meanings and identities – by rejecting the ascriptions as 'whore' or 'Germanized' from parts of the 'Turkish' communities, or the ascription of being 'insufficiently emancipated' by their German environment, they articulated identities as (feminist) migrant women who claimed the authority to articulate their own gendered ethnic identities. In this sense, the 'running away from home' stories played an important role in constructing alternative and oppositional repertoires of identity.

The telling of life-stories is a truly social process in which those who coax the story tellers and listen to and interpret their story all take part (Plummer 2000). With the different roles, positions and intentions of the audience the meanings of a story change too. A story about 'running away from home' takes on different meanings, according to whether it is told to a feminist migrants group or for example, a social worker to be seen as needy and worthy enough to merit receiving e.g. housing benefits.

*Narrations of self between surveillance and resistance*
A crucial level of discourses enunciating migrating women are legislative: immigration, residence, employment, welfare, sometimes mediated by social work or community service agencies. These expert knowledges often mis-recognize and mis-represent the women's subjectivities, but in any case have discursive and material effects on the women's enunciation (cf. Gutierrez 1999). These expert knowledges themselves elicit self stories, whose function is often to survey and control the women's legitimacy. These expert knowledges form a powerful intertext in dialogue with which the women tell their stories. Thus, Nilüfer pointed out to me that the research interview reminded her of her interview at the Canadian Embassy, when applying for family reunification with her father:

> N: (…) it's too much bureaucracy in the Canadian embassy – so by the time they decided that I can emigrate there – they had my life-story as well there, and the woman said 'Write a book' (laughs). I said 'What am I gonna do? I'm waiting'. She said 'Write a book' (laughs).

Giddens[5] argues that the generalization of the telling of life-stories as an everyday epistemology of the self is a response to 'ontological insecurity'. He points out the crucial functions of narrations of self in late modernity: on the one hand as personal strategies for making sense of life, and striving to maintain a

---

5   Giddens' (1991) argument is not about biographical research methods; it pertains to epistemological and ontological aspects of life-story telling in everyday life. Contending that these different forms of knowledge inform each other, his arguments' implications for the use of biographical research methods are examined.

sense of 'ontological security' (1991: 3) despite the general culture of risk, time-space compression and accelerating colonization of life worlds. These personal projects of self reflexivity are however not one-dimensionally resistant de-colonizations of the life world, but deeply permeated with regulatory mechanisms. Techniques of self narration and identity formation are informed and elaborated through expert knowledges. Personal strategies of defence from abstract systems are not only individual projects, but are generated by, and feed into, collective life styles that form the basis of what Giddens terms 'life politics' that holistically engages persons in the negotiation of their life worlds with the abstract systems of late modernity.[6] Indeed, Gültekin (2003) argues that migrant women as narrators of their life-stories demonstrate a particular type of self reflexivity that relies on at least a double perspective of 'values and orientations of the country of origin and that of immigration, in which both *traditional* and *modern* orientations of both countries are expressed' (2003: 214, my translation from German, emphasis in original). She argues that migrant women have developed a particular ability of viewing and evaluating processes in their lives from multiple perspectives, an ability that at once requires and fosters '*intellectual and emotional mobility*' (2003: 215, emphasis in original).

The telling of a life-story, or a self story, is required of people in different contexts of regulation, normalization and surveillance. For migrants, this practice often entails the implicit demand to justify why they are here, when they are going back, what the basis for their entitlements (e.g. to education, benefits, housing or jobs) or participation (in social, political, cultural practices and organizations) is. Thus, the kind of self-reflexive construction of self-identity that is required of them on an everyday basis does not centre on Giddens' assumed question of recuperating personal meaninglessness. Instead, the 'ontological insecurity' can indeed be heightened by the repetitive demand to legitimate their presence, their requests and their right to participate, this can be felt as a disempowering intrusion transgressing a boundary of intimate self knowledge that is not voluntarily shared.

---

6   I find some problems with Giddens' theory of self-reflexivity and the ensuing unresolved 'life politics'. The re-appropriation of meaning and identity from abstract systems may be a precondition for challenging class, gendered, racialized and other power relations. However, there is no necessary logic that will lead the empowered subjects to engage in such politics as 'Subjective feelings of empowerment and autonomy ... cannot be the full criterion for evaluating the politics of a certain action' (Yuval-Davis 1994: 186). I remain unsatisfied by Giddens' suggestion that self-reflexive narratives and 'life politics' recuperate a central problem of subjectivity in late modernity – 'personal meaninglessness' (Giddens 1991: 9). Giddens' approach emphasizes the adaptation of selves and subjects to disembedding circumstances. Instead, I would like to stress that these selves may proceed to challenge these disembedding circumstances. Though Giddens' model does not preclude such challenges, his emphasis on coherent self-identity suggests he displaces responsibility onto the self for reconciling in narrative, what cannot be reconciled materially.

Indeed, the surveillance of migrants already in the country has become a powerful tool of migration control so that the policing of external borders ('Fortress Europe') is complemented by the constitution of internal border zones: streets, points of contact with social service provision or indeed the public transport system can become policed as 'border-zones' where those who are thought to be potential illegal migrants are subjected to spot checks (cf. Bosniak 2008) and indeed people whose primary role is not that of border patrols, like school teachers, GPs and their receptionists, etc. are incited to survey the legitimacy of migrants. This surveillance is based on rendering migrants as transparent objects of knowledge and Engbersen (2001) has suggested that the metaphor of 'Panopticon Europe' to understand this. This enforced transparency differentially targets migrant populations according to 'race', ethnicity, class and gender; yet these techniques of surveilling legitimacy produce particular forms of subjection/subjectification as 'migrant'.

In response to these surveilling forms of expert knowledges, another important intertext of expert knowledge for the migrant women presented in this study were collective writings and theorizations of migrant women, to which they themselves contributed also. Thus, the boundary between 'expert knowledges' and self-reflexive constructions of self-identity is multi-directionally permeable and indeed the status of 'experts' can be challenged by fostering new forms of (self-)knowledge production. This process was self consciously initiated by the migrants' and migrant women's movements, referred to earlier, and is ongoing. Pınar for example emphasizes how she co-organized and spoke at local, national and international workshops and conferences of Black and migrant women as enabling her to articulate a claim for political and social participation as a migrant woman (see Chapter 6).

> P: In this context migrant women really struggled against the white structures here to say we do not want to be researched about anymore by white Germans. Instead we want migrant women to do research about us, you know. And we don't want to be seen as objects anymore on whose backs others create a name for themselves but we want to participate creatively and actively and we want to participate politically and legally and on every level.

*Self-representations as subjugated knowledges*

Migrant women's knowledges can be described with Foucault as 'subjugated knowledges', that

> have been disqualified as inadequate to their task or insufficiently elaborated: naïve knowledges, located low down on the hierarchy, beneath the required level of cognition or scientificity. (…) [these] disqualified knowledges (…) which involve what I would call a popular knowledge (le savoir des gens) though it is far from being a general commonsense knowledge, but it is on the contrary a particular, local, regional knowledge, a differential knowledge incapable

of unanimity and which owes its force only to the harshness with which it is oppressed by everything surrounding it (…) (1980: 82).

Foucault argues that subjugated knowledges can point beyond the limits of truth established by dominant discursive regimes, thus unfolding a transformative power. In this sense, the migrant women's life-stories can produce accounts of their selves alternative to or contesting the ways in which dominant discourses and practices (of citizenship, immigration legislation, public discourses of gendered ethnicization as well as those of community-leadership) position them (cf. Mirza 1997).

During the interviews, the women repeatedly referred to stereotyping discourses on migrant women from Turkey, positioning their own experiences and their interpretation *vis-à-vis* these. Education was an important part of this stereotyping. Introducing herself and her family Birgül states:

> B: My father is a farmer and my mother was a housewife. But my father was not a very rich farmer, he had a small property. Everyone in the family studied. All of us seven girls. Everybody studied with their own efforts. All of them are graduates. I think maybe it was the influence of the older siblings that we studied, also.
>
> U: Have your parents supported you in that direction?
>
> B: Of course, this question always arises, as if in Turkey girls did not study. My mother and father were not against our studying, it was not a conservative family at all. They had beliefs, but they did not prevent our studying.

Birgül identifies my question about parental support of education as casting her into the stereotype that assumes Turkish parents curtailing their daughters' education. She also makes reference to religion as this is stereotypically assumed to be the motivations for parents curtailing daughters' education. By asserting her own experience as valid, she critiques these stereotypes, arguing in detail about the regional, local, religious, economic and gendered as well as idiosyncratic aspects affecting her education. She thus frames her explanation of 'who I really am' to address misrepresentations of women from Turkey.

This example relates to the extent to which subjugated knowledges can shed critical light on power relations, but of course, migrant women's self-presentations do not only critique dominant knowledges but can also be complicit with these aligning themselves with subordinated or dominant discourses, or indeed be implicated in both.

> For a woman, claiming the truth of her life despite the awareness of other versions of reality that contest this truth often produces both a heightened criticism of officially condoned untruths and a heightened sense of injustice. …

> But it would be short-sighted for us to ignore the narrative models of acceptance and conformity, since these, too, must be analyzed, interpreted, and understood. (…) Women's lives are lived within, and in tension with, systems of domination. Both narratives of acceptance and narratives of rebellion are responses to the system in which they originate and thus reveal its dynamics (Personal Narratives Group 1989: 7–8).

As argued in Chapter 6, we need to analytically distinguish between social location, identification and the values the women ascribe to. Thus, their value systems and the ways in which they align themselves with various 'epistemological communities' (Assiter 1996) also need to be taken into account as influencing their self-presentation and their knowledge of the social worlds in which they participate. Thus, the migrant women's life-stories presented here contain elements of compliance as well as transformative knowledges disrupting dominant notions of identity, belonging and citizenship. In the process of interpreting and presenting them, as a researcher, I highlight particular aspects that I believe I can help transform our theorization of citizenship.

## The Biographers

The migrant women whose life-stories are presented here were chosen for being skilled or professional as well as being useful informants about exercising agency, and presenting a variety of experiences. They were approached through personal contacts and through snowballing in London and a German city. Six interviews were conducted in the German city and four in London between January 1998 and April 1999. The book also makes limited use of some material from interviews conducted in the German city in 1996. The sample includes first and second generation migrant women. In London, there were no second generation interviewees. The migration from Turkey to Britain began in larger numbers only in the late 1980s. This meant that second generation migrants were not yet at the age to have significant professional experiences. The generation of migration constitutes differences in terms of socialization experiences, in relation to the countries of residence and Turkey. Despite these differences in their life-course, the interviewees also constructed significant similarities and commonalties across generations of migration, as Mandel (2008) points out in a context of ongoing migration, generations of migration cannot be neatly delineated from each other. At the time of interview, none of the women were married, I interviewed 1 single lesbian, 1 lesbian mother living with her partner, one single heterosexual and one divorced heterosexual mother in London and in the Germany city I interviewed four divorced heterosexual mothers, one divorced woman without children and one woman 'living apart together' with her partner, i.e. they did not share a home. Within this sample, the explanation for the divorces/separations of interview partners were varied: dissatisfaction with partners, being single as a lifestyle choice, the difficulty of finding a partner as a single mother, prioritizing time for children over partnership were some of the reasons mentioned. Yet, while these were the reasons the women volunteered, this issue was not probed or problematized in the interviews. The current occupations of the migrant women were: self employed (2), medical professional (2), property developer, social worker (2), social pedagogue (2), architect/ postgraduate student. The ages ranged from 34 to 60.

The cross-cultural character of the study will be discussed in more depth in Chapter 2. Germany and Britain were chosen to examine the conditions of differential racialization that the country of residence provides. The research focuses on the German side of the study and uses the British interviews to make a point about the historical and social specificity of racialized and gendered subjectivity constructions. The structural impact of gendered racialization can become clearer in a cross cultural perspective in which Turkishness holds very different meanings *vis-à-vis* the society of residence. The sampling does not produce a typology of skilled migrant women, or in any way aim at statistical representativeness. This is a problematic assumption in particular with reference to marginalized groups, since the notion of representativeness is often imbued with homogenizing theoretical assumptions. Skilled and professional migrant women, particularly those of Turkish background, are an understudied group (Kofman 2000, Kofman et al.2001, Kürşat-Ahlers 1996, Tan and Waldhoff 1996, Gutierrez Rodriguez 1999). Therefore this book contributes new empirical ground to the study of migration, ethnicity and gender. However, this study can also help to make more complex our theoretical understanding of the social construction of skill. Furthermore it contributes an exploration of the role of skilled and professional women as gendered actors in processes of community building. Generally, it hopes to elucidate the theoretical and empirical underpinnings of migrant women's commonalties and differences of class, education, ethnicity and cultural capital.

**Interviewing**

The interviews were based on an open-ended, semi-structured interview guide. I began by introducing myself and the research project and explained that I was most interested in learning about the interviewees life-stories around themes of migration, growing up, education, work, family and social, political and cultural activities, though I encouraged them to set out what they themselves considered important, and that they were welcome to introduce those topics they felt I had left out. Moreover, I assured confidentiality and stressed that if there were any issues they did not want to discuss, I would not probe them. The interviewees chose the locality for interviewing, and most interviews took place in the interviewees' homes, one in my home (Nilüfer) and two at the interviewees' workplace (Ayten and Pakize). The interviews lasted between 1 and a half to 6 hours. Some of the interviewees were previously known to me, others not. Some researchers suggest that a previous relationship with the interviewees is crucial to establish mutual trust (Lejeune 1980, Plummer 2001). While I found that those interviewees who I previously knew were very open with me, also experienced this with some interviewees she met for the first time.

As a second generation migrant from Turkey, I grew up in Germany and moved to Britain in 1995 for postgraduate study. Thus, I share some biographical commonalties with my interviewees. This created particular issues of intersubjectivity for the research process. While in research on migration, ethnic matching of interviewer and interviewee has become common practice, sharing other characteristics, such as based on educational status, is not that common. As the exploration of these characteristics formed key research themes, methodology and research questions become complexly intertwined.

Matching of interviewer and interviewee in terms of gender and ethnicity is often discussed as enabling mutual trust and a common understanding of the research questions, as well as breaking down hierarchical boundaries and unequal communicative relations (Rhodes 1994). Yet, same-gender, same-ethnicity interview relationships do not automatically lead to non-hierarchical communication and shared meanings. Instead, ethnicity (cf. Song and Parker 1995), and gender, constituted points of reference that were dialogically negotiated in the interview situation. Commonalties and differences were not simply 'facts' but were negotiated intersubjectively: gendered life styles, age, generation of migration, motherhood or non-motherhood, as well as ethnically specific resources such as language or knowledge of cultural practices were factors along and across which the interviewees presented themselves situationally as similar or different from me and vice versa. Language was an important marker of similarity, difference and willingness to cross boundaries. I emphasized to each interviewee that they could choose the language in which they felt most comfortable and were welcome to switch (English, German or Turkish). However, retrospectively I noticed that I tended to start off the initial conversation in Turkish with the first generation interviewees and in German with the second generation interviewees. This was based on my assumptions that first, they would be more comfortable in Turkish and second that I had to prove my linguistic competence as a second generation migrant and thus signal that I was willing and able to cross any linguistic and generational boundaries. Indeed most first generation interviewees chose Turkish as the interview language, and most second generation interviewees chose German. All interviews also involved language switching. Sometimes this switching was initiated by the interviewees to accommodate my own limitations in Turkish, thus signalling a willingness on their part also of crossing boundaries.

While the process of interviewing gives space to migrant women to elaborate, during the analysis and presentation of the life-stories, their words on paper could not argue back to my interpretations, thus requiring self-reflexivity. It was at times a daunting task to bring out the women's self-presentations with due respect to their meaning, while combining this with my research interests by selecting and highlighting particular themes and aspects of the life-stories. For example, for some of the interviewees, the concepts of subjectivity and agency, or citizenship seemed rather abstract and they themselves may have preferred a different conceptual frame for their life-stories. A key intellectual and political project for me was to understand and counter social divisions and power relations from an intersectional perspective. Therefore I foreground gender, ethnic and class relations in the life-stories. My interviewees may not all agree with this project, or my particular take on it. Thus, I am cautious of assumptions that shared social characteristics automatically produce shared knowledges of the self and the world. Such knowledges cannot be directly read off the social positions of their bearers, but are articulated as projects of building 'epistemological communities' (Assiter 1996) that dialogically construct knowledge across identities and experiences. My positionality gave me specific resources for carrying out this research, such as ability to communicate in different languages, having lived in Germany and Britain gave me a certain familiarity with some discourses and practices relevant for this research, allowing and requiring me to travel between different systems of meaning and enquiring about the material and institutional constitution of these.

The interviews were fully transcribed. The system of transcription is not based on linguistic conventions, but instead tries to enhance readability, I mark pauses with '-', render a loud voice in bold script and special emphasis in italics. I follow Lejeune's (1980) argument about transcription, that turning spoken language into written word should avoid reifying a voyeuristic gaze and 'condescending behaviour destined to produce an "anthropological" effect by constructing in the interior of a written system the image (…) of a kind of "savage" state of the language' (1980:291, my translation from French), suggesting that respect for the narrators requires rendering the life-stories to reconcile the vividness and informality of spoken word with the conventions of written language.

In the analysis, I employed what Ifekwunigwe (1997: 134) terms the 'artichoke method', that is reading the transcript carefully several times and noting questions to the text. I analysed the interviews first in terms of how each individual interviewee constructed her life-story, which key themes and key topics emerged, what where the underlying knowledges and how the interviewees presented themselves in the interview situation. Subsequently I looked at how these key themes and topics and self-representations related to the other interviewees' life-stories, as well as to the academic theorizations. The interview material is presented in thematic order rather than preserving fully the narrative sequences or even the full life-stories. This is due to restrictions of space; a thematic presentation allows me to explore the diversity of experiences in-depth in a relatively smaller space. I have provided narrative and biographical contextualization in my comments. Lengthy quotes enable the migrant women's self-presentations to be read alongside my interpretations.

Plummer names three major ways in which life-stories can be related to theories: 1) to take a story to challenge some overly general theory; 2) to take a story to illustrate and illuminate some wider theory; 3) to take a story as a way of building up some wider sense of theory (Plummer 2001: 159), in this book, I use life-stories at varying degrees for all three tasks. In particular, I argue that life-stories of migrant women are a particularly useful epistemological starting point for an intersectional analysis of the meanings and transformatory potential of citizenship. In the following chapter I introduce the theoretical and conceptual context in which the life-stories are produced, presented and interpreted.

# Chapter 2
# Citizenship, Identity and Culture: The Contexts of Britain and Germany

This chapter critically introduces theoretical debates on multicultural and postnational citizenship and their relation to gendered migration. In the first part it is argued that articulations of citizenship, nation and identity are contextualized with different national practices. Therefore I begin by examining conceptual, institutional and policy issues of 'race', ethnicity, and migration in Britain and Germany. It is argued that the British multicultural model addresses the experiences of post-colonial migrants but is less effective in understanding other groups, particularly the increasing number of so-called 'white' ethnic minorities including asylum seekers and undocumented migrants. In Germany by contrast, while multiculturalism forms a powerful discursive point of reference, it is not institutionalized. Instead, migrants are incorporated through a system, where paternalistic German institutions mediate between them and state interests. However there are also important points of convergence between the two countries which have been neglected in previous analyses: The British patriality rule and the German constitutional right of return of ethnic Germans both essentialize membership in the nation and citizenship rights by 'race' and descent. The representation of 'race' and ethnicity in both countries is based on a homogenization and construction of a black-white dichotomy in Britain and a German-foreigner dichotomy in Germany. Moreover, emerging agendas on integration policies are likely to lead to further convergences.

The following section sets out how Orientalist views have constructed the migrant women from Turkey as the 'Other Other' of Europeanness, going on to discuss the interlocking of gender, ethnicity and class and how these affect gendered migration. It argues that the experiences of migrant women, marginalized from citizenship rights, can provide analytically central insights for theorizing citizenship. Theoretical debates on citizenship should be combined with an empirical grounding in the lived experiences of everyday life with its hybrid cultures.

## National Identity, 'Race', Ethnicity and Citizenship in Britain and in Germany

The literature on nationalism and racism in Britain and in Germany initially presents a picture of contrasts (cf. Layton-Henry and Wilpert 1994, 2003).

Britain and Germany have different histories of nationalism and racism. For British nationalism, the empire has been constitutive; however the 'trauma of de-colonization' has been excluded from narrations of the nation in the post-colonial period (Smith 1994). The very absence of working through British colonialism has led to a 'post-colonial melancholia' (Gilroy 2004) and is mirrored in the construction of the post-colonial immigrants as the distinctive, racialized Other (Mirza 1997, Hall 1992, Smith 1995, Ware 1992, Layton-Henry and Wilpert 1994). For official German nationalism in the post-war period, the fascist period constitutes an important point of reference seen as an internal Other. It is a historical phase against which post-war German identity is delimited at all cost, this period which is constructed as a 'gap', shapes national identity through the absences and boundaries it imposes. The Holocaust has become the most powerful symbol of German fascism, an important historical point of reference for all debates of racism in Germany. The specific ways of the invocation, remembering and forgetting of this event are constitutive of German national identity in the post-war period. Despite the centrality of the remembrance of the Holocaust for a post-war national identity, the official assessment of the Holocaust has also circumscribed debates on racism. Continuities in personal and public histories become unspeakable or trivialized (cf. Räthzel 1994a, 1995, Rommelspacher 1994) and the image of the end of the second world war as 'liberation' from fascism that led to a new start, with a clean slate, the 'Stunde Null' (hour zero), are part and parcel of constructing the Federal German Republic's national identity. The re-unification of the two German Republics in 1990 constitutes another point of reference for the construction of 'internal Others'. The differences between East and West Germany have been constructed as dichotomous hierarchies in public discourses, including gendered imaginations (Räthzel 1995). Despite these internal differences within the construction of Germanness, the boundary with foreigners as external Others remains constitutive. Despite contradicting evidence of up to 10% of Germany's population being non-citizens, Germany was held to be 'not an immigration country', until the Social Democrat and Green government begun debating the need for immigration to consolidate the German economy and social security system in 2000. Setting in motion changes to the nationality laws and a new law about the 'regulation and limitation of to-migration', i.e. a law, explicitly not on 'immigration' but 'to-migration'. The choice of words is significant: despite a shift in the evaluation of migration to Germany as long-term and in some cases as permanent, this wording falls short of an acceptance of immigration as part of the national identity and migration is only seen as something that requires limitation and regulation.

*Contrasting Models of Citizenship*

The British colonial legacy and the fact that many Black British people hold formal citizenship have led many authors to identify a different model of incorporation here, than in Germany or other countries whose colonial history has not been as salient (cf. Rath 1993, Brubaker 1989). Until January 2000 in Germany, the definition of citizenship was purely ethnic: the previous citizenship law, dated from 1913, had based the *right* to German citizenship exclusively on *ius sanguinis*, granting non-residents of German origin the right to citizenship while all non-Germans, even if resident in Germany did not have any entitlements to naturalization. Their naturalization was made contingent on 'German interests' and was seen as an exception. In 1999, the new Social Democrat/Green government amended the citizenship law against vehement opposition of the conservative Christian Democrat parties and their popular mobilization. The principle of *ius sanguinis* has been given up in favour of a form of *ius domicilis*: from 1 January 2000, children born in Germany have the right to German citizenship if one of the parents has been living in Germany for eight years and has secure residence status. While this constitutes an important shift in the symbolic meaning of citizenship, the practical effects of this amendment are not as far reaching as the debates indicate (Hell 2005). Yet, there have been about one million naturalizations of migrants since the new citizenship law became valid, in 2006 about a quarter (26.8 %) of the 33,388 persons naturalized in the previous 12 months were previously Turkish citizens (Migrationsbericht 2006: 173).

In Britain, on the other hand, most colonial immigrants hold formal citizenship and until 1981, birth on the territory facilitated automatic access to British citizenship (Dummett 1986). This is an important difference to Germany.[1] Together with multiculturalist policies and institutions that do not exist in Germany, such as specific anti-discrimination laws, official equal opportunities policies and official multiculturalist policies in many institutions (cf. Modood 2007, Parekh 2008, Vertovec 2007), facilitating and regulating the political and social participation of ethnic minorities. These, of course, are important factors for the development of certain forms of agency. Recognition – even if partial – through state institutions has effects on the ways in which ethnic minority people can formulate demands on the state, claim resources, and access decision making. In Germany, these processes almost exclusively operate through German mediators since the *'Ausländerbeirat'* (Foreigner's Council), the only officially legitimated bodies of political representation for migrants have consultative functions only. A small number of ethnic minority people who hold German citizenship have very recently begun to access decision-making positions as MPs, MEPs and local councillors. For these reasons, some authors suggest that both countries represent opposites of 'ethnic' versus 'multicultural' models of migrant incorporation and citizenship (Brubaker 1989, Kofman et al. 2000, Radtke 1994). The British multicultural model recognizes a certain degree of cultural and ethnic difference. Ethnic community organizations are recognized as representatives of ethnic groups, and thus accorded participation in the formulation of social policy. This has made a difference in the

---

1   Although there are also some ideological and practical convergences in the two countries' citizenship legislation, in particular since the erosion of all British citizens' right to settle in the UK (cf. below).

incorporation of migrants, particularly refugees, since these organizations were responsible for their provisions. This has positive effects, such as a greater input of migrants' and ethnic minority people into social policy and the formulation of specific social and cultural needs. At the same time, these multiculturalist policies tend to problematically reify static notions of culture and community. Thus, in a study on recent Bosnian refugees, Kelly (2003) argues that British multiculturalist government practices incited the development of 'contingent communities' (Kelly 2003) on the basis of ethnicity, despite the refugees' reluctance to identify thus. She critiques that the British reliance on ethnically bounded community groups elevated ethnicity into the master-identity script, without which individuals cannot access resources and enter a relationship with the state. Moreover, there is a lack of democratic representativeness and accountability of community organizations and their leadership. These factors can lead to a reification of hierarchies and oppressions of ethnicity, gender and sexuality[2] (cf. Anthias and Yuval-Davis 1992, Kofman et al. 2000, Sahgal and Yuval-Davis 1992). Existing multiculturalist policies in Britain are, however, modelled on post-colonial 'Black and Asian' migrants and do not sufficiently respond to the needs of more recent groups, such as migrants from Turkey (cf. Uguris 2001, Vertovec 2007). Moreover, 'Turkish and Kurdish migrants are not represented sufficiently in the workforce of the local councils even in those wards where they form a large minority despite the equal opportunities policies of these authorities' (Uguris 2001: 9). Therefore, the full extent of differential systems of incorporation in Germany and Britain does not manifest itself in the case of migrants from Turkey.

Another important difference is the extent, quality and history of resistance against racism from racialized and ethnicized people. While Britain has a long history of visible resistance against racism, and more recently also of Black feminist resistance against gendered racialization, in Germany this resistance has been less visible. One reason for this is that post-colonial migrants from Africa, the Caribbean and Asia hold formal citizenship in the UK. They had all formal political rights and did not have to fear deportation for their political actions. This underlines the importance of formal citizenship for migrants' political participation (cf. Kofman et al. 2000, Layton-Henry 1991). Yet, anti-racist knowledges travel, thus in the German context many debates of the 1980s in Britain and the USA on political Blackness and Black feminism have been formative for migrants' self-representation and organization in the 1990s. More recently, the formation of migrants' and ethnic minority networks on the European level has also fostered the transnational use of such resistant knowledges (Anthias and Lloyd 2002).

*Similarities: Ethnic Germans and Patrial Britons*

Yet, there are some important similarities in the *framing* of issues of race, ethnicity and racism. One such similarity is the construction of nationals and

---

2    This is examined in more detail in Chapter 6.

immigrants through legislation. Germany is often, and rightly so, criticized for its legislation that gives automatic access to citizenship to anyone who can prove German ancestors.[3] This practice of according automatic citizenship to ethnic Germans is in stark contrast to the difficult procedures of acquiring citizenship for other migrants, which remains conditional. While since the late 1990s, German authorities' practice of recognizing German ancestry has become stricter, severely reducing immigration of German ethnics (*Aussiedler*), the conceptual basis of Germanness remains intact. Yet, this ethnic and racist basis for accessing citizenship is not exclusive to Germany. British changes to immigration laws have successively eroded the right of New Commonwealth and Pakistani immigrants to enter the country. The patriality rule that allows full British citizenship, including the right to settle in the UK, only to those with a parent or grandparent born in the UK, has not been formulated on explicitly racist terms. However, the 1968 law was designed in such a way that the 'vast majority of British citizens, free from immigration control are white people (at a rough estimate, 54 million of a total 57 million)' (Dummett 1986: 146).

For much of the post-war period, dichotomized representations of ethnic identity have been prevalent frameworks for understanding difference in both countries, despite highly complex ethnic and national compositions of both 'native' and 'immigrant' populations, the Black-White divide in Britain and German-*Ausländer* dichotomy (for critiques, cf. Aziz 1997, Anthias and Yuval-Davis 1992, Radtke 1994). Yet, in the past decade or so this has been changing, as there has been a diversification of the ethnic background of migrants to Britain, yet only recently has this begun to be addressed in research and policy debates. In particular with the emergence of widespread and rampant racism against asylum seekers who do not easily fit with the pre-existing notion of Blackness but have been targeted by 'xeno-racism' (Sivanandan 2001) and other migrants, including from the European Accession countries (cf. Kofman et al. 2000, Parekh Report 2000, Vertovec 2007). The group of migrants from Turkey in Britain comprises a large proportion of asylum seekers (cf. Küçükcan 1999), and in particular Kurds from Turkey have been targeted by racist press campaigns on asylum seekers (Parekh Report 2000). However, most data collection or theorizing on ethnicity does not take so-called 'white' ethnic minorities into account adequately.

*Avoidance of 'Racism'*

Although legally anyone without German citizenship is an *Ausländer*, socially the term coincides with racialization so that white West-Europeans are only

---

3   During the early 1990s, accepted proof of German parentage for many applicants from Eastern Europe has been the membership card of the National Socialist Party of the father or grandfather, while those who had been stripped of German citizenship on racial grounds during the fascist period were often not recognized as German for the purposes of immigration (Wilpert 1993).

occasionally regarded as *Ausländer* (Forsythe 1989). On the other hand, for example Black Germans may experience being labelled as *Ausländer*, despite their formal German citizenship and cultural competence (cf. Oguntoye et al. 1991). While class, educational status and generation of migration are factors that may qualify the racialization of an individual *Ausländer* situationally, this does not render the categorization ineffective. The '*Ausländer* research paradigm' (Blaschke 1992) constructs the *Ausländer* as problems for different areas of social policy and social work and does not consider racism. Indeed, the concept of 'racism' was refuted as 'too ideological' until the mid 1990s. Instead problems were attributed to 'hostility to foreigners' (Kalpaka and Räthzel 1990, Lutz 1991, Piper 1998). Therefore, the focus was on promoting 'friendliness to foreigners' as an interpersonal attitude based on the better mutual understanding of each other's culture. State and civil society organizations promoted cultural campaigns to foster such 'foreigner-friendly' attitudes (for critiques cf. e.g. Jäger 1992, Kalpaka and Räthzel 1990, Leiprecht 1994, Lutz 1991).

In the British context, the race relations paradigm has long dominated the social sciences and social policy. There was space in the race relations paradigm for structural discrimination to be acknowledged, and racism to be named. However, racism was not recognized as a pervasive phenomenon that structured the whole society and construction of the nation (for a critique, Gilroy 1987). Racism was reduced to economic exploitation and discrimination in education, the labour and housing markets (cf. Rex 1994) and the Black and Asian population constructed as an underclass (e.g. Rex 1988). These discourses promoted similar strategies of mutual understanding and friendliness, to counter racism, as the German 'friendliness to foreigners' (cf. Brah 1996). In Britain, owing also to the interventions of Black and ethnic minority academics and activists, the race relations or multiculturalist approaches have been challenged from a wide range of positions (Anthias and Yuval-Davis 1992, Brah 1996, CCCS 1982, Gilroy 1987, Miles 1989, Phizacklea and Miles 1980, Phizacklea 1983, Sivanandan 1982).

Both concepts of 'friendliness to foreigners' and 'good race relations' miss out the complex and shifting hierarchization of different ethnic groups. Moreover, both accept the categories of 'race' or *Ausländer* as givens, the groups thus designated appear to be unproblematically assignable. The shifts in the construction of ethnic groups, such as the different meanings of the category 'Black' cannot be recognized and accounted for (Anthias 1992). The focus of politics based on these paradigms is the promotion of 'good race relations' or 'friendliness' in the context of Germany. This calls on the Other to integrate, to adapt to the norms of the 'host society', while the dominant populations are called upon to be tolerant. The basic premise of (white) Britishness or Germanness as the national norm is not questioned (Gilroy 1987, Räthzel 1994).

*'Multiculturalism is Bad for Cohesion'*

Discourses about the end of multiculturalism have become a Europe wide feature, both in countries with and without multiculturalist institutions, feeding into new policy based on the assumption that multiculturalism is bad for social cohesion. Multiculturalism is far less established formally in German institutions than in Britain; still, it constitutes the hegemonic discursive framework for articulating critiques of racist practices and institutions.[4] Despite its absence from most institutions, multiculturalism functions as a powerful 'bogey man' for culturalist racist discourses: thus, in 1997, there was a prominent debate in the media on the 'failing of the multiculturalist society' (Der Spiegel 14 April 1997). The debate on a German *'Leitkultur'* (German Leading-Culture in 2000 and regularly revived thereafter) was another prominent attempt to cement the centrality of a culturally and politically homogeneous Germanness.

In Britain, the official turn away from multiculturalist policy won ground with the disturbances in Northern cities in 2000 and in both countries, the view that young Muslims, some of whom were citizens or second generation migrants, had become involved in Islamist terrorist activities was based on the existence of parallel structures and lack of social cohesion that was supposedly precipitated by multiculturalist policies' emphasis and valuing of ethnic difference (cf. Bourne 2007, Modood 2007, Parekh 2008). These arguments against multiculturalism are very different from the critiques put forward above. This new emphasis on social cohesion or revival of 'assimilationism' (Back et al. 2002) is based on essentializing ethnic minority and migrant communities and identities, in particular those labelled or self-identified as Muslim, and juxtaposing it to national cultures or European values that are constructed as essentially liberal and based on the progressive incorporation of human rights: 'Muslim people as a whole are now being stereotyped not just as terrorists but also as backward, sexist, homophobic bigots whose intolerance and values threaten all our freedoms' (Bourne 2007: 6). These anti-multiculturalist discourses in both countries feed into a renewed emphasis of integration and migration policy. This makes both formal and substantive citizenship rights conditional to integration, often narrowly conceived. Indeed, the emphasis on culture that some versions of multiculturalism have promoted is reiterated, only this time with the promotion of civic, national culture rather than cultural pluralism. This is problematic as it undermines the promotion of equal rights for migrants and ethnic minorities, which is not viable without

---

4   Kürşat-Ahlers (1996: 114) analyses the shift towards multiculturalist discourses in the late 1980s Germany as 'semantic shift' that leaves the existing societal structures of exclusion intact. She analyses multiculturalism as a strategy to culturalize social difference and discrimination, and as argued earlier for the British context states: 'Paradoxically, public-opinion leaders within the Turkish minority readily adopted this concept of cultural segregation since it enhanced their social influence within the Turkish community' (1996: 115).

the acceptance of cultural pluralism and the interaction of cultural elements and practices of both majority and minority citizens and migrants.

## Migrants from Turkey in Britain and Germany

Commonality and difference are never assessments of 'objective' given situations but are constructions which give meaning according to social and political purposes. One of the major difficulties of comparative research is to either construct ideal typical differences or render differences invisible. My approach does not attempt to build a comparative framework to measure degrees of difference and sameness; rather, by using two national contexts, this book aims to shed light on the contextual and place specific nature of giving meaning and constructing identities. This involves looking at aspects of identity like 'being from Turkey' around which a continuity of identity is organized across contexts and places, borders and boundaries. While there may be many similarities between migrant women in both countries, such similarities are not self evident but have to be discursively constructed. The commonality of gender and country of origin does not override differences in current living conditions or vice versa.

*History*

There has been large-scale migration from Turkey to Germany since the late 1960s, mostly as 'guest-workers', yet, those who entered under the formal label of guest-worker had diverse motivations, including political or ethnic persecution. After the recruitment stop of 'guest-workers' in 1973, family reunification became the main mode of entry. After the coup d'etat in 1980 asylum seekers, first political activists and, from the mid-1980s, Kurdish refugees, constituted other significant groups. The number of Turkish citizens in 2006 was 1,738,831, accounting for 25.8 % of the foreign population (Migrationsbericht 2006: 158). This group is ethnically diverse, reflecting the multi-ethnic composition of the population of Turkey (Zentrum für Türkeistudien 1998). The migration to Britain started in the mid 1960s, as a small number, comprised of students, professionals and migrants on the work permit scheme, entered (Dokur-Gryskiewicz 1979). By 1974, there were about 4,000 migrants from Turkey in London. This small scale migration continued during the 1970s. The military coup in 1980 lead to an increased politically and economically motivated migration to Britain, mainly undocumented. From 1989 onwards, the number of asylum-seekers from Turkey, mostly Kurds, increased significantly. The exact number of migrants from Turkey in Britain is difficult to determine: the Turkish Ministry of Employment and Social Security gives the number of Turkish citizens in Britain as 65,000, this excludes the number of asylum applicants, 13,783 until 1995 (Küçükcan 1999: 62–63). The problem of statistical data is further compounded by the category of the 'Turkish-speaking community', operative in social policy provisions and ethnic monitoring

(King et al. 2008). This includes Turkish Cypriots, many of whom, as post-colonial migrants, hold British citizenship. Despite their divergent migration histories, these groups are viewed as one community. Küçükcan estimates the number of Turkish Cypriots and migrants from Turkey in Britain to be 130,000 (1999: 63). From existing data, it is however clear that migrants from Turkey are concentrated in the Greater London area, where they are ranked as the 15th group of those born outside the UK, numbering 39,128 (GLA quoted in Vertovec 2007: 1032). The notion of Turkish-speaking communities has been challenged recently and local authorities have begun to include the category of Kurds and Kurdish-speaking into policy and ethnic monitoring, though only haltingly (Holgate et al. 2008).

*Economic Incorporation*

The economic incorporation of migrants from Turkey differs significantly in Germany and Britain. Thus, most migrants from Turkey entered Germany as guest-workers and have been employed in the heavy industries. As these declined, unemployment among Turkish migrants soared (cf. Faist 1995). The number of skilled, white collar or professional workers among Turkish migrants is low, although with increasing numbers of second generation graduates this is changing. Since the 1990s, self-employment is increasing and diversifying (Şen and Goldberg 1994, Ausländerbeauftragte 2000). In Britain, in contrast, migrants from Turkey tend to be concentrated in small and medium ethnic enterprises. In the 1980s to late 1990s, this was mainly in the textile industry, often owned by Turkish Cypriots, and later by Turks and Kurds. With the increasing outsourcing of textile production from sweatshops in the UK to other countries, this is now a negligible employment sector. Currently the restaurant and retail industries are main sources of employment, and self employment in these sectors is significant (Küçükcan 1999, Holgate et al. 2008). While the existence of an ethnic (niche) economy is helpful, in particular for new arrivals, it has contradictory consequences. As highlighted in Chapter 4, while it may allow the circumvention of restrictions on migration status and work permits, it often goes hand in hand with economic exploitation (cf. Erdemir and Vasta 2006) and sexual harassment. The availability of many low paid, low skilled jobs in the ethnic economy also contribute to some young people self-restricting their ambitions to these jobs (Enneli et al. 2005).

*Differential Salience of Ethnic Identity*

While 'Turks' are often viewed as the most distant ethnic group in Germany (Finkelstein 2006, Mandel 2008, Wilpert 1993), in Britain, they are ambiguously positioned as 'invisible ethnic minorities' (cf. Holgate et al. 2008). Therefore, ethnically specific anti-'Turkish' or anti-'Kurdish' racist public discourses are barely articulated in Britain.[5] Instead, this group is racialized by association with and representation as 'Muslim', 'asylum seeker' or 'refugee'. Public representations of migrant women from Turkey differ in both countries. However, the ways in which the migrant women made sense of their positioning in the society of residence, were similar. The interviews in Britain indicated that despite the absence of public representations of migrants from Turkey in Britain, the interviewees were faced with stereotypical representations of Muslim women and had to position themselves *vis-à-vis* these. This constitutes an important convergence with the migrant women in Germany. A significant difference was in the extent and frequency of direct racist verbal and physical abuse and violence they encountered. While this was a significant problem in Germany, it did not seem as widespread in Britain. This may be due to the differential construction of 'visibility' in the two national contexts.[6] Yet, other forms of racism were common to the experiences of women in both countries. The migrant women themselves also made comparisons between Germany and Britain during the interviews. Both groups concurred in the view that racism is more widespread in Germany than in Britain. This echoes public representations in the Turkish language media (available in both countries) as well as those of British or German media. My aim here is not to confirm or reject this view, nor to generate indicators for measuring racism, instead this chapter aims to call attention to the concurring or divergent dynamics of racialization.

These institutional and economic differences between Britain and Germany are reflected in the life-stories. While my initial expectation was that the experiences of the migrant women in Britain and Germany would be significantly different, in the course of the study it turned out that this view was mistaken. The differences between Britain and Germany do not present themselves clearly within the life-stories. As this study focuses on skilled migrant women, the similarities in living and working conditions are more significant. The period in their life, when they worked as guest-workers or in the ethnic niche economy,

---

5   Between 1995 and 2001 I followed the *Guardian*, the *Observer* and the *Times* regularly. This revealed that Turkish or Kurdish people in Britain are rarely mentioned. Turkish or Kurdish people become a topic in the following contexts: an underage British girl marrying a Turkish man in Turkey and converting to Islam, British women being raped on holiday in Turkey, Kurdish protests in Europe and London against the kidnapping of Abdullah Öcalan (PKK Leader), Kurdish and Turkish gangs in London in drug trafficking, Kurdish asylum seekers in Britain, and violence between Turkish and British football fans, both in Britain and Turkey. Although these were not systematically analysed, the discursive repertoires in the media coverage clearly refer to Orientalist representations. Elements of this included: representations as pre-modern and folkloristic, Islam as overdetermining cultural identity and behaviour, political radicalism and a lack of democratic political forms, the image of the (Muslim) terrorist, Oriental despotism, the oppression of women as overdetermined by Islam, nationalist violence, irrationality.

6   However, Enneli et al.'s (2005) study on young people found that especially young people of Kurdish background reported experiences of ethnic discrimination. Thus, gender, age, class and other factors mediate the experience of racism.

as well as accessing residence rights (as undocumented or irregular in Britain, as guest-workers or guest-workers' spouse) most clearly exemplify the different systems of incorporation. However, the current situation of the interviewees, as skilled or professional, informed and structured the telling of their stories. A study focussing on communities or community organizations may show such differences more clearly, I believe, since the most striking differences are in the ways in which multiculturalist or foreigners' policies construct migrants as a group. In the following this chapter theoretically locates the arguments, starting with an examination of the stereotypical representations of Muslim women, that the migrant women are faced with.

## Theorizing Boundaries and Cultures

### The 'Other Other'

A basic assumption of most research on migrants from Muslim countries, particularly on Turkish migrants in Germany has been that their identity and behaviour can mainly be explained on the basis of their culture of origin. Women in ethnic majority groups, as well as in ethnic minority groups are regarded as the Other, while maleness is seen as constituting the norm. This has for a long time been replicated within research on migration by ignoring women migrants or by constructing them as the 'Other Other' (Lutz 1992): gender relations and gender roles are conceptualized one-dimensionally as oppressive to women and women are portrayed as passive and victimized. This image relies on a reductionist view of 'Muslim culture' as simply enacting religious and cultural paradigms, defined in an Orientalist manner by the researchers. This construction of migrant women is relational to the image of the woman national, whose forms of femininity are reduced to ideal types (emancipated, democratic, progressive) and posited as the ideal (Anthias 2000, Huth-Hildebrandt 2002, Lutz 1992, Ochse 1999).

The underlying concepts of culture, identity and ethnicity are problematic on various levels. Identity is reduced to cultural identity which is collapsed into ethnic identity. Other aspects of identity (e.g. gender, sexual, class, political, etc.) are regarded as negligible. Moreover, this view does not take into account that culture is in its very nature hybrid, constantly changing and subject to political and social processes of signification (Bhabha 1990). The equation of culture and ethnicity makes it inconceivable that different interest groups within an ethnic group may give different meanings to cultural resources and use them for different ends (Yuval-Davis 1989, 2006).

### Gender, Nation, Ethnicity

To avoid the traps of these hegemonic representations, I begin by clarifying the terms and concepts used. I am arguing from a point of view which regards gender, 'race', ethnicity and class as intermeshing social divisions (Anthias and Yuval-Davis 1992, Hill-Collins 1990, Yuval-Davis 2006a). The focus of this book is on the interrelated constructions of the migrant women's femininity and ethnicity. This book does not view ethnic and national groups as inherently distinct. Both national and ethnic projects construct and maintain a collectivity. These collectivities claim to be based on common origin, culture, territory or destiny. Barth (1969) has made the point that ethnic groups are defined by their boundaries and not so much by the cultural contents. He argues that although the contents of a culture changes, the group holding this culture regards itself as continuous. And although in some cases cultural differences within one group are just as, or even more significant than the cultural differences to another group, the boundaries continue to be constructed along ethnic lines. These boundaries, however, are not a given. They have to be actively upheld by specific sets of prescriptions and proscriptions for inter-ethnic contact. These boundaries may be flexible and shifting, still they remain constitutive for the collectivity. 'Although the boundaries are ideological, they involve material practices, and therefore material origins and effects. The boundary is a space for struggle and negotiation' (Anthias and Yuval-Davis 1992: 4). The same group can be constructed (by its own members or externally) at varying times and in different situations as an ethnic or a national group. Anthias and Yuval-Davis argue that the most significant difference between ethnic and national groups is that the latter claim or struggle for a separate political representation.[7] Throughout, the term nation and national is used to point to projects referencing the nation-state or projects for a nation-state. The term ethnicity is used to refer to both ethnically dominant and subordinated groups within a nation-state. It is important to call attention to the particularity of ethnic majorities, too as one way of de-constructing their normalization and dominance. Processes of boundary construction, inclusion and exclusion are a focus of the book. They are closely bound up with racist practices. By racism I mean discourses and practices which exclude and subordinate people who are constructed as a 'race' or ethnic group. Racialization means the social process by which a group is constructed by means of a biologistic or culturalist[8] language (cf. Anthias and Yuval-Davis 1992). Ethnicization refers to the social construction of ethnic groups.

*Cultural Nationalization*

Cultural forms that exist in a nation-state are not automatically national cultures. Instead, certain cultural forms are selected, evaluated in a positive way and claimed

---

7    To those denied it, claiming a national identity, in a world organized in nation-states, is of course an important strategy of legitimization of political self-representation and independence.

8    Racism is increasingly legitimized not with reference to biological but naturalized, cultural differences (Yuval-Davis 1997). By 'culturalist' I mean the ascription of a static notion of essentialized cultures to ethnic or national groups, that functions to legitimize racist discourses and practices.

for national projects. This takes place on various levels, be it in the frame of far-reaching public institutions such as the education system, media, advertisements, literature or in a more local framework in everyday habits, family life or personal relations, etc. (Johnson 1993: 167). Gender relations are a central element of the 'national culture' and competing versions of this: women's role in ethnic or national projects is often examined only in relation to and depending on men. They are viewed in family metaphors as mothers, sisters or daughters. As mothers and wives women's role as biological and ideological reproducers of the nation or ethnic group and its boundaries is pre-eminent. On another level women and their appropriate (sexual) behaviour serve as signifiers of ethnic and national difference. The construction and guarding of the boundaries of ethnic groups is a constitutive element of ethnicity; thus the construction of gender roles is central to the construction of ethnicity both, materially and symbolically. Moreover, women are also social actors in their own right in ethnic and national processes (Anthias and Yuval-Davis 1989). Despite the assertion of a homogeneous national culture, diverse and even contradictory cultural forms exist and are constructed as representative for the nation by different groups. Political and social groups attempt – with different means and on different levels – to hegemonize their version of a national culture and to use it for their own interests. In such national cultural projects diversity may well be recognized in some respects. However the unifying element of attempts to construct a national culture is the construction of an external Other against which boundaries are drawn. The transgression of these boundaries, such as in the form of sexual relations with a person who is imagined as racial or ethnic Other, is often viewed as treason, in particular for heterosexual women (cf. Yuval-Davis 1997, Wobbe 1995). Internal differentiations and inequalities are often legitimated and naturalized with reference to the image of the 'national family', using heteronormative gender and age based hierarchies within the family to naturalize those within the nation, while maintaining the claim to unity and solidarity within the nation and the family (Appiah 1990, McClintock 1993).

National culture itself is represented as being based on a long history, being naturally grown and homogeneous. An important means in this representation is the repeated narration of the nation (Bhabha 1990a). However, in order to produce the nation as homogeneous, the forgetting of disruptions and heterogeneity is as important as remembrance (Anderson 1993).[9] National culture is represented as whole, spanning high culture and everyday culture, being modern, pure and historically authentic (Bhabha 1990b). Ethnic minorities and their cultural forms are juxtaposed to this as deviant, partial and mostly limited to everyday culture, often as traditional and backward. They do not have at their disposal the cultural

---

9   Both Anderson (1993) and Bhabha advocate a constructionist approach that does not view nations as primordially given but as historically constructed. Both emphasize that cultural affinity among members of a nation did not pre-exist the nation-state but rather that the creation of cultural norms, in particular with reference to language and narration of history, produced a national consciousness.

authority bestowed by the status of the national. At the same time, their cultural forms are denounced as 'impure' and containing elements of the so-called national majority cultures. Multiculturalist discourses differ in some respects from this claim to a pure national culture; what they nonetheless share with this is the assumption that cultures are bounded ethnically.

*Culture as a Means to Identification*

Nationalization of culture is closely linked with processes of cultural identification. By identification it is meant processes in which subjects form their identities, both personal and in relation to collectivities. This is never simply a 'free choice' but always takes place under conditions in which one is ascribed identities and social positions. These are grounded in material power relations. In this sense, identification is always a process in which resistances and contradictions are negotiated and struggled over. Conceptualizing identities as multiple acknowledges that people identify in various, sometimes contradictory, ways which may be weighted differently depending on the situation.

An important moment in the formation of identification is the recognition of identity through authoritative instances on different levels such as family, school, media, etc. There are different versions of national culture struggling for hegemony, but there are also different identities that articulate in relation to national identity, be they political, professional or sub-cultural identities. This does not always happen in a nationalist form, it can take place in opposition or as an alternative to national identity or simply in a non-nationalist form. Within the nation-state and its institutions, that regulate many areas of life and legitimate or de-legitimate different practices, national identity is not simply one among many.

> National identity is a meta-discourse or grand narrative that regulates or polices other identifications. Discourses of the nation are only one source of recognition, but they have a particular power because often associated with citizenship, law, and legitimized violence. The power of national agencies to recognize citizens is one side of the condensation of powers which is the nation-state (Johnson 1993: 209).

For ethnicized and racialized people, cultural identity is complicated as their legitimacy to claim belonging to the nationalized culture in which they live is ambiguous and struggled over (cf. Stevenson 2003). National institutions of authority do not recognize parts of their cultural identity. Moreover, ethnicized identities can be systematically mis-recognized (cf. Johnson 1993). Hall, writing about the Caribbean history of colonization and the effects on migrants from the Caribbean, states:

> The ways in which black people, black experiences, were positioned and subject- ed [sic!] in the dominant regimes of representation were the effects of a critical

exercise of cultural power and normalisation. Not only, in Said's 'Orientalist' sense, were we constructed as different and other within the categories of knowledge of the West by those regimes. They had the power to make us see and experience *ourselves* as 'Other' (Hall 1990: 225).

Such representations are part of a national culture that constructs its dominance (among other things) through the exclusion and mis-recognition of ethnicized and racialized identities. Of course ethnicized people also produce their own representations of themselves that can contribute to an alternative, 'positive' identification. However such 'self-representations' are also contested. They construct specific forms and boundaries of community and prescribe exclusions. As the second generation migrant women pointed out, as young girls or women, they were faced with the threat of exclusion from the Turkish community, when exploring sexuality before or outside marriage, and aspiring to live independently as single women. While some of them felt these transgressions meant that they could not lay claim to identify as 'Turkish' anymore, they subsequently began to question these versions of ethnic identity and construct shared meanings of 'Turkishness' with other second generation women that would better represent themselves and accommodate their gendered choices of lifestyles, as will be discussed in more depth in Chapter 3. Different articulations of a politics of belonging construct divergent notions and ideals of gendered ethnic identities, as Chapter 6 explores. Non-national and anti-national cultural practices and identities formed through self-representation are not simply equally valid alternatives to nationalized identities. No one can simply choose identities to fit; instead they are always contested and negotiated.

## Gender and Migration

In a review of representations of migrant women from the 1960s to the 2000s, Huth-Hildebrandt (2002) argues that the themes highlighted in representations of migrant women have changed. Yet, the prevalence of themes such as crime among young migrant men, forced marriage, and wearing scarves at school, in the 2000s exemplify that gender is still central in constructing the ethnicized Other. In this sense, gender relations are used as an argument to polarize debates on migration. Research on women who migrated from the 1960s to 1980s (as those presented in this book) has long relied on the modernity-difference hypothesis (Apitzsch 1996) that constructed migrants as backward and in need of catching up with modernity in Europe (cf. Ochse 1999). Migrant women's family care work was seen as representing the traditional culture of origin and thus a particular obstacle to modernization (Apitzsch 1996), a notion that is challenged in Chapter 5. This view analytically locates migrant women firmly within the domestic sphere, often seen as a privileged site for passing on the 'essence' of an ethnicized or nationalized culture (cf. Yuval-Davis 1997). Factors such as the lack of rights to work as legally dependent spouses, formal and informal gendered racism in the labour market (cf. Erdem 2000), as well as in civil society (Akashe-Böhme 2000, Gutierrez Rodriguez 1999, Toksöz 1991) were neglected in these analyses. This book argues for emphasizing the perspectives of migrant women and taking them seriously as subjects with agency (e.g. Gölbol 2007, Gültekin 2002, Gutierrez 1999, Lutz 2007) whose experiences can contribute to our understanding and theorizing not only of migration but wider social phenomena.

Women have often played a crucial role in individual as well as household[10] migration decisions, even if this was not always visible (cf. Lutz 1998, Phizacklea 1998). The interconnection of economic and other motivations for migration is particularly significant for women. Among the women whose life-stories are presented here, gender-specific motivations for migration were the financial need to provide for children as single mothers, as Chapter 4 discusses. Furthermore, the wish to escape gendered social control as divorcees, single women or lesbian women, as well as to shift the power balance in or escape from an unsatisfactory marriage is discussed in-depth in Chapter 5. The wish to experience and get to know a different society was also an important factor, intimately linked with a wish to access different forms of socially recognized gendered lifestyles and constructions of self.

The institutional regulation of migration, such as immigration legislation, recruitment contracts and intermediaries, plays a crucial enabling and constraining role. For women who enter under family reunification legislation, this severely constrains their possibilities to take up work in the first years. Those who enter as tourists, students, au pairs, undocumented or asylum seekers, also face restricted (or illegalized) access to the labour market, and social rights. Often these immigration statuses increase their gendered vulnerability as will be shown in Chapter 4. Transnational ethnically specific networks are an important resource in negotiating the structural constraints of migratory regimes providing informal support to migrate and find work (Anthias 2000, Kofman et al. 2000, Faist 1998, Cohen 1997). Migrants who are positioned differentially in terms of ethnicity, gender and class have differential access to these resources (Erdemir and Vasta 2007) and differential capacities of actualizing these resources as 'capital' (Anthias 2007), as Chapter 4 elaborates.

While the migration of women in earlier flows was hardly recognized, since the 1990s there has been a growing recognition of the 'feminization of migration' (Lutz and Koser 1998). Thus, by 1960 women constituted nearly 47% of migrants globally. This grew to 48% by 1990 and in 2000 nearly 49% (Piper 2008: 3). While the vast majority of migrant women work in unskilled jobs and in the informal sector, it is important to recognize the diversity of migrant women (Anthias

---

10   While the household has constituted a focus of analysis in gendered migration studies, it is important to examine women's role both with respect to their strategies as part of the household, as well as their strategies of negotiating the power relations within the household (Carling 2005, Kofman et al. 2000, Prodolliet 1999).

2000, Carling 2005, Kofman et al. 2000). Indeed, among the key policy concerns identified by Piper is the '"bifurcation" between skilled and less skilled migration in ease of migration between countries' (2008: 5). The three key principles of regulating migration (family reunification, economic and humanitarian concerns) are increasingly being 'diluted' by concern for current labour market needs, so that guest worker type migration regimes are re-emerging. While women are concentrated either in undocumented, informal or low skilled work, this is often a consequence of their entry routes or of the (gender specific) ways in which their labour is valued. Thus, sexist laws might channel female entrants under family migration but 'this does not mean that migrant women are inherently non-productive' (Carling 2005: 8). These channelling effects of migration legislation can have particularly detrimental effects for women in the current climate where policy and public discourses strictly distinguish between 'useful' and 'abusive' migrants (Erel 2007), with gender differentiated effects on entitlements and opportunities of active social, political and economic participation. In the following, these issues are explored through the lens of contemporary citizenship studies. How can an excluded or marginalized category, migrant women, enhance our understanding both of the processes the structures of citizenship?

*Migrant Women and Citizenship*

Citizenship is a contested concept, promising equality and inclusion, while it also constructs boundaries and contains inherent exclusions:

> Who can be regarded as a citizen? Which boundaries separate citizens from those partially or wholly excluded from citizenship? Thus citizenship is not only seen as changing and evolving over time, but as a contested concept, which can at any stage of social development be invoked by those excluded, if the rights of citizens come to be seen as merely privileges lacking legitimation (Bauböck 1991: 15).

While formal citizenship is undoubtedly significant, especially for migrants, examining formal citizenship alone is insufficient for making sense of the position of migrant women. Instead, I shall discuss citizenship in its wider meaning, as 'membership in the community' (Marshall 1953), yet the very concept of 'community' is in question. On one hand, the boundaries and basis for making communities are defined and negotiated within ethnicized and gendered power relations and hierarchies, on the other hand various overlapping or competing constructions of community lay claim to bestowing the rights of citizenship. This section, rather than aiming to define citizenship explores it as a 'momentum concept' that we must 'continuously rework … in a way that realizes more and more of [its, U.E.] egalitarian and anti-hierarchical potential' (Hoffman 2004, p.134, quoted in Lister 2008, 48).

*Critical epistemologies*

Most debates about both formal and substantial aspects of citizenship are structured by a dichotomizing logic: on the one hand, there are the migrants and their interests, on the other hand, there is the receiving society and its interests. While supporters of an inclusion of migrants may argue that the societies' of residence and the migrants' interests converge in certain respects, the epistemological basis for distinguishing these interest groups on the basis of nationality and/or ethnicity is taken for granted (cf. Carens 1995). Thus, such accounts weigh up the benefits and costs of immigrants to a society. These benefits include: economic gains, the possibilities for nationals to social mobility, at times even the values of cultural diversity. The costs on the other hand include loss of social or cultural cohesion, growth of unemployment and strains on the welfare system. In these approaches, migrants remain marginal to conceptualizations of citizenship. As for migrant women, academic debates on citizenship tend to exclude migrant women by focusing one-dimensionally on migrants generically defined as male (e.g. Bauböck 1991, Mackert 1999), or by focusing on citizenship of women nationals (e.g. Philipps 1995, Appelt 2000). By putting the subjective accounts of women of Turkish background centre stage, this book takes a contrasting epistemological starting point.

*Cultural capital and the ideal citizen*

Most theorists agree that citizenship is a status that bestows rights and obligations. At the same time, each system of citizenship also constructs its ideal-typical subject as those who are best able to fulfil their obligations and are presumably thus best equipped to exercise their rights. As Léca points out, 'those individuals who consider their interests as properly served through citizenship are recognized as the best citizens, and those who possess the most "capital" (material, cultural or technological) are recognized as the most competent' (Léca 1992: 20).[11] This is one aspect of an increasing responsibilization of citizens that has gone hand in hand with a reduction in the welfare provisions of welfare states (cf. Isin and Turner 2008). Yet, much of the cultural and social capital of migrant women is not recognized in their society of residence (see Chapter 4; cf. Lutz 1991, Kofman et al. 2000). As argued above, migrant women are not seen as fully competent

---

11   Lister (1990) critiques the concept of 'active citizenship', used in 1980s Britain, in a similar vein, arguing that the concept puts the obligations and economic self-reliance of citizens centre stage and at the same time constructs the poor as constituting a 'culture of dependency'. She argues that this glosses over inequalities in access to education, training and good quality jobs. In terms of political and social activity, too there is an inequality in who is constructed as the ideal, active subject and who is constructed as merely a recipient: 'it seems clear that the government regards the poor as the objects, not the subjects, of active citizenship. There is a tacit understanding that while the philanthropy of the middle classes is the hallmark of active citizenship, the campaigning of welfare rights groups and the like constitutes the undesirable face of political activism' (Lister 1990: 19).

participants in national cultures of the societies of residence. One key aspect of cultural citizenship therefore pertains to the recognition of, and valuing of, marginalized cultural identities: 'Full citizenship involves a right to full cultural participation and undistorted representation' (Pakulski 1997: 8). Thus, culture is a key site of contestation, where issues of symbolic challenge and exclusion come to the fore. These contestations take place both inside and outside of formal administrative power structures. Stevenson argues that 'we should seek to form an appreciation of the ways in which "ordinary" understandings become constructed, of issues of interpretative conflict and semiotic plurality more generally' (2001: 2). This pertains to struggles around the representations of migrant women as the 'Other Other' or indeed as subjects with agency (see above). Challenges to representations of ideal or 'normal' citizens are important to making citizenship more inclusive (Stevenson 2001: 4).

*Multilayered and multidimensional citizenship*
Citizenship is a multidimensional concept and theorists have pointed out different levels of citizenship i.e. legal, social, political (Marshall 1953), different aspects of citizenship: i.e. active/passive and public/private (Turner 1990), as well as different tiers of citizenship (local, regional, national, transnational (Yuval-Davis 1997b). Despite the universalist claims of contemporary European democracies, members of the community are positioned differentially with relation to all of these dimensions of citizenship, according to class, gender, ethnicity, 'race', ability and legal residence status (cf. e.g., Bauböck 1994, feminist review 1997, Lister 2008, Soysal 1994).

*Postnational citizenship*
For different categories of citizens (or denizens[12]), different capacities and statuses *vis-à-vis* the state and society are prioritized. Soysal (1994) argues with respect to migrants in Europe, that although they may not be formally citizens, they share in the same social rights as full citizens. She views this as an example for the emergence of 'post-national citizenship', which privileges human rights over nationally bounded citizenship rights. While agreeing with her normative view I do not see the basis for such a development put into practice yet: political rights are indispensable to ensure and sustain migrants' status and redefine the substance and form of rights and obligations, including the rights of denizens. Further, migrants' social rights are still contingent on their employment, political and criminal record. (cf. Anthias and Yuval-Davis 1992, Mackert 1999). Moreover, in practical terms the nation-state remains responsible for their realization, though e.g. European institutions may require to balance 'the competence of the national state in granting admittance and residential rights' with 'respect of

---

12   Hammar (1989) defines denizens as non-citizen residents, with secure resident rights who have similar rights to work and welfare. This claim is critically examined below.

fundamental human rights' (Rigo 2008: 155). Furthermore, those countries who ratified conventions on the rights of migrant workers or refugees tend to be the sending rather than the receiving countries. Migrants' access to transnational or supranational institutions to claim their rights *vis-à-vis* the nation-state they live in is limited and shaped by their relation to the nation-state of their residence or formal citizenship (Morris 1997, Anthias 1998, 2001, Rogers 2000, Kastoryani 1998, Kofman 1997, Kofman et al. 2000). Yet, a very important aspect of the framework of postnational citizenship is that it re-focuses attention from nation-states as agents of citizenship to supranational organizations on one hand and migrants as collective and individual actors on the other.

*Social rights, social contributions*
Migrant women's citizenship has primarily been explored in terms of their access to social rights. While, undoubtedly, the attainment and realization of social rights is an important basis for realizing other aspects of citizenship, It is argued that our theoretical framework for studying migrant women's citizenship needs to extend beyond a focus on social rights. Approaches that reduce migrant women to bearers of social rights structurally fix them as *recipients* of services, ignoring the ways in which migrant women, e.g. as health workers in the UK, as mediators and community workers, as cleaners in public offices are part and parcel of *providing* public services (not to mention the ways through which they provide services that replace the public services that have been cut, such as in formal and informal employment in caring for elderly, sick, disabled and children. Thus, a focus on migrant women's citizenship as articulated mainly through their social rights neglects the active economic aspects of their citizenship practices. They contribute economically both through their labour and tax paying as well as through unpaid labour in the home. Indeed for many who work in family businesses in the ethnic niche economy, an entrepreneurial activity that has often been hailed as revitalizing the societies of residence economically, the boundary between paid work outside and unpaid work within the home is blurred. The notion of 'global care chains' (Hochschild 2000) has recently drawn attention to the transnational aspects of women's unpaid caring labour: Thus, many migrant mothers (often working as carers in rich nations) have to rely on childcare in their countries of origin and do not have the choice to bring their children with them.[13] The low paid labour of these women at once subsidizes the economies of the rich countries of residence, but more than that, it subsidizes public services and employers' inaction in realizing unfulfilled promises of substantiating formal equal opportunities for women citizens. In this sense, migrant women are part of re-articulating spaces of citizenship, (i.e. public sphere participation for citizen women), and modalities

---

13    Reasons for their inability to live with their children include the irregularity of migration status, inadequate and unaffordable childcare, inadequate housing and working conditions. This 'outsourcing' of caring labour implicates mostly other women in the sending countries, in global care chains (Hochschild 2000).

of citizenship (i.e. through remittances and through challenging existing forms of doing family in the countries of origin and transnationally). As remitters of money, ideas, and participants in transnational flows, migrant women also create new forms of community and belonging. Furthermore, the view of migrant women's citizenship mainly as bearers of social rights structurally reifies what Avtar Brah calls 'minoritization': the construction of ethnicized or racialized groups as 'minors in tutelage' (1996: 187) rather than as active, though not always recognized subjects of citizenship practices. Thirdly, a reductionist view of migrants' citizenship as primarily social does not take account of migrants' cultural, political and social contributions to civil society. Finally, all of these contributions can only be fully taken into account if we do not collapse national identity and citizenship but instead conceptualize migrants as part of the civil society (cf. Anthias 2000, Bauböck 1991, 1994, Yuval-Davis 1997b).

I approach citizenship as a 'set of practices (juridical, political, economic and cultural)' (Turner 1993: 2) as opposed to legalistic, state centred and static notions of citizenship (cf. Stasiulis and Bakan 1997). Such a view accepts that citizenship is a dynamic process of inclusion and exclusion that takes place across a range of social relations. A broadened notion of citizenship, not entirely contingent on the nation-state in its conception, could also serve the argument to question the exclusivity of the privileges conferred by formal citizenship (cf. Bauböck 1991, 1994).

*Engaging Citizenship with Life-stories*

There is no self-evident way of engaging the concept of citizenship in the life-stories of migrant women. Debates on citizenship are wide-ranging and often centre more on political philosophy than on the experiences the concepts engender or the practices by which the concepts may be challenged. Indeed, more empirically grounded studies into what 'lived citizenship' might mean to people, to improve our knowledge of 'how people understand and negotiate rights and responsibilities, belonging and participation' (Lister 2008: 54) is needed. Kabeer suggests that academic debate about citizenship needs to strive to incorporate the 'views and perspectives of "ordinary" citizens ... We do not know what citizenship means to people – particularly people whose status as citizens is either non-existent or extremely precarious –or what these meanings tell us about the goal of building inclusive societies' (2005: 1).

*Multicultural citizenship*
How might we engage migrant women's life-stories in academic debates of multicultural citizenship? These debates suggest that multiculturalist citizenship can mediate between groups, individuals and the state (cf. Van Dyke 1995, Kymlicka 1995, Radtke 1994, Rex 1994). Multiculturalist citizenship rights are proposed as an intermediate level between individual and state where oppression and disadvantage of marginalized groups can be remedied. Thus, Kymlicka (1995)

argues that group rights should protect the cultural difference of ethnic minorities from encroachment of the ethnic and cultural majority.[14] He views different ethnic groups' cultures as changing, but distinct. Culture, in his view is a precondition for exercising freedom of choice, since a cultural framework is necessary to make sense of one's experiences. He views the protection of minority cultures therefore as essential for safeguarding the liberal tenet of freedom of choice, since even if the contents of cultures changes, he argues, the concept of (ethnically) separate cultures should be maintained. Critics caution that group rights may lead to the oppression of 'internal minorities' (Green 1995) or individual dissenters (Waldron 1995). Kymlicka integrates these critiques, arguing that cultural group rights are justified in so far as they protect the ethnic minority from the majority, but the majority society should limit its tolerance of practices that place internal restrictions on its members. This raises the issue of which (culturally specific) values of the dominant ethnic group are used to judge practices of minority groups (Yuval-Davis 1997). Moreover, such a static concept of culture as ethnically bounded needs to be deconstructed to acknowledge that culture is hybrid, processual, unfinished and dialogic (Bhabha 1990). This view on culture as open to interpretation sheds new light on the issue of cultural authenticity and authority in the context of ethnic power relations. Thus, the interpretation of cultural forms is not neutral but often constitutes a struggle for hegemony within and across ethnic groups. So that most often conflicts in the name of cultural authenticity represent conflicts about the authority over such cultural forms and practices. By de-coupling cultural forms and practices from their dominant nationalized meaning and constructing other meanings, ethnicized people can disrupt the normalization of nationalized cultural forms and practices. Such a disruption, according to Bhabha, also has deeply destabilizing effects on dominant identities (Bhabha 1996). Hybridizing strategies of destabilizing nationalized cultural practices challenge multiculturalist concepts of cultural mixing. While multiculturalist policies might recognize cultural diversity within particular, regulated parameters, these policies also survey its boundaries. Moreover, multiculturalist strategies do not question the legitimacy of the power relations between majority and minorities. Multiculturalisms fix cultural forms and practices to an ethnic group in a 'musée imaginaire', they catalogue, hierarchize and separate these cultural forms from each other (Bhabha 1990: 208). A hybrid notion of culture moreover has a destabilizing effect on power relations and dominant identities within ethnicized groups. Unlike many multiculturalist practices, it

---

14   Kymlicka differentiates between three types of group-differentiated rights, which should be accorded situationally:

'-self-government rights (the delegation of powers to national minorities, often through some form of federalism);

-polyethnic rights (state support and legal protection for certain practices associated with particular ethnic or religious groups; and

-special representation rights (guaranteed seats for ethnic or national groups within the central institutions of the larger state)' (Kymlicka 1995: 6–7).

does not view the most 'culturally distant' claims to ethnic identity as the most authentic. Such policies and practices often result in what Shachar describes as the 'dilemma of multicultural vulnerability', whereby the state empowers religious and often socially conservative groups to become representatives of the ethnic group. This is not based on democratic principles of representativity and often reinforces oppression of vulnerable people and groups, such as women, sexual minorities and children (Shachar 2000). Kymlicka's view of culture has been criticized for the foundational status it gives culture for constituting personal and political subjectivity (Modood 2007). Kymlicka's conception neglects the ways in which minority and majority cultures become entwined (Parekh 2008), pluralized and deterritorialized (Bloomfield and Bianchini 2001). Indeed, '(t)he capacity to gain autonomy from your own culture, open yourself to other cultures, take and incorporate into your own symbolic repertoire selective elements ... is an integral part of everyday life ...' (Bloomfield and Bianchini 2001: 107). Thus, the argument that we need ethnically defined cultures to make sense of the world around us and participate in it, as a legitimation of group rights is problematic.

While most theorists focus on group rights of marginalized, disadvantaged or oppressed groups, Bauböck reminds us that in most liberal democracies group rights are already enshrined, however as corporate rights of privileged groups:

> Many collective rights in modern states are in fact corporate rights of socially privileged groups, which reinforce their dominant position in society by institutionalizing them in the political sphere (take as examples the privileged position of dominant religious congregations enshrined in state law, or the special social rights for higher ranking civil servants in many Western states). Alternatively, however, collective rights may also have the opposite effect of compensating for social discrimination. Whether a collective right enhances or diminishes equal citizenship will depend on its contribution to the equalization of opportunities for social action within a highly unequal structure of class, gender, ethnic and other collective differences (Bauböck 1991: 22).

This argument crucially brings power relations back into discussions of multicultural citizenship. Furthermore Kymlicka's argument that 'culture' enables agency and choice is put into perspective. A unified and reified notion of ethnically bounded cultures underplays first the significance of social divisions of class, gender, sexuality and others within an ethnic group as constitutive of inequalities. Second, it reduces inequalities to systems of meaning, without taking the material and economic sources of inequality into account. Moreover, it is important to be cautious of the 'nominal or partial recognition of universal human rights and trans-border citizenship rights' as they 'have coincided with tightening restrictions on the rights of new immigrants. These tendencies are contradictory and create a dynamic terrain of struggle' (Bakan and Stasiulis 1997: 118). In contrast to Kymlicka's approach which combines communitarian and liberal arguments, Bauböck endorses an egalitarian conception of citizenship. His model of group rights, does not justify the extension of rights to residents through tightening access to newcomers, instead taking inequalities on an international scale into account. Bauböck also formulates a normative demand for the establishment of migration rights, arguing that migrants' rights as individuals to cross-border mobility, should be as normatively binding as those of nation-states to limit entry and belonging (for a contrasting view cf. Hailbronner 1989). These aspects are all too often bracketed out of discussions of migrants' group rights in favour of a culturalist focus. While debates on multicultural citizenship raise the issue of tensions between group rights and individual rights, this rarely takes into account the ways in which individuals construct their own relation to a group, how they position themselves in relation to it and how they view its boundaries.

*The structuring absence of migrant women's agency*
For the particular group of skilled and professional migrant women who are the subject of this book, such debates of citizenship hold very little space. Where participatory aspects of citizenship are discussed, it is often within the frame of multicultural citizenship and group rights, assuming a homogeneous group with clear-cut, pre-determined boundaries. The debates on citizenship present women's rights and ethnic minority rights as clearly delimited, and at times in opposition to each other (Kymlicka 1995). Attempts to conceptualize group rights, that is women's rights and ethnic minority cultural rights, often end up essentializing both groups and their interests and 'needs'. The intersection of women's and ethnic minority rights is then retrospectively debated from a supposedly 'neutral' all-knowing liberal authorial point of view. This contributes to making the dominant ethnic group invisible and normalizing its standpoint as universal. The dominant ethnic identity is tacitly identified with liberal values thus conflating liberal political and ethnic identification (cf. Yuval-Davis 1997). Crucially this discursive strategy achieves the construction and maintenance of the myth of objectivity and non-partiality of both liberalism and a Eurocentric perspective. Neither the material, economic, political, institutional, nor the discursive power bases of this authorizing/authorial strategy can be questioned from within this epistemological and ontological framework.

Citizenship debates focus on gender mainly in terms of welfare provisions, and posit both ethnic minorities and women as receivers of social citizenship rights rather than examining their participation in shaping citizenship. The current positioning of the migrant women who form the subject of this book as skilled women puts them in a privileged position where they do not depend to the same extent on welfare provisions as working class ethnic minority women. Yet, over their life-course, some of them depended on welfare provisions. On the other hand, their active citizenship consists in participating in and changing social structures of their countries of residence. These participatory elements of citizenship are only beginning to receive sociological attention with respect to minority women (Kofman et al. 2000, Lister 1990). The participation of ethnic minority women/ migrant women in shaping the debates and substance of citizenship is barely recognized, both politically and academically. This is a *structuring absence* that is both a product of and productive of the centrality of the liberal, ethnically neutralized subject position that is authorized in political and academic debates on citizenship. By putting the migrant women's life-stories into the debate on citizenship the debate is shifted on two different levels:

First, many of the migrant women actively participate in shaping the substance and boundaries of citizenship through their professional activities, often in roles of mediators in an everyday manner. Moreover, through their professional, political and social commitment they participate in policy-making debates. They contribute from within institutionalized and authorized structures (such as local authority consultative committees, professional bodies, etc). These contributions of ethnic minority women are rendered invisible by the discursive construction of a neutral ethnic, gender and class position of the people constituting these bodies. Their presence as ethnic minority or migrant women is discursively effaced. This is based on the construction of professional positioning as neutral in terms of gender and ethnicity. When they disrupt such neutralization strategies, they are singled out as 'trouble-makers' (cf. Chapter 6). Alternatively, they are offered an authorized subject position as an 'ethnic/gender' expert. This is based on an essentializing identity-politics-cum-clientelism-paradigm which allows and 'burdens' (Mercer 1990) migrant intellectuals to speak for 'their' respective ethnic group. This is mirrored in the employment opportunities of migrant women which are often restricted to serve an ethnic minority clientele (cf. Lutz 1991, Gutierrez Rodriguez 1999, Bundesausländerbeauftragte 2000[15]). This problematically reduces their remit and competence to work with other ethnic minority people. This intellectual segmentation confines them to the margins. On the other hand, the migrant women themselves may feel compelled to represent the views and issues concerning other ethnic minority people, if they want them to be addressed at all. However, the 'burden of representation' (Mercer 1990) that these intellectuals carry positions them in a political and discursive paradox: on the one hand, it encourages the construction of a constituency, since they have to legitimize their right to speak on behalf of a specified clientele. However such a construction inevitably entails reductionist elements. Especially the wish to speak for those least likely to make their own voices heard, such as migrant women experiencing domestic violence (see Chapter 6) fosters the disjunction of the (independent, articulate, empowered) Self and the subject of discourse (dis-empowered, victimized) while at the same time relying on the identification of speaker and subject as a mode of authorization/ legitimation of representation through the paradigm of shared gender and ethnicity or migrancy.

These problematic aspects of representation, essentialism and legitimity can be addressed more adequately in the context of the migrant women's social and political commitment, outside of policy-making structures, that is trying to

---

15   This is generally truer in Germany, however the interviews in Britain suggest a similar tendency.

lobby these policy-making structures from outside. In this site they may be most productive in shifting the terms, concepts and underlying logic of the citizenship debate. Even if such emergent challenges may get incorporated and significantly re-interpreted once they do become part of the policy-making debate.[16]

Thus, this book addresses one of the questions Turner identifies as key to analysing citizenship, that is in how far the migrant women are part of the 'social forces that create such [citizenship, U. E.] practices' (1993: 3). He argues that:

> ... social citizenship is both a condition of social integration by providing normative institutionalized means of social membership, which are based upon legal and other forms of entitlement, and citizenship is also a set of conditions that promotes social conflict and social struggle where the social entitlements are not fulfilled. This ambiguity in the character of citizenship is also reflected in its history either as a form of social incorporation or as a set of conditions for social struggle (Turner 1993: 11–12).

Putting migrant women in the picture as participants in debates and struggles on citizenship, challenges tacit precepts of the conjunction of identity, authority and citizenship. This contribution to the citizenship debate rests on my analysis of their stories on their social, political and cultural activity; that is the *participatory* dimension.

Secondly, analysing the level of migrant women's *experiences* of gendered and racialized inclusion and exclusion allows for a critique of the absences in citizenship debates. The link between identity, ethnic group membership, rights and citizenship is crucial in determining the substance and boundaries of citizenship (Anthias 2000, Yuval-Davis 2001, Kofman et al. 2000, Soysal 1994, Holmes and Murray 1999, Isin and Wood 1999). The debate on multiculturalist citizenship posits the cultural group rights of ethnic minorities and women's rights as distinct. It takes essentialized and most culturally distant notions of 'the ethnic community' as the basis for its argument (Anthias and Yuval-Davis 1992, Yuval-Davis 1997a). The subject of women it constructs is based on majority citizens. Women's role as symbolic border guards, reproducing the ethnic group symbolically, biologically and culturally is essential to representations of ethnic community. The notion of ethnic community rights thus risks reproducing and reinforcing patriarchal rights over women's (sexual) behaviour within the framework of multiculturalist democracy (cf. Shachar 2000).

The experiences and agency of the migrant women presented here challenge essentialized and homogeneous constructions of community and ethnic minority

---

16 Pınar gives the example of her participation in a campaign to remove paragraph 19 that prevents women from divorcing since they face deportation. While some German Länder introduced guidelines to protect victims of domestic violence from deportation when they divorce, the practical application of these guidelines is not always satisfactory argues Pinar.

femininity: by choosing to live as single women, to divorce, choosing non-Turkish partners, or living lesbian relationships they do not conform to hegemonic representation of 'Turkish' women's sexual behaviour and role as markers of ethnic difference. By mothering in ways contested by 'the ethnic community', they, at times self-consciously, at times reluctantly, disrupt the naturalization of the mother as the transmitter of national or ethnic identity. By questioning ethnic identity, engaging in feminist politics, challenging gender and age based hierarchies in 'Turkish/Kurdish' political organizations, challenging ethnic hierarchies and racism within the migrant ethnic community and by building cross-ethnic personal and political identifications and networks, they interrupt the equation of identity and belonging as ethnically bounded.

The migrant women's presence in the societies of residence, their claim to recognition of their difference and commonality with majority citizens, their refusal to submit to representations of themselves as 'Other Other' and their active interventions in everyday practices of education, work, mothering and socio-political activism 'reconstitutes the distinction between citizens and aliens' (Rigo 2008, 158) thereby transforming the meaning of citizenship.

In the following chapters on these life-stories the ways in which the migrant women's experiences and practices relate to constructions of citizenship are discussed. This includes contradictions, since resistance and challenges to some structures of domination may go hand in hand with privilege, acquiescence and participation in other structures of domination. Such contradictions and conflicts between different group memberships and the intersection of privilege or oppression, are however not exceptional borderline cases, as the literature on multicultural citizenship suggests (e.g. Green 1995, Waldron 1995). Instead, it is argued that these conflicts are central to the social divisions constitutive of communities in general. Thus, this book is making a case for treating multiple, overlapping and contradictory constructions and negotiations of community as central to understanding the meanings of citizenship rather than an exceptional situation that does not concern the 'normal' or 'ideal' citizen. The next chapter explores how migrant women constitute themselves as subjects with agency, looking at their negotiations of gendered ethnicized identitification in the site of education.

# Chapter 3
# Developing Agency: Schooling and Family

The process of becoming a citizen, a member of society capable of actively participating in it, is mediated through the key institutions of family and schooling. For those migrant women who grew up in Germany,[1] this has often entailed contradictions between different expectations of parents and school about the kind of person they should become. These contradictions have often been described in terms of a 'generation clash' (Otyakmaz 1995) between young migrant women eager to adapt to the lifestyles of majority citizens and the parents who are assumed to want to see their daughters grow into gender roles that do not allow them a full participation in the society of residence. Here, a more nuanced picture emerges. The migrant women introduced the topic of education and family to position themselves as agents: taking educational decisions, negotiating institutional and familial expectations and obstacles and positioning themselves *vis-à-vis* public and more personal meanings of gendered ethnicized identities. In the second part of the chapter the discussion turns to the first generation of migrant interviewees. Although they value education, for most it was not a key site of developing agency; indeed only where access to education was barred it became a key focus for the life-story narrative. This chapter then explores education as a site where migrant women construct themselves as subjects with agency.

## Second Generation Migrants: Education as a Site of Developing Agency

The interviewees' present occupational positioning is of a higher status than that of the majority of migrant women from Turkey, who are concentrated in unskilled jobs. In this sense, this chapter looks at how education relates to their occupational 'exceptionality'. However, the ascription of an exceptional degree of success is itself a problematic concept, as will be elaborated below.

In a review of the literature on explanations of migrant pupils' problems at school, Teunissen finds that 'the vast bulk (...) concentrated on learner characteristics as the primary explanatory source of low school results, yet the outcomes of these studies are disappointing. They are often no more than an unsubstantiated catalogue of pathological symptoms' (1992: 97). One key theme in the literature on the education of migrant girls has been that of culture clash, which posits that

---

1   The sample of second generation interviewees is located only in Germany, since the timing of migratory flows from Turkey to Britain made it difficult to find adult second generation interviewees in Britain.

the girls experience different expectations, and form distinct and irreconcilable identities at home and at school (Otyakmaz 1995, Thornely and Siann 1991, Mirza 1992, Basit 1997, Teunissen 1992). This thesis has trickled down into teachers' attitudes and understandings of their migrant pupils. Basit argues that the thesis of culture clash and female pupils leading a 'dual life' (1997: 429) at home and at school is based on a misrepresentation particularly of Muslim family life as oppressive of girls and restricting their freedom. It ethnicizes generational and age based differences dichotomously and ignores those areas where parents and daughters share values. The explanatory framework of the culture clash especially fails to take into account positive parental attitudes towards education (Basit 1997, Mirza 1992, Lutz 1990, Bhachu 1991). Moreover, the culture clash thesis reduces the real dynamism of family values to an image of fixed power relations. Among the institutional and structural factors impacting on migrant girls' education, low teacher expectations, poor advice on career options, and the labeling of their aspirations as unrealistic or over-ambitious are significant for the context of this study (Mirza 1992, Thornely and Siann 1991). A further important factor that is little recognized in Germany is the impact of racism as a pervasive phenomenon, as well as of racist incidents (cf. Mirza 1992).

The second generation migrants in this study share some commonalties. Many of their parents explicitly justified their decision to migrate through the availability of better educational opportunities for their daughters. Thus, in most families, education was valued and encouraged. In contrast to this familial support, many of the girls came up against formal and informal gendered racism at school. This included bullying by pupils and sometimes teachers and being stereotyped as low achievers. This, together with their parents' lack of information about the German educational system meant that they often started their schooling in lower level schools and had to access higher level schools at a later stage against institutional resistance. Only Pınar's family viewed female education as superfluous. What is common to all of them is that they began at a young age to take educational decisions for themselves, against institutional and/or parental obstacles. Another commonalty is that the higher the level of schools they attended the more they were positioned as 'exceptional' both by German and by migrant people. An important tension during their secondary education was that between ethnicized notions of education and sexuality (cf. Lutz 1990). Many of them dealt with this tension by adopting dichotomous ethnicized gender images that were dominant in public German discourses: they identified more strongly with Germanness, since they felt an identification with Germanness promised them access to education and gender roles that included female independence. They juxtaposed this to Turkishness as embodying restricting gender roles and a bargain between either living sanctioned sexuality in marriage or gaining education and developing a desexualized gender role. These issues became particularly pertinent as ethnicized measures of female freedom. Thus, the 'German'-identified behaviour of having a boyfriend and going out is posited as representing freedom. This gendered ethnicized discourse structured the life-course of all interview partners as they were required to position themselves *vis-à-vis* this conflict in their adolescence. Interestingly, this played a role even for those interviewees who subsequently did not identify as heterosexual, thus pointing to the pervasiveness of this heterosexist Orientalist gaze. However, the interview partners found different ways of challenging the premises of ethnicized and gendered dichotomizations inherent in this.

The British literature discusses the pressures on 'Western' girls to carefully balance being involved romantically without spoiling their reputation as sexually 'loose'. This may make it difficult in particular for working class young women to pursue education (Tett 2000). In this context, the gender specific expectations about delaying romantic involvement among ethnic minority girls of Muslim background can enhance migrant girls' educational opportunities (Basit 1997, Bhachu 1991). Yet, in the German public discourse, these tensions of becoming sexual subjects in a 'Western' frame are not problematized. This absence can be viewed as a measure of the hegemonic constructions of the normativity of 'German' femininity as an unproblematic ideal representing freedom.[2]

Until recently, a hegemonic research paradigm identified parental attitudes to education as the main obstacle for second generation migrant women's education (cf. Faist 1995). Yet, other studies found that despite high motivation and academic success, migrant girls are not rewarded with the access to vocational training or jobs matching their achievements (cf. *Bericht der Ausländerbeauftragten* 2000). The role of personal and institutional racism in education remains neglected in the literature.[3] Except for Canan, all second generation women come from working class families, where parents had low levels of education. They were the first generation in the family to gain higher education. Parental encouragement of the daughters' education was thus, if implicitly, experienced as an expectation of social mobility.

---

2    One exception to this is Lutz's (1990) study that conceptualizes the realization of sexuality and education as different forms of freedom, arguing that her respondents concurred with parental expectations of delaying sexuality for the sake of education. The young women agreed with their parents to delay sexual relationships in order to gain educational qualifications first, and were in turn granted freedoms such as living apart from their parents.

3    For example Lindo argues that although Turkish migrants in the Netherlands experience racism in schooling it should not be seen as an obstacle to their education. According to him, the existence of friendships with Dutch people makes the difference that enables pupils to 'take extremely insulting confrontations with racism and discrimination in their stride. (…) they did not let such incidents affect their attitude towards Dutch society at large, nor their motivation to continue schooling or their search for a good job' (Lindo 2000: 218). Yet, I would argue, that whether or not migrant students successfully deal with racism, it constitutes an obstacle for them. Moreover, as in the examples of teachers' racist ascriptions in this sample, the necessity to resist them constitutes an additional difficulty that racialized pupils do not have to deal with.

*Giving Meaning to 'Exceptionality': Canan*

In the following we turn to a figure of speech that most interviewees use in discussing their schooling: 'being an exception'. This notion of exceptionality is related to the small number of girls of Turkish background in Realschule and more so at Gymnasium during the time of their schooling (late 1970s to 1980s).[4] Moreover, the topos of 'being an exception' negotiates ethnicized gender images that the girls where confronted with at school, through their peers and teachers as well as through friends of Turkish background outside the school environment and their family. In the interviews, this notion is not uniformly elaborated and interpreted. What is interesting about the notion of being an exception is how it gives meaning to categories of ethnicity and gender, referring to both personal and collective aspects of identification as well as the ways in which self-representation relates to ascribed identities.

Canan is a 36 year old property developer born in Germany. Her father was an entrepreneur who left Turkey for political reasons, and lost all his property. Thus, the migration to Germany was an experience of declassing for her parents who became unskilled factory workers. Canan appreciates the emotional, intellectual and financial support of her parents for her education, which she sees as fostering her independence and ambition. She values her parents' tolerant upbringing that encouraged her to choose whatever she liked from her cultural environment. Her brother who was 16 years older did not live with the family but continued to help them with educational decisions. Canan spent her childhood and schooling years in a small southern German town with a large population of Turkish background.

Canan strongly develops the theme of being exceptional in her life-story with regard to her exceptional status at Realschule as well as the positive relationship with her parents.

*Racist victimization as a motivation to assert oneself*
Canan begins her life-story thus:

> C: Well, the discrimination began already in the second grade, when I was 8
> or 9 years old, in any case when I started school. And it began with these two

---

4    The three tiered school system in Germany separates pupils after primary school according to achievements into 1) Hauptschule – providing a minimum qualification after grade 9; 2) Realschule – providing qualification for vocational training, including white collar jobs after grade 10; 3) Gymnasium – providing qualification enabling higher education.

In the city where most of the second generation interviewees attended schools, the percentage of girls of Turkish background graduating from Realschule was as follows: 1983: 10.0%; 1984: 12.9%; 1985: 16.6%; 1986: 21.1%. The percentage of girls of Turkish background acquiring access to higher education was as follows: 1983: 0.9%; 1984: 1.7%; 1985: 1.6%; 1986: 2.8%.

girls who beat me up as a dirty Turk, because they claimed I had head lice, because there were lice at school. And this was my first experience. Through this I developed my personality, to defend myself for the first time.

In recounting this experience as formative, Canan does not point out the aspect of her victimization in her narrative. Instead she focuses on the agency she developed following this incident. '(....) I had to defend or protect myself as a foreigner. Everywhere, I was an exception, my personality was exceptional, too. Because somehow I made myself stronger'. Canan affirms the subject position of exceptionality and articulates it as achieving an exceptional personality, beyond the experience of racism.

This first incident had long-term effects. Although the teacher had not taken her injuries seriously, refusing to send her to hospital it turned out that her jaw and teeth were severely shattered, requiring repeated surgery and medical care until the age of 19. Canan is hard of hearing; in conjunction with this disability, the injuries contributed to a speech disorder. Despite recognizing that in the long-term she had 'this burden to carry', Canan emphasizes her parents' resourceful support. 'My parents tried to lift this burden financially (...) they hired a German teacher for me'. So that she could both overcome her speech disorder and improve her German. Additionally this private tuition enhanced Canan's self esteem.

*'Taking away place from German students'*
In the fourth grade of primary school, when children are selected for the three tiered school system, Canan's teacher argued that she was not suited to go to a higher level school 'as a Turkish pupil (...) [she said] I would only be taking away place from German pupils'. Canan's brother, who 'is a psychologist, got stuck into this, so that it became known in this school that we as Turks do not remain submissive, but they knew that we can defend ourselves'.

The teacher's argument does not take into account either Canan's academic achievements or her needs, instead privileging nationality as a criterion for access to education. Canan's Turkishness, in the teacher's eyes, disqualifies her from higher level education, a privilege reserved for German pupils, expressing a racist exclusion. Canan and her family deployed a multi-layered strategy to counter this discrimination: First, the fact that her brother who was not even living in the same town, and not her parents went to see the teacher is significant. He could assert his educated, professional status and thus prove that he as a person from Turkey had achieved what this teacher wanted to withhold from his sister. Second, as a psychologist involved in educational research, he held some authority as an 'expert'. Third, the brother's getting involved was meant to shatter any assumption that 'Turks are subservient' to teachers' authority. This assertion of Turkishness reaffirms the centrality of ethnicity for Canan's identification *vis-à-vis* the teacher, as opposed to accepting an exceptional and 'less Turkish' identification as some other interview partners described for their interactions at school. To make it known that '*we* can defend ourselves' conflates Turkishness as a collectivity with the family. It emphasizes that Canan is not just an individual but that she can draw on her family's support, which is indeed exceptional among the second generation interviewees. The emphasis of Turkishness strategically embeds this family as part – and representative – of a national collectivity. Thus, Canan's brother's intervention is meant to demonstrate the education, professional expertise, family solidarity and spirit of self defence at their disposal as an ethnic or national characteristic.

This intervention was successful, so that Canan was offered access to Realschule and Gymnasium. Although her father would have preferred her to attend Gymnasium she decided to attend Realschule since already at the time she knew she wanted to get a vocational qualification.

*'Marking' 'Difference'*

In Realschule, she was a successful student. However this success became a contested issue: Canan describes two situations where a teachers' conference had to be called to decide upon a controversy about her grades. In year five, Canan's grades in German improved through the help of a very supportive teacher. However, his colleagues did not accept his marking. 'And therefore, they especially had a conference (…) whether they should give me an A in German or not'. Finally the mark was changed to a B. The second incident was with a different German teacher a few years later, when Canan had been marked with an E for the whole term but doubted the validity of this. She took the essays to the liaison teacher for second marking. This time the especially convened teacher's conference upgraded her marks, accepting the second marking, so that she achieved a C.

Both these conferences, convened especially for Canan, constituted an exceptional situation. Characteristically, German is the subject in which her achievements are contested. This subject is thought to be a preserve of German students and migrants' success or failure in this subject is often attributed to ethnicity. Thus, not only the mark was at stake here but also the authority to judge her competence in a language assumed at the time[5] to be 'foreign' to second generation migrants. While the first time her competence was contested successfully by the teachers, the second time Canan herself used the same procedure to contest an unfair marking. This story lends weight to Canan's self-representation as an assertive and ambitious person, it is a story about successfully using the tools with which she felt unfairly treated (a teachers' conference to decide on her marks) for claiming her rights the second time around.

---

5    By now this may have partially and locally changed since the emergence of the hyphenated identity marker of German-Turks in the late nineties. However, the contention that pupils of Turkish background are low achievers due to language difficulties still remains a powerful topic of public discussion, scandalizing the multilingual pupils rather than an education system that fails them.

C: I have to say that I have often in my life been confronted with discrimination, I know many [Turkish, U.E.] women who have *never* been confronted with that.

U: Yes, that's right.

C: Maybe because I always wanted to assert myself, to represent myself as a Turkish girl.

U: Hmm.

C: I have experienced many negative things. And then I have always worked my way up from below again.

Canan rejects racist ascriptions attached to the subject position of 'the little Turkish girl' as a low achiever, who is passive and incapable of defending herself. Instead, she claims the subject position of Turkish girl, values it positively and demands recognition for her version of Turkish femininity.

*'My parents were something very special'*
Canan's relation with her parents was very close and supportive. She attributes this to their occupational and class status:

C: This is a very different basis, well, in human terms, my parents used to be entrepreneurs (…) that means liberal minded, tolerant thinking. Well, they think in a very tolerant way, and were very tolerant to me and my brother (…)

Especially her father was important to Canan. He encouraged her self esteem and belief that 'you can assert yourself'. Canan also describes him as a very 'cultured' person who taught her 'a lot about Turkish culture'. Her parents wanted Canan to be educated in both Turkish and German. Thus, during her primary school while she had private tuition in German she also attended Turkish school in the afternoon.

C: In the area where I lived with Turks, I only spoke Turkish. And talked to Turkish people, that is Turkish children who didn't even know proper Turkish. In order to prevent this, I should learn proper German, too.

Here it is interesting to note the slip of meaning from the knowledge of proper Turkish to proper German. This emphasizes the importance Canan and her parents place on standard language. This is one way in which the class difference of her parents' social origin is reproduced in the family's interaction with the neighbouring families.[6] Moreover, by educating Canan at a Turkish school and sharing his knowledge of a class specific 'Turkish culture', he transmitted this class differentiated cultural capital to her, too. So that Canan grew up conscious of class difference as well as national and ethnic difference of 'culture': 'I was given several cultures. That is, I have the German culture and then the Turkish culture. And they said I should appropriate for myself, what I think is right'. The underlying concept of nationally-bounded culture is embedded in the common sense knowledge that separates and labels cultural forms along lines of nationality and ethnicity (cf. Chapter 2). Her parents' suggestion that a cultural synthesis is possible, even desirable and their emphasis on her independent choice are very different from other parent-child relationships of second generation interviewees, where nationalized 'cultural' attributes were clearly polarized. Canan's parents did not regulate Canan's behaviour or moral notions of sexuality, along ethnic boundaries, either. She told her parents 'who is my first boyfriend, and who's in love with who and so on (laughs) (…) We spoke about everything, *no* topic was a taboo at home, *that didn't exist'*.

Her parents' tolerant attitude was put into relief by the 'very conservative' views of the Turkish people in their environment who tried to pressure her and her parents by spreading 'primitive rumours' about Canan. However the family did not submit to this mechanism of social control. This prioritizing of individual liberty can be contextualized with her parents' social origin: the respect and reputation the family and Canan had in the neighbourhood was not as crucial to their identity, as the liberal values which Canan attributes to their former life as entrepreneurs.

Some of her peers respected and admired Canan for her liberties, finding it difficult to accept their own parents' control:

> C: For example there was a friend, I used to smoke and she also smoked. And she got caught by her father and he said 'I'm going to kill you' and so on. Then she said 'Before you kill me, I'd rather kill myself'.
>
> U: Hmm.
>
> C: And that's what she did. But this death, she committed suicide … [Before her suicide she said, U.E. ] 'Canan is allowed to smoke, but not me, why' she didn't understand that. And- and- and one cannot – why you, and school trips, and why is she allowed to go on school trips and not me, and ah it is the home, the parents are different.
>
> U: Hmm. Yes.

---

6   For a fuller discussion of the symbolic significance of 'speaking good Turkish' as a key element of cultural capital, see Chapter 4.

C: And I knew that my parents (…) are something special. Therefore I protected them.

The experience of her friend's suicide drastically illustrates to Canan, but also in her life-story, the 'specialness' of her upbringing. This made her value the liberal educational attitude of her parents, but also made her feel responsible for 'protecting' them from gossip: 'of course, I took care that I don't meet anyone when I smoked or so. (…) simply that they don't talk about me'. However, what was most important to Canan was the knowledge that her parents were on her side regardless of any gossip.

*How (Not) to be Exceptional*

The theme of being an exceptional migrant appears in many of the second generation migrants' narratives on schooling. Across the life-stories, there are some common interpretations of what the status of being special meant, such as going to a higher level school (i.e. Realschule or Gymnasium). That meant that the school constituted a predominantly German environment. Another common element across life-stories was that as migrant girls they had to negotiate and challenge teachers' ascriptions and assumptions about being low achievers and often negotiate racist ascriptions or verbal and physical abuse from fellow students. However, there are also differences in the meanings of being an exception and the strategies the migrant women used retrospectively to integrate this 'exceptionality' into their life-stories. Let me exemplify this by contrasting Canan's approach to that of Deniz. At the time of interview, Deniz was in the final stage of her law training. Her father was a factory worker and her mother a housewife from a small town in Turkey. While Deniz's parents encouraged her education at Realschule and Gymnasium, which was exceptional for the neighbourhood, they nonetheless expected her to conform to their norms of socializing: this meant avoiding friendships with German peers. They wanted to prevent a 'contamination' with perceived 'German' sexualized gender identities. Deniz reflects about the notion of being an 'exception' as a label that stuck to her since school and finds that as an aspiring professional young migrant woman it is still often invoked by Germans. Deniz was one of only four other migrant students at her small-town Gymnasium. Thus, she felt at first that her classmates' construction of her as an exception seemed appropriate to Deniz herself:

D: I must admit that sometimes I felt I was something special, you know.

U: Yes, yes.

D: I was recognized and so on, and I believed [that I was an exception] myself at the time. Retrospectively of course, the older I grew the more I saw through what's happening. And they always said 'I don't mean you' when they spoke about migrants and I was present. When they talked about the things they didn't like about migrants on the side they mentioned that they didn't mean me, you know. (…) I felt funny, what does this signify that I am supposed to be somehow different, but I really only understood later what they meant.

In contrast to her earlier years of schooling at Hauptschule, where she experienced open racism, at Gymnasium Deniz felt recognized. However, this inclusion was conditional and partial.[7] The ascription of being an exceptional migrant still remains powerful and Deniz challenges this:

> D: Many things that I do are not self understood because I am a migrant woman. Always, since the school I was an exception. To be an *exception*, to be a migrant girl and then to be an exception. Well there is – in inverted commas – a mass; the majority. I don't think this way, it is the view of the others, the migrants, the normal migrants, and then there are a few exceptions who are not that important, one mentions them in passing.

The construction of a subject position as an exceptional migrant implicitly presupposes a majority or mass of migrants against the backdrop of which her specialness is made visible (cf. Walkerdine 1997). The problematic enunciation as an exceptional subject that Deniz experiences, ascribes otherness to the 'mass of migrants'; they lack the positive attributes of an educated subjectivity that is admissible in a predominantly German, educated context such as her schooling and, at the time of interview, professional life. At the same time, it constructs Deniz's subjectivity as only peripheral, not constitutive, of what it means to be a female migrant from Turkey. Deniz's self-presentation negotiates this dichotomy of mass and exception. Deniz's present strategy of identification as a migrant emphasizes her solidarity and commonalty with the 'majority of migrants' and refuses to accept the ascription of exceptionality. This is on one hand a way of refusing to relinquish her identification with her parents and other migrants, who, as working class migrants, do not fit into the admissible category, on the other hand, it is part of her political strategy of choosing an identity as 'migrant' (see Chapter 6).

Canan presents her schooling as initiating the development of her personality as particularly ambitious and assertive, against the ascribed stereotype of 'the little Turkish girl', implying passive acquiescence. One way of proving her assertiveness

---

7    Parker (1995: 30) coins the term 'conditional belonging': 'The claim [to Black or Asian British identities, U.E.] is the right to a form of conditional belonging, whereby the qualified sense of attachment is throwing the onus onto the British to change themselves, rather than locating all the "problems" within the new generations of black and Asian young people'. Here, the term 'conditional and partial inclusion' is used to examine the other side of the relationship; that is the admission of the Other into a nationalized collective identity by those who can unproblematically claim to define the conditions for belonging.

was through the affirmation of her Turkishness, for example by gaining a special permission to choose Ottoman history as her examination topic. In contrast to Deniz, Canan's exceptional position extended to her Turkish environment, where she enjoyed more liberties than her peers. This may be a reason why Canan embraces the label of exceptionality and values it positively: she shared with her parents an educationally higher status and different values from those of their Turkish working class environment. Thus, the notion of exceptionality did not estrange her from her family, unlike in Deniz's case, where education was a shared aspiration with her parents the practice of which brought her, however, conflicts of loyalty in terms of class and ethnicity. Canan's parents aimed at an education that would enable her to appropriate elements from both 'German' and 'Turkish' culture, moreover, they shared with Canan a relatively higher educational status to their Turkish peers. Therefore she did not feel pressured to choose either of them, as many other interviewees experienced in their youth, especially relating to parental expectations of ethnicized gender roles. Thus, Canan experienced heterogeneous notions of Turkishness, as the discrepancies between her parents and the Turkish families around them showed. However, her loyalty to her family was reinforced by this.

An important difference in Canan's and Deniz's negotiation of 'exceptionality' is the use of ethnicity or nationality. Throughout the interview Deniz uses the concept of migrant, as an inter-ethnic political identity and questions homogeneous Turkish national identities. In contrast, Canan claims Turkishness for herself and, in a strategy of reversal imbues it with positive meanings.

## Pınar: Education as Resistance to Parental Expectations

In contrast to most of the second generation interviewees Pınar's parents did not want her to access education but instead wanted to prepare her for the life of a married housewife. In the following, the relation between family and education in Pınar's narrative is examined, focussing on the identificatory moments that family and school held for her. Like Canan, Pınar presents her schooling as a time of learning to take decisions on her own, to resist oppression and to develop agency. In contrast to Canan however, Pınar felt the parental home to be mainly restrictive and saw this as a site of oppression. She viewed her school environment as a site of liberation and as enabling. She points out that at school, her achievements were recognized and that she could position herself as a 'passionate intellectual' in her school environment. These are key elements of her self-presentation throughout the interview.

Pınar is a 34 year old social worker in a managerial position. She was born in rural Turkey. Her father migrated to Germany shortly after she was born; thus she grew up only with her mother until the age of five when the father brought them to Germany. She is the second of five siblings. Her father worked as an unskilled worker at first in factories, than as a postal worker while her mother was a housewife.

When Pınar began primary school, she didn't know German. This, and the racist bullying that she suffered from her peers made her first two years at school very difficult. Moreover her first teacher was very strict and treated her language difficulties as 'stupidity'. Both the teacher and her schoolmates at times openly discriminated against her. One experience that was shared by other interviewees relates to the tradition of dyeing the hands with henna on festive occasions. Often, the children were punished for this at school as the German teachers and classmates interpreted their dyed hands as 'dirty'. However, in the third grade, Pınar began speaking German fluently so that she could follow the lessons better. She also began defending herself physically against the racist bullying.

*Fashioning the self through education*
A turning point for Pınar was entering secondary school, she emphasizes that the meaning of school changed for her: Her ability to speak German and a very supportive teacher spurned her interest in education. The teacher engaged the migrant children's experiences of difference in the classroom, he took their specific situation seriously by talking to them separately and by including the migrant children's experiences into the teaching topics. This contributed to Pınar's change of attitude towards school and this teacher acted as an educational gate-opener for her. By the end of the sixth grade, she came top of the class. This indicates the importance of gaining recognition by the teachers. Pınar felt that his recognition compensated her for her parents' lack of interest in her academic achievements.

Her parents did not value female education, so, when she got a recommendation for Realschule, they wanted her to attend the lower level Hauptschule instead. Pınar decided to secretly register for and attend Realschule against her parents' wishes. This act of defiance, enabled her to attend Realschule for four years without her parents' knowledge. Their indifference towards her schooling – they never asked about her school reports or got in touch with the teachers – made this possible. However, at the end of year nine they found out accidentally.

> P: And somehow my school report was lying around. And that's when he saw it, it said Realschule not Hauptschule ... And for this huge lie I got a beating that I haven't forgotten to this day (laughing).

> U: Yes.

> P: (…) But somehow I continued. But at the time it was like this, that school had actually become my home, you know. It was the area where I had my freedom, where I had ideas, where I could [relax from the things going on at home]. There were always tensions at home. Because the relation between my parents was always classical, my father took it out on my mother, psychologically and physically.

> U: Yes, yes.

P: And we were always the mediators ... My father attacked my mother and I always hated being at home.

U: Uh-hum, yes.

P: That was somehow a place where anything could happen at anytime. It was enough for my father to be in a bad mood. ... And, uh, the mother had somehow lost our respect in our eyes, because she had to suffer so much and did not defend herself. And that is what we had been watching for years.

## *Violence and private public boundaries*

Pınar was victimized by the tensions at home as well as being subjected to her father's and mother's beatings, however she was not only a victim but, with regard to her education developed strong agency. As Pheterson argues, 'victimization and agency are not mutually exclusive. Women may at times be victimized in their quest for greater agency and at other times be compelled to take transgressive initiative in their attempt to escape constraint' (1996: 18). This extract also raises issues of the link between family life and school. Pınar's pursuit of education was a resistance against her parents' projected future for her as a housewife. While Pınar herself at the time was dreaming of a love marriage it 'didn't mean that it was an alternative to an independent professional development'. Her parents' lack of interest in her education on the one hand hurt her, but she used it for her own ends by circumventing their restrictions to attend Realschule. Pınar re-interpreted her life in the public space of school as her real 'home', where she could be free and relax from the tensions and domestic violence that she experienced in her family home. This radically puts into question liberal notions of the home as a private place of safety, comfort and relaxation free from intrusion, such as Turner (1990) posits when discussing the private axis of citizenship. For many women, the home does not constitute such a sphere of individual freedom (Walby 1994). Instead it is the place of their domestic and caring work, and may be the place where their civil citizenship rights to physical integrity can be protected least. When Pınar describes the family home as a place where 'anything could happen at any time', she gives expression to the arbitrariness of domestic violence. The family home was an unsafe place for the children and the mother. Contextualized with debates on citizenship, this radically calls into questions the conceptualization of the private and the public. Walby qualifies Turner's (1990) notion that the private is a place needing protection from state or public intrusion: 'The male-dominated family household is incompatible with full citizenship. Social citizenship for women is incompatible with and unobtainable under women's confinement to the family and the vagaries of a dependency relationship upon a private patriarch' (Walby 1994: 391). The importance of not conceptualizing the home or household entirely as a private space, where the state should not interfere become more urgent when considering multiculturalist concepts of the private and the public. Thus, Rex (1994) advocates a

> multicultural society in which there is on the one hand a shared political culture of the public domain and, on the other, a world of private communal cultures. The former will be based upon the notion of equality of opportunity (...), and the latter on the acceptance of the right of separate communities to speak their own languages, to practice their own religions and to follow their own family practices (Rex 1994: 7).

Such a vision of family practices as a matter of communal rather than state protection and regulation risks an implicit acceptance of double standards of protection against domestic violence through the state (cf. Shachar 2000). By locating her 'real self' in the public space of schooling, Pınar resisted the consequences of domestic violence as controlling her personality (cf. Mama 1993). The deprivation of other forms of agency through domestic violence can render the imagination an important site of resistance. Christian (1990) argues that domestic violence aims at depriving the victims of their subjectivity. In this situation, to express one's self, even through imagination, means resisting this victimization. Pınar points out how she and her sisters used to decorate and re-decorate their bedroom over and over again. She felt that having to be at home at the weekends, without the legitimate possibility to go to school, felt like a 'prison', and therefore she felt that decorating the room gave her an opportunity to effect at least a visual change: 'if one can't tear down the walls, one can paint them in new colours'. However, Pınar's agency did not remain on the level of imagination and she chose the space of education as the site of fashioning a self outside the direct reach of her parents. In her life-story Pınar presents her successful maintenance of this site of an independent self despite the violent punishment as representative of her ability to overcome obstacles and take decisions independently as well as her perseverance.

In the interview Pınar explains her father's domestic violence by recourse to his problems at a racist workplace. He shared these experiences of discrimination with his family but did not seek any redress, instead presenting his suffering as a sacrifice for the sake of his family:

> P: I remember that the man always sat at home all alone and read. He never smoked, he never drank he *never* compensated in a different way, he didn't go out, he never met any friends. He *only* was at home and worked.
>
> U: Hmm.
>
> P: That was all his life. And somehow I think that his life revolved around us, the reason why he went to Germany was to earn money and to provide for his family.

U: Hmm.

P: and he didn't enjoy [life]. My mother for example was very sociable, she always said 'Let's do …' whatever and he always repressed that in her. … 'Where do you want to go, haven't you had enough'? And everything in terms of social life that she had, he always nipped it in the bud, *always*. With sanctions, with beatings, or other things, he didn't talk to her anymore, or he threw her food out or so. He was *very* malicious with her.

While Pınar and her sisters had to mediate between the parents, they did not identify with their mother either. Pınar describes her behaviour as 'being subservient to the stronger one and kicking those below'. Delineating themselves from the mother, Pınar and her sisters defied the violence to build independent lives. They oriented themselves towards the outside world, which they identified as German and split off from their experiences of home, which they saw as representing Turkishness.

P: Everything that was going on at home was the roots, but [we] rejected it. That was also the phase when we forgot how to speak Turkish.

U: Yes.

P: Although before that time we spoke Turkish very fluently … But then we only responded in very short sentences and sometimes in German. Always when my mother nagged, we said 'Yes, it's alright'. Or when the father said something 'Yes, daddy'. …

Language use is an important way in which resistances can be conveyed. By using a language that was beyond the full grasp of her parents, Pınar and her siblings shifted outside the field of their control. Moreover, the use of language is crucial for creating a sense of self. Thus, using German also implied constructing a self independent of and in opposition to the parents' projections. Despite her parents' prohibitions and punishments, including beatings, Pınar continued to attend Realschule. Moreover by lying to them about her school schedule, she managed to do many other activities outside school.

### 'We can't keep her from doing what she wants'

When Pınar's older sister left home against the parents wishes without marrying, this was a turning point for Pınar. She began to realize that despite his violence, the father's authority had its limits. This realization and her excellent marks at Realschule reinforced her determination to attend high school to qualify for higher education against the parental wishes.

P: And I was somehow always waiting and looking for a moment at which he would be at his most peaceful. And then I stood before him, because I couldn't hold back anymore and just shouted it out 'I'll go to Aufbaugymnasium,[8] there and there' and then I went straight to my room.

U: Yes.

P: Of course, he went straight after me and shouted and nagged. And the whole thing escalated so that he beat me very heavily.

U: Hmm.

P: Because he said 'First you start doing your own thing, making your own decisions, then you start smoking, then you start drinking and then you go prostitute yourselves'.

U: Hmm, yes.

P: And um, I think there was nothing that could humiliate me as much as this 'whore', you know. Everything that girls did that was unrelated to sex is being described in this way, anyway. And I don't know, I let it happen because I was programmed to expect that it is going to happen anyway, you know.

U: Hmm, yes.

P: And at one point you lose any relation to your body. You know it's going to happen, and at one point he will cool down, um, but I notice it to this day, emotionally.

This clearly expresses how her father linked any form of female autonomy to sexuality. She also expresses her mechanisms of dealing with the violence: she had accepted the beating as a fact of life and begun to understand its mechanisms, thus making it more predictable. The disengagement from her as a reaction to domestic violence is described again when Pınar returns from her first day at the new school, after escaping from home despite being locked in and guarded by her mother.

P: I got home with the attitude I'll get a beating. (sighs) And then it happened. And then I went to my room – I don't know, it was so schizophrenic the way I dealt with it, you know. I could leave it behind *immediately* and continue with what I was doing.

---

8  Aufbaugymnasium is a special school for Realschul-graduates to do their A-levels.

U: Hmm.

P: I started preparing files and notebooks for school, etc.

The word schizophrenic captures the coping mechanism of splitting off the corporeal experience of victimization. The splitting off of the victimized self at least partially allowed Pınar at the time to maintain an independent construction of self. As Walkerdine points out, 'routine humiliation, exploitation and oppression produce circumstances which themselves can be met with complex defences, defences which may indeed be crucial to survival' (1997: 41). A universalized discourse on psychological development which views splitting as pathological, she argues is not tenable since it does not pay attention to splitting as a sometimes necessary survival strategy. Instead of pathologizing the reaction of splitting, therefore it should be contextualized with 'the conditions of survival and oppression' (1997: 37).

Post-structuralist theories of identity often invoke a notion of the self as fragmented and multiple. This contains liberatory aspects in that it reveals the regulatory discipline involved in constructing a life-story free of contradictions. Such a notion of self as fragmented can moreover de-centre the normalization of dominantly gendered and ethnicized subjectivities by revealing the narrative effort in the construction of their wholeness. However, a hailing of the self as fragmented risks obscuring the traumatic aspects of fracturing the self as experienced in violent transgressions of corporeal boundaries. Such experiences make the narrative construction of a coherent self more difficult for victims of domestic violence. The industry of self-help guides, and other public sources such as consciousness raising groups, counselling, politicized identities as survivors of domestic violence, offer frameworks for enabling the telling of a life-story as whole. Elsewhere in the interview Pınar refers to consciousness raising groups of women of colour that enabled her to collectively make sense of her experiences of domestic violence. She views this retrospective process as central in allowing her to speak about these experiences, also in the interview situation (cf. Chapter 6). At the time however the splitting off of the domestic violence reinforced a notion of her self as dichotomized in gendered ethnicized terms.

Despite the parents' opposition and subsequent punishments Pınar enjoyed Gymnasium, she felt proud of her academic achievements. Moreover being at Gymnasium enabled her to elaborate an identity as an intellectual. This identification was opposed to the stigmatizations and victimizations she was subjected to in her family. The two worlds of family and school to her thus held very different identificatory moments. Ethnicity was one aspect of this dichotomy and she conflated her family with Turkishness, and rejected any identification or relation with this:

P: I remember, I felt so great, when we had a free period and I was at a café with my friends, discussing. For me that was … I used to discuss passionately. I felt so … I don't know, I felt so intellectual at the time, you know.

U: Hmm.

P: And at the time it really was the case that I had nearly only German friends. And somehow I wasn't prepared to get involved with Turkish people, because I always thought it was this narrow world.

This dichotomy of Germanness and Turkishness as holding very different subject positions for her was reified by Pınar's fear that if she told her German friends and teachers about her problems with her family 'it would be bad for my image'. Pınar here refers to the widespread discourse of the 'Other Other' that portrays women of Turkish background as objects of either Turkish male violence and oppression or of patronizing German 'emancipation'. Neither subject position holds space for her construction of an independent, passionate intellectual. By withholding her experiences of domestic violence, Pınar took control over the image she projected of herself to her friends and teachers at school.

When in her second year at the school, Pınar decided to share her experiences at home to some extent with her friends and with a school employee, she focuses on the consequence, that she was given the opportunity to use the school as an excuse to gain more free time from her parents. This shows how she resolved the tension between a split and contradictory experience of self as both victimized and agentic. The element that holds together the story of her contradictory experiences is her emphasis on her resourcefulness, even in sharing experiences of victimization. The tension between a fragmented notion of self and the incitement to construct a coherent self that better fits the demands of a biography to live by is partially resolved by Pınar through centring her agency in the life-story. Thus, she points to the fear of a mis-recognition by her German school friends and teachers, to explain her reluctance to share her experiences with them.

*Beginning to get recognition from the parents*
With time, her parents grew to grudgingly accept Pınar's schooling. One reason was that they gained approval and respect for Pınar's achievements by neighbours and acquaintances. Another factor that reconciled the parents was that Pınar compromised with them and attended a Turkish school run by the consulate. Moreover, Pınar had made friends with some schoolmates of Turkish and Kurdish background. For Pınar, these girls were 'totally different, and their families were different, too'. The parents of one of her friends were divorced and had entered new relationships, they gave her a lot of freedom. Another friend was Kurdish and her parents were left wing activists, who had fled Turkey after the coup d'etat in 1980. Pınar's parents allowed her to visit these friends. Making friends with these girls from Turkey gave Pınar access to versions of Turkishness and Kurdishness

which she was curious about and with which she identified more. Her friends were active in Turkish political organizations, and Pınar developed an interest in them, too. She spent a lot of time studying for her A-levels, either at home or with her friends of Turkish background, where she sometimes stayed for two or three days. She says she had 'arranged herself' with the situation.

> P: And then I think I broke through the whole thing. Beating did not always work –sometimes I would let myself be beaten in advance, and then went on to do what I wanted, you know.

> U: Hmm. Hmm.

> P: Somehow this is a totally crazy game one lets oneself in for. And then I started simply not to come home. I went off, I knew they couldn't do more than beat me. For two days I did what I wanted, came home, it happened, I was beaten but I had also started defending myself, you know. That I would push, or that I pushed my mother or took something out of her hand and threw it away, or broke things.

> U: Hmm.

> P: Hmm, well, and then it came to the point when they didn't dare beating me at all. I said 'if you beat me again I'll leave'. And that was … that was the weapon number one, you know, that I had discovered. That was [their] greatest fear. All those years I never guessed that. To loose face in front of the Turkish community (…). It was possible to blackmail them with this. And although I always said to them I will never allow you to loose face, there were nevertheless moments when I said 'I'll leave'.

In this extract, it does not appear as if Pınar simply 'arranged herself' with her parents' restrictions. On the contrary, it seems she combined appeasement, negotiation and open resistance. Pınar used the cultural values of her parents, such as the shame related to a young woman leaving the family home and laying herself and the family open to reproaches of having failed the respectability expected of her. Pınar's growing awareness of her parents' vulnerabilities *vis-à-vis* a wider Turkish social environment enabled her to realize her own power in relation to them. When she describes her threat of leaving home as 'blackmail', it is important to keep in mind that loosing face in such a situation would of course primarily refer to Pınar. While gaining awareness of her own power was important, through her friends' support she increasingly gained the means to actually stay away from the family home for some time.

When Pınar graduated as the best of her year, her mother's attitude towards her education changed. She regretted having stood in the way of her daughter's education and supported her against the initial resistance of the father to pursue higher education.

In contrast to Canan's life-story, for Pınar the main site of developing agency was the struggle against her family in order to access education. While the topics of conflict around sexuality and freedom of movement are common to many second generation migrant women's life-stories, Pınar's experience of sustained domestic violence made this conflict particularly salient. As opposed to other parents, who encouraged education while maintaining control over the girls' freedom of movement, Pınar had to fight for access to education. This reinforced her splitting off the spheres of home and school. She identified the school as her 'real home' where she had a certain degree of control over her self-representation and gained recognition through her academic achievements that she was denied from the parents. The gendered and ethnicized dichotomization of these spheres led her to reject Turkishness and to refuse to speak Turkish for some time.[9] The contradiction between Pınar's favoured self-presentation as an independent intellectual and her victimization through domestic violence as well as the associated feelings of shame and the fear of being patronized made it difficult for Pınar to reconcile the spheres of education and home. In her life-story, she emphasizes the aspect of her resourcefulness and agency in circumventing parental control and restrictions. Only by accessing alternative versions of Turkishness and Kurdishness through her friends could she resolve the ethnicization of the dichotomy between home and school. The social validation and recognition of her academic achievements finally brought her parents around to accepting her wish for education.

### The First Generation: Formal and Informal Education in the Tension of Work and Schooling

At first glance it is striking that among the first generation migrant interviewees the theme of schooling is most often treated very briefly. Rosenthal (1995) suggests that the lived experience underlying life-story narratives makes certain experiences more difficult to narrativize in a life-story. Among the criteria she gives for the tellability (Erzählbarkeit) of life-stories, two are particularly relevant for explaining why the first generation interviewees do not elaborate on their schooling. One of the preconditions for giving Gestalt to lived experience through narrativizing it in a life-story is a 'biographical need to tell' (1995: 99, my translation from German). The second, possibly more relevant precondition is a certain scope in decision making and agency, as well as changes in time and space. For the first generation

---

9    This is something I commonly found in other second generation interviewees' life-stories. The dichotomization of Turkishness and Germanness could only be resolved by accessing alternative concepts of Turkish femininity and thus putting the parental notions into perspective.

respondents, their schooling seems to fit into a pattern of 'normality' and thus is not deemed worthy of elaboration:

Biographical thematization is 'not provoked by a self understood normality of the life-course but through experiences of contingency – by events and acts that call for departmentalizing, digesting, normalizing' (Kohli in Rosenthal 1995: 108–9, my translation from German).

Yet, one story on education stands out among the first generation migrants. The significance of education in Selin's life-story is through its absence. Although the context of Selin's upbringing is very different from that of the second generation migrants, there are parallels, in that family needs took precedence over Selin's wish for education (cf. Basit 1997, Tett 2000). Moreover, Selin's educational trajectory reveals the articulation of gender, ethnicity and education in the Turkish context for a Kurdish woman. While her life-story, as the others, is not meant to be representative, it points to the differentiating category of ethnicity within Turkey and its articulations in the context of international migration.

### Selin: Challenging Education as a Marker of Distinction

Selin is a 36 year old entrepreneur in London. She is Kurdish, and migrated to Britain as a refugee in 1989. She is the fourth of six children of a well-off farmer's family, in a Kurdish village in southern Turkey. The quest for respect and recognition of the stigmatized and marginalized identities such as her Kurdishness, Alevi religious background and her feminist commitment are a key theme in her life-story. This quest has led her to develop herself and look for community against hierarchical structures that she eloquently critiques. Reflecting on her positioning within power relations in diverse places and spaces and re-evaluating commonalties and differences along various axes of power relations structures her narrative. She presents herself as multiply discriminated and victimized, but maintaining her agency through being 'continuously involved in struggles' against this victimization.

### Struggles for Education

Selin was a very successful student at primary school and very much wanted to continue her education, however there was no middle school in the village. So she was sent to stay with her older sister with the promise that she would attend school there. However, it turned out that both her sister and her husband worked outside the home and Selin, at the age of eleven was expected to look after the new born baby.

> S: And I stayed with them for six years. They had fetched me to send me to school but for six years they didn't send me to school.

> U: Hmm.

S: Of course, as I grew older, that is as I grew more conscious of myself, you know I always watched the children when they went to school in the big city. I got very sad 'send me [to school] too, send me too!' They didn't send me. I knew their situation – that they couldn't send me and so on. Telling me that they would send me to school was just an excuse to take me with them to the town. And then I resisted a lot. I started to fight with those at home, when I went to the village – 'send me to school'.

U: Hmm.

S: 'If you don't send me to school, I won't look after my sister's children' and so on I said.

U: Hmm.

S: Well, this fight took a long time. Even in my childhood I had this struggle. I used to say to my mother and father 'if you want, you can kill me. I won't go to my sister's house. Because if they don't send me to school I won't stay with them'.

In this instance, Selin's unpaid labour was used as a familial resource that did not however benefit Selin. This is a case in point to challenge a unified notion of the household that disregards the unequal, gender and age hierarchical use and access to resources[10] (Kofman et al.2000: 27). 'The household (…) has its own political economy, in which access to power and other valued resources is distributed along gender and generational lines' (Hondagneu-Sotelo quoted in Kofman et al.2001: 27). Like Pınar, Selin threatens her family with disregarding even violence, claiming that even if her father tried to kill her she would struggle for education.

---

10    Actually, the unequal control over labour power within the family may become clearer, if we compare this unpaid domestic work with the phenomenon of evlatlik (fictive adoption). Özbay (2000) researched domestic work in Turkey, in particular the institution of evlatlık – domestic servants which were taken on as young children and treated like members of a household. She conceptualizes their role as 'mixtures of slaves, servants and adopted daughters in terms of their position in urban middle class households' (2000:3). She emphasizes that their position as 'non-kin members of the household' need not mean they were treated well, but instead reflects that 'maltreatment may well exist among the family members as well' (2000: 3). Thus, I would argue that the use of Selin's domestic work can be compared to that of domestic workers. Of course, the crucial difference being that her sister and brother-in-law's household was not middle class. However, the commonality is that (fictive or not) kinship served as a legitimation of the unpaid domestic work. While there are certainly aspects of reciprocity in the relationship, this should not distract from the exploitative and unequal control of resources. Yurtdaş (1995) also mentions a case, where the promise of education was used to persuade a girl to agree to become an evlatlik. This promise was not realized, however.

This alerts us to the desperation of her situation and to the very limited scope of agency that left nothing but her own physical integrity as a bargaining tool. Finally, the family consented to send Selin to school, however this time they were unable to overcome the bureaucratic obstacles. Selin sees this as a consequence of structural and interpersonal racism and argues that as a Kurdish student one needs a sponsor within the institution:

S: First of all it is a problem to get permission from the family to go to school.

U: Yes.

S: Second, to be enrolled at school is another problem.

U: Really?

S: Of course, they don't just take you in at school. You need to know someone, and then they take you. That's the way it is.

U: Hmm.

S : I continuously – not being Turkish […], that identity was always with me anyway. For that reason, wherever you go, you must definitely find someone [a sponsor, U.E.] for them to accept you. Of course that influences a person's development, prevents it.

A number of structural factors influenced Selin's educational trajectory: the unavailability of secondary education in the village is a consequence of uneven development between rural and urban areas in Turkey. This is compounded by racist state policy towards Kurdish areas and villages that have been characterized as forms of 'internal colonialism' (Wedel 2000: 111). This underdevelopment (e.g. inadequate services such as road building, electricity, provision of health centres or schools, etc) combines with nationalist ideologies and practices of female education: The Kemalist ideal of the educated, Western-oriented woman as the ideological reproducer of the nation constructs Kurdish women as particularly backward.[11] To Kurdish people, education and access to the public sphere at once hold the threat of racism and assimilation as well as opportunities for social mobility and political intervention. This is articulated in nationalist terms by both the Turkish state and Kurdish nationalist movements, who particularly target Kurdish women in their symbolic role as reproducers of the national collectivity:

---

11 This can even mobilize Turkish women's identification with a civilizing mission to educate girls in the Kurdish areas, which are depicted as backward particularly in their gender relations (ibid.).

either to assimilate them into Turkishness through 'civilizatory' national education, or through hailing them as the true bearers of the Kurdish national culture to be protected and thus reify their exclusion from the Turkish dominated public sphere. In Selin's life-story, this nationalized conflict around female education is implicit. Therefore, Selin's education took place informally through working in different contexts: she worked for her sister as an unpaid childminder in the city and then re-migrated to the village when she was 17.

### Deconstructing educational power

Selin put up a rigorous struggle to access formal education as a young girl. Retrospectively however, she points out the contingency of formal education as a privilege on the basis of gender, class, ethnicity and the rural-urban divide. Having been excluded from this privilege, she continues to feel the consequences. For example she still finds it difficult to concentrate on reading long texts, such as books, which evokes a feeling of inadequacy. However, she goes further than recognizing the racism and sexism inherent in differential access to education by critically examining the value of the written word, and educational qualifications as powerful tools for reproducing hierarchies. Thus, referring to her experiences in Britain in the Turkish dominated women's movement, where she feels she has been patronized and discriminated against because of her lack of formal education (cf. Chapter 6) she states:

> S: They were always putting other women down because of their [lack of] education … But this is not education or anything: to attend schools within this system is not education, really.

> U: Mmm (smiles).

> Selin: (emphatically) I mean it seriously, a person can develop themselves through reading – of course through reading. But if I went to such and such school of Kemal Atatürk in Turkey under such and such circumstances I studied at university and was educated after Atatürk's principles … I don't call that education or anything. I don't even consider them having graduated from university.

> U: Mmm, mmm.

> S: I don't even want to go to that university, why should I go to this Kemalist, to study at Kemal's school?

> U: Mmm.

> Selin: I didn't used to feel that way, I wanted to go and study. But once I know how to read and write, I can read for myself. I will study at life's school, learning with people, I can study through living.

On the one hand Selin here critiques the nationalist character of the Kemalist education system: Thus, statues of Mustafa Kemal (Atatürk), the founder of the Turkish Republic, in schoolyards underwritten with the words 'Happy those who call themselves Turks' have been attacked by Kurdish schoolchildren. The nationalist character of the curriculum as well as regular rituals such as the daily singing of the national anthem, the importance of the flag and many more performances of 'banal nationalism' (Billig 1995) can be seen as supporting Selin's argument.[12] The Turkish supremacist character of the education system and materials has also been critiqued by the teachers' union. Moreover, she critiques the use of education as a distinguishing marker of ethnicity and class. She analyses her experience of being labelled and disqualified as an 'uneducated' woman by Turkish feminists as a form of indirect racism,[13] as Kurdish women are disproportionately excluded from education. Although she values education and reading as a tool for 'developing oneself', she does not see 'book learning' as privileged knowledge. Examining the experiences of African American women, Hill Collins[14] argues that they value 'wisdom', concrete knowledge enabling their survival, before 'booklearning'. Booklearning, she argues rather than helping to solve everyday problems and conflicts tends to cover them up, avoiding viable solutions (cf. Tett 2000). Other elements of Hill Collins' theory that resonate with

---

12    Other interviewees, both first and second generation migrants who had part of their schooling in Turkey, also criticize the nationalist character of the Turkish school system. The daily oath may serve as an example here:
'I am Turkish/ I am honest/ I am hardworking/ my principle/ to protect the younger ones/ to respect the elder/ to love my country, my nation/ more than my self./ My ideal/ to rise, to progress/ my existence/ shall be dedicated to the existence of the Turkish nation./ Oh great Atatürk/ who has created our life of today/ I swear/ to continue incessantly/ on this path that you have paved/ according to the ideals that you have created/ following the aims that you have set./ Happy those who can say "I am a Turk"!' (quoted in Kurt 1989: 268, my translation from Turkish)

13    I term actions, structures and discourses racist, if their outcome excludes or subordinates people on the basis of racialization, even if the intention is not racist (cf. Anthias and Yuval-Davis (1992), Kalpaka and Räthzel (1990).

14    Hill-Collins' concept of Black feminist thought is related to other, feminist and Afro-Centric epistemologies. Although developed in a specific historical and national context, it contains elements that can be used in other context when developing and evaluating knowledges. Hill-Collins' emphasis is on the positionality of knowledge and its empowering or disempowering potentials. Her notion of partial knowledges which need to be enhanced through dialogue and exchange with people whose experiences and knowledges give another perspective on interlocking systems of oppression. Therefore, I think it is justified to transpose her epistemological theory to this context.

Selin's critique are the importance of dialogue in validating knowledge and the relevance of an ethics of care that 'suggests that personal expressiveness, emotions and empathy are central to the knowledge validation process' (Collins 1993: 215). This is particularly salient to Selin's anger at her exclusion from education and the subsequent devaluation of her informal learning. So, rather than viewing her anger as distorting her judgement, these emotions can be seen as motivating her critical perspective (cf. Chapter 6).

**Conclusion**

The migrant women's life-stories presented here elaborate how they position themselves as subjects with agency. Already at an early age they resisted open and indirect forms of racism, challenged teachers' low expectations and negotiated the right to enter higher level schooling. As most parents did not have an understanding of the school system, these girls often accomplished this by themselves with moral but little practical parental support – in Pınar's case despite her parents. For the second generation of migrant women, an important discourse *vis-à-vis* which they had to position themselves was that of the clash of gendered and ethnicized familial culture and school culture. Many did indeed experience tensions between their families' and the teachers and fellow students' expectations regarding appropriate ethnicized gendered behaviour. These girls were furthermore positioned as 'exceptional' in that they were academically successful and attended higher level schools. Yet, they negotiated the meanings of 'exceptionality' and the identities ascribed them to accommodate themselves as subjects with agency. Selin's story of being denied access to education through her family but also structurally as a girl in a rural setting who is part of an ethnic group experiencing racist exclusions, shows the intersections of gendered and ethnic power relations. It also illuminates the interrelationship between familial and social power relations. While Selin was able to wrench the promise to go to school from her family, she could not overcome the obstacle of racist school admission policy and rural-urban differences.

An important form of agency that Selin and the second generation migrants in Germany have in common was their refusal of a subjecting gaze: Canan challenged the ascription of being the 'little Turkish girl', Pınar 'controls' her image by disclosing only partially her experiences at home and Selin challenges the value of formal 'Kemalist' education. Her validation of wisdom gained through life experiences not only allows her a positive self identification but also challenges the use of education as a marker of gendered, ethnicized and classed hierarchy. Canan's strategy of revalidating her 'Turkish' female identity as assertive and powerful reverts its devaluation. These ways of telling their life-stories against the grain do not simply show narrative agency, but it is argued that the ways the migrant women tell their selves are at once enabling moments that helped them negotiate and overcome their experiences of victimization. Thus, Pınar managed to survive the racism in her early years of schooling and eventually re-defined the school as the place where she could be her 'real' self as opposed to the domestic violence she experienced at home. This chapter discussed in-depth the ways in which migrant women developed agency, countering Orientalist representations of themselves as passively enduring victimization that have been discussed in Chapters 1 and 2. This sets the ground for the wider theme of this book, that is, how migrant women transform practices of citizenship. The struggles around formal education, its gendered, classed and racialized aspects which formed the focus of this chapter are important in understanding how, through contesting their positioning as 'exceptional', the migrant women claim belonging and recognition of aspects of their identity which cannot be easily reconciled with Orientalist representations, such as being independent, sexually autonomous, academically or professionally successful young women. Yet, formal education and qualifications are not enough to explain the experiences of migrant women's incorporation into the society of residence. The role of informal cultural capital and how this is validated in the society of residence by mainstream institutions as well as within the ethnic minority community are also crucial in understanding the occupational trajectories of migrant women as the following chapter will discuss.

# Chapter 4
# Women at Work

The previous chapter discussed how migrant women established themselves as subjects with agency in the setting of education, thereby challenging preconceptions of women from Turkey as less skilled. This chapter discusses in more depth how they realize their skills in the site of paid work. While the chapter problematizes some aspects of the relation between paid and unpaid reproductive work, for the sake of clarity the main discussion of unpaid work can be found in Chapter 5, which focuses on mothering. Paid work is important for an understanding of how migrant women transform citizenship in two ways: on one hand, paid work often is key in enabling migrant women access to social citizenship rights, including the right to stay or to bring over family members (cf. Chapter 5). On the other hand, migrant women's access to skilled work is also conditional on the degree of their legal inclusion through migration and labour market regulation. While such regulations tend to limit, or at the very least regulate, their ability to realize their skills, they also find ways of overcoming the non-recognition of their skills. One way is by transforming the social construction of what is valued as cultural capital giving access to skilled employment, another way is by challenging the legal and institutional racism that limits their access to skilled employment.

It is argued that social and cultural capital on the one hand, and institutional structures, such as immigration legislation and (mis-)recognition of professional qualifications in the countries of immigration on the other hand form the restrictive and enabling framework for the women's professional development. An important aspect are the issues of skilling, de-skilling and re-skilling. The literature on migration has for a long time neglected the category of skilled migrants. Only since the 1980s has a new interest in skilled and professional migration emerged in migration studies. Despite the findings of a wide range of typologies of skilled migrants, much of the research has focused on those working for transnational companies (Kofman 2000, Favell et al. 2006). Additionally, the literature on globalization, transnationality and to some extent that on diaspora has looked at skilled migrants, often casting them as a new type of migrant, intrinsically different from the presumably unskilled post-colonial or guest-worker labour migrant. Here, this chapter challenges such a clear cut distinction between the 'global' professional, taken to be emblematic of an unproblematic transnational community on the one hand, and its juxtaposition with the 'ethnic' unskilled worker who is either rooted in her culture of origin or uprooted from it and unable to deal with diversity on the other. It is argued that gender and ethnicity articulate the professional developments of migrant women, albeit differentiated according to immigration status, formal and informal qualifications and class positioning.

Therefore, three interrelated aspects of working life are examined: institutional and interpersonal gendered racisms at work, (non-) recognition of skills and the role that migration specific social and cultural capital play for migratory and occupational trajectories. Instances of these can be found in all life-stories in varying forms and degrees. For the sake of clarity, these issues are discussed by focusing on one of these aspects in each life-story.

## Paid Work and Citizenship

Paid work is an important aspect of citizenship since participation in the labour market is a central factor in attaining social rights (Faist 1995). This is particularly relevant for migrants since in many cases their residence status or ability to initiate family migration is contingent on their ability to support themselves financially without recourse to the state. However, unrestricted access to paid work is a privilege of citizens so that immigration legislation controls migrants' access to the labour market in general, and to specific professions. Moreover, informal mechanisms contribute to the hierarchical organization and gender and ethnic segregation of the labour market. One of the most important obstacles to migrants realizing their skills is the non-recognition of their qualifications through state and professional bodies (Krahn et al. 2000). Coupled with legal obstacles through immigration legislation, this makes it difficult for migrants to access skilled employment. Recent research on refugee employment in the UK also confirms the importance of a lack of recognition of skills (Bloch 2002, 2004, Dumper 2002). The current debates on the recruitment of skilled migrants do not pay attention to the experiences of previous flows of migrants. Instead, they suggest that skilled migrants will encounter inherently different conditions, or that they constitute an inherently different group of migrants that will be more useful and more easily integrated (cf. Kofman 2007: 244). Indeed, the new Path to Citizenship (Home Office 2008) proposed by the UK government suggests allowing a transition to citizenship status for skilled migrants while unskilled migrants are relegated to a temporary status.

While the women whose life-stories are discussed here have of course migrated in earlier periods under different conditions, it seems useful to consider the experiences of previous migrants, examining the obstacles to the recognition of skills and the mechanisms of de-skilling.

## The Social Construction of Skill

The regulation of occupational and professional skills not only establishes a standard of service delivery, but also constitutes a mechanism of social closure and occupational protectionism. Based on a case study of medical occupations, Witz urges scholars to give up a 'generic concept of profession' as this obscures the gendered processes underlying the concept: 'It takes the successful professional projects of class-privileged, male actors at a particular point in history to be the paradigmatic case of profession' (Witz 1992: 64). Instead she suggests studying concrete 'professional projects', i.e. projects of occupational groups to achieve professional closure through credentialist and/or legalist tactics. This seems a useful approach for dealing with the diversity of occupations in this study as it questions reified boundaries of professionality. Migrant women, in particular if they are third country nationals, do not have an adequate representation in the public sphere and have limited means of realizing their individual occupational projects. Thus, the stories told here are often those of limiting the negative effects of de-skilling and continuously struggling for recognition of their qualifications and skills.

In Germany, vocational and professional training are highly regulated (cf. Faist 1995) and non-recognition of qualifications acquired abroad is common (cf. Nohl et al. 2006). In some professions, such as medical doctors, even if the qualification is recognized, a specific 'professional permit' is required of migrants. Moreover, the self-employment is not a right but dependent on the local labour market conditions for migrants with temporary residence permits. Labour market legislation privileges first Germans, then EU citizens have to be given priority over third country nationals with job vacancies. In Britain, vocational and professional training are less formalized and 'on the job training' is more common. With respect to the migrant women in this study, the most important obstacles in the initial phase of working in Britain were their irregular residence status and lack of UK work experience. Another important obstacle was the overseas student status, which means that only after three years of being a regular resident in Britain could they study and pay the same fees as home students, thus making re-skilling very costly both in terms of time and financially.

## Migration and Transnational Social and Cultural Capital

Debates on the social mobility of migrants, individually or collectively often rely implicitly or explicitly on notions of cultural and social capital. Thus explanatory frameworks that rely on the culture of migrants to explain how well they adapt to living in the country of migration explain educational or economic success or failure of migrants with recourse to the appropriateness of their cultural capital to the society of residence. These culturalist[1] arguments are often invoked to 'blame the victim' for their economic or educational failure, and avoid examining the structures of the society of residence (Vermeulen 2000).

---

1   By 'culturalist' I mean approaches that foreground the supposed culture of the migrants' country of origin as an explanatory variable for how well they fare in the adaptation process.

Schiller et al. (1992) usefully propose viewing migrants as participants in two societies, within a globalizing system. They attempt to redress nationally bounded approaches, as well as the economistic focus of world systems theory, instead focusing on migrants' social relationships and positioning as 'fluid and dynamic' (1992: 8): 'A transnational perspective on ethnicity must be developed that includes an examination of culture and agency within this expanded social field' (1992: 17). They argue that one of the ways in which migrants use these new spaces of agency is by translating 'the economic and social position gained in one political setting into political, social and economic capital in another' (1992: 12). However, they caution against cultural reductionism, arguing that culture and cultural capital are always negotiated in struggles over hegemony. In a system of nation-states, these forms of cultural capital always risk being appropriated into nationalized versions of culture. Here, the focus is not on transnational aspects of *forming* cultural capital, but on the intra-group processes of *distinction within* the country of migration. These intra-group processes, it is argued, are important to understand the differential validation of particular cultural practices and resources and their mobilization into capital.

In contrast to Schiller et al.'s (1992) suggestion, not all theories of transnationalism or diaspora pay enough attention to the contested and dynamic character of cultural capital. Instead, ethnicity is often reified as the determining basis for social solidarity, without taking intra-ethnic divisions and differentiated cultural capital into account (cf. Anthias 1998, 2007). Thus, with reference to diasporas, Cohen argues that '(t)he combination of cosmopolitanism and ethnic collectivism is an important constituent in successful business ventures' (1997: 171). Faist's (1998) proposition that migrants make use of transnational networks of reciprocity and patterns of social exchange puts particular emphasis on kinship and family as resources that can be mobilized for economic benefit. In a similar vein Nee and Sanders (2001) suggest that the family should be the unit of analysis as it is key in constituting migrants' human-cultural capital, which they see as key in explaining economic incorporation. Both of these approaches take the male migration experiences as normative. They ignore women as actors in their own right, viewing them as resources either for the family or the ethnic group. Firstly, this results in ignoring the migration experiences of single women or those whose lifestyles challenge heteronormative gender roles (cf. Chapter 5). But, more generally these approaches do not pay sufficient attention to the internal hierarchies and power relations within ethnic groups.

I additionally problematize a notion of 'human-cultural capital that is fungible in the host society' (Nee and Sanders 2001: 386) as a heuristic device,[2] by drawing

---

2   Werbner (2000) also critiques such a notion, arguing that cultural capital takes on different culturally and context specific meanings. An ethnocentric use of the concept does not sufficiently take the value systems of the migrants themselves into account and therefore produces and reifies an ethnocentric notion of success. Moreover, assuming that there is a neutral and objective type of cultural capital fungible in the host society conceals both open

attention to the processes by which particular actors seek to validate particular versions of ethnically specific cultural practices as migration specific cultural capital and seek to further gain recognition within the society of residence for these.

In the following I examine how processes of migration and the constitution of cultural capital work for women as social actors, rather than viewing them as constituting the social capital to be used as a resource. The focus is on how different actors within the migrant group constitute versions of ethnically specific cultural capital. This underlines that ethnically specific social capital cannot be viewed as a unitary category, but instead includes unequal control and denial of resources as well as solidarity.

## Towards a Bourdieu'an Framework for a Gender-nuanced Analysis of Multi-ethnic Transnational Societies

Most migration scholars employ human capital models of cultural and social capital or do not indeed situate the models of capital they use, often implicitly relying on the widely circulated concepts of Putnam or Coleman. I would like to suggest that a Bourdieu'an notion of social and cultural capital, which leads to quite a distinct understanding of power relations, is useful for furthering our understanding of migrant women's geographical and social trajectories. In the wider social sciences, an interest in Bourdieu's ideas has been revived. Thus, his ideas of capital have been suggested as a fruitful way of taking account of the role of capital, asset and resources in the study of social stratification (Savage et al. 2005). Furthermore, feminists have critically explored uses of Bourdieu's ideas for understanding gender (e.g. Adkins and Skeggs 2004, Silva 2005 and 2008) and Yosso (2005) has critically assessed the potential of Bourdieu'an theorizing for re-validating the cultural capital of people of colour in the US. I am particularly interested in looking at *how* gender, ethnicity and class intersect in positioning migrant women vis-á-vis cultural practices in migration. As many feminists have stated, cultural capital theories tend to insufficiently engage with women as subjects producing and using cultural capital, Lovell (2000: 22) suggests a need for exploring:

> What kinds of 'investment strategies' do women follow in what circumstances? How may the existence of women as objects – as repositories of capital for someone else – be curtailing or enabling in terms of their simultaneous existence as capital accumulating subjects? The answers to these questions must be relative to historical and cultural contexts, and to positions occupied within 'the social field'.

---

and subtle mechanisms of legal, institutional and informal de-valuation of migrants' skills and qualifications (cf. Kofman et al. 2001).

Here, the discussion critically engages with Bourdieu's (1986, 1997) framework of cultural and social capital. Taking individual women rather than a preconceived group as the unit of analysis[3] enables me to examine in detail the transformative and processual nature of cultural and social capital. Moreover, I will show how women migrants, who at times have transgressed gendered norms, do not fit into *a priori* notions of cultural capital but rather have participated in creating new categories of validation.

Cultural capital, according to Bourdieu appears in three states: embodied, institutionalized and objectified, of which only the former two are of interest here. In the embodied state 'cultivation, *Bildung*' is incorporated. The notion of embodiment is maybe best expressed in the concept of habitus, which includes a way of bodily comportment and speaking as markers of distinction. This implies an investment of time and 'work on oneself (self-improvement), an effort that presupposes a personal cost' (1986: 244). Cultural capital includes both formal education but perhaps more importantly informal education transmitted through the family, in which sense it has a quality of inheritance. Other sources of cultural capital can be political parties, social movements, cultural groups, etc.

> Because the social conditions of its transmission and acquisition are more disguised than those of economic capital it is predisposed to (…) be unrecognized as capital and recognized as legitimate competence (…) (1986: 245).

This is particularly salient in the context of migration, where the migrant by virtue of her ethnicity is constructed as less competent over the nationalized cultural resources of the society of residence. In its institutionalized state, cultural capital consists of formal institutionalized qualifications which are 'formally independent of the person of their bearer' (1986: 248).

Social capital consists of a 'durable network of more or less institutionalized relationships of mutual acquaintance and recognition' (1986: 248). Social capital is not a given, but requires a constant effort of institution. This effort need not be consciously aimed at deriving benefits and includes affective elements such as friendship, gratitude, respect etc. In Bourdieu's argument, social and cultural capital can be converted into economic capital, e.g. through advantageous access to the labour market which is of concern here. Bourdieu's conception of different forms of capital critically engages with power relations and the constructedness of cultural and social capital. While Bourdieu's analysis of various fields in which forms of capital get activated opened up significant insights, he has paid less attention to ways in which these forms of capital are activated for resistant purposes. Here, I am concerned with these aspects, in particular how migrant women challenge

---

3    cf. Portes' 1998 critique of overstretching the application of social capital to groups or even nations. Also, Silva (2006) argues that qualitative methods reveal a complex picture of the formation and meaning of social and cultural practices as capital.

and transform existing classificatory systems of cultural validation, by articulating differential ways of doing gender, ethnicity and migrancy.

Although referring to gender and ethnic differences in passing, Bourdieu's model is based on a nationally closed cultural universe.[4] Yet, migration is located at the conjuncture of different class, social and especially nationally and ethnically bounded systems and their gendered articulations. Migrant women navigate[5] these boundaries and transgress them and this complicates the levels of analysis.[6] Moreover, migrant women are positioned not only *vis-à-vis* the national formation of their country of residence, but also *vis-à-vis* the different sections of the ethnic minority population and the country of origin. Rather than taking the status of certain cultural practices for granted, let us explore the meaning the women give them. Rather than classifying cultural and social practices, the aim is to show the processual, negotiated trajectory with an emphasis on movement within and across classifications.

I am particularly interested in drawing attention to the variety of social and cultural capital *within* a migrant group as it is differentiated according to gender, class, educational status and ethnic affiliation within this migrant group. These differentiations pertain not only to the resources available to individual migrants but also have an impact on the ways in which social and cultural capital can be mobilized (cf. Anthias 2007) and indeed which kinds of migration specific cultural capital are produced.

*Undocumented = Unskilled?*

The interplay between restrictive migration legislation and/or occupational closure mechanisms often lead to a de-skilling of migrants. If their skills and qualifications are not recognized, the labour market in the country of residence leads them to re-skill in different professions; that is the trajectory of Nâlan's migration. Nâlan comes from an educated middle class family in Istanbul. Her professional and educational aspirations in her youth were determined by two important factors in her life. The first is the early loss of both her parents, which traumatized her intensely so that her brothers, with whom she grew up, did not push her towards academic achievements. The second factor influencing her professional trajectory

---

4   The experiences of ethnic minorities are mentioned only with respect to their curtailment through a cultural, social and economic system that is organized in a national and class-hierarchical manner.

5   Indeed, Yosso (2005:80) argues that people of colour create a specific type of 'navigational capital' to find their way in racist institutional environments.

6   As Silva (2005) has pointed out, Bourdieu's static notions of gender and the family have not allowed him to take account of the increasing diversity of family forms and gendered articulations creating new types of normalcy. Silva calls for an exploration of the new forms of cultural capital that these new articulations of gender and household give rise to.

was her involvement in political groups, which meant that political activity was 'the most important thing' in her life at the time. This political involvement formed her own value system and Nâlan ruled out occupations she had previously considered attractive, such as acting, as 'a bourgeois thing'.

After graduating from high school, she enrolled in vocational courses in computing and afterwards immediately found employment, because she learned a skill that enabled her to work in an expanding professional area with little competition:

> N: At the time computers were very new. In Turkey there was only one [big international company]. (…) Of course it was very easy to find work at the time. You could get into any company that you applied for. Very few people had computing skills. At the time there were still these small cards. (…) It was probably around 1973.

Although she only had vocational qualifications, the specific conditions of supply and demand for her novel skills, her on-the-job training and increasing experience, provided her with job security and good working conditions.

Nâlan lived with her partner (cf. Chapter 5). As the main breadwinner, she went back to work straight after the birth of their child.

> N: I worked, of course [my husband's] parents looked after the child. 40 days after [the birth] I went back to work. For Turkish standards my work was very good. But despite this, women's rights were very bad. You had to go back to work after 40 days, there was no maternity leave. Or you had to quit work and I didn't want to do that. It was as if I was going to give up my independence.

Nâlan's independence, however, was also curtailed by the necessity to accept childcare from her in-laws, for whom this provided a lever for social control. During her husband's military service, Nâlan started getting involved with the new women's movement, which was the only progressive oppositional movement able to organize in the aftermath of the 1980 coup d'etat.

*De-skilling as an undocumented migrant*
When she divorced from her husband, Nâlan began to experience increasing social control through her brothers, and her freedom of movement was restricted (cf. Chapter 5). Moreover, she began worrying about the future of her childcare arrangement with her in-laws. Her activism in the women's movement, as well as contacts through her old political organization, gave her an opportunity to make connections with individuals in Britain. When a close friend of hers in Britain suggested that she should migrate, she left her son in the care of the in-laws and migrated. She saw the migration as an opportunity to escape the social control of her family, economic dependence on them, as well as the stigmatization of the status of divorcee. Despite the support of her friend, with whom she lived at first,

she experienced the initial period in Britain as very difficult. Especially her lack of knowledge of English made her very vulnerable.

While Nâlan wanted to learn English she was also compelled to earn money: Another friend of Turkish background, whom she had known through their political organization, took her by the hand, introducing her to a Turkish-owned textile factory, where she started working as a finisher.

> N: I started work the next morning at 8, looking forward to earning money and being able to find a flat of my own. But then I realized the bad working conditions – very unhealthy, the building was damp, no health and safety regulations were in place. We worked till ten at night, around four in the afternoon my feet began hurting very badly.

She worked in this factory for nearly a year. To her, the worst thing was the humiliating treatment of the workers. She gives an example of a relative of the owner also working in the factory:

> N: He was a real macho, always looking at the women from behind, at their behind and everything, disgusting. And I was working, putting something on the shoulders of the garments (…) I had the things in a box. He passed and dropped the box. He didn't even say sorry or anything, he didn't have any manners at all. And he told me to pick them up. I looked at him and at that moment I would have liked to hit him on the head. But I didn't have anywhere else to go, I depended on this job.

Her undocumented status, her lack of English proficiency and formal professional qualifications led to Nâlan's de-skilling. She felt caught in a vicious circle: the low pay necessitated long working hours, which, in turn, made it impossible for her to attend language classes. Her transnational social networks through her political organization and the women's movement were essential in supporting her migration project and in giving her access to ethnically specific job networks. These jobs in Turkish-owned textile factories did not necessitate knowing English or having residence and work permits. On the other hand, being dependent on the ethnic community's economic niche because of her lack of English and an undocumented immigration status, Nâlan could not realize her professional skills. The textile factory as an economic niche for migrant newcomers in Britain has a long tradition – Jewish immigrants occupied this niche at the beginning of the century, followed by different Asian communities, and more recently also migrants from Turkey. As Nâlan's and others' testimony show, the benefit of an ethnic economic niche is very ambiguous for the workers. Unsafe and unhealthy working conditions, little job security, working regulations or workers' organization are often the trade-offs for being able to work in an undocumented or semi-documented way (cf. Vasta 2004, Erdemir and Vasta 2007). Moreover, sexist harrassment is commonplace (cf. also Anthias 1992). This ethnic economic niche, either in the textile factories or in restaurants, has been a source of employment for many new migrants, especially if they are undocumented.

After a year her boyfriend from Turkey, also a computer specialist, joined her, experiencing the same problems. 'In the beginning you have only one choice and that is working in a factory, you cannot even work in a restaurant if you don't know English. Because you don't know the language it's very difficult.. Living with her boyfriend allowed her to share the expenses and enabled her to quit the factory.

> N: We had rented a flat together [...] and I started to go to school and worked in a café. At that time I didn't have problems with immigration, after three months I got a residence permit, at the time it was easier I guess. [...] When that happened I tried to bring my son over. I researched a bit and they told me you have to pay taxes, [...] that's why I went to work in a hotel, which was the easiest work to get. [...] I started to work as a chambermaid, to clean the rooms, change the bedding. I worked there for a year, then Ugur [her son] came. That was very hard work, also. For five years I was there, every day I changed the bedding, it was very hard work (...) they treated you very badly, not the workers, but the guests. Very, very weird things, in general at a five star hotel it was men on their own who came on business trips. They left pornographic pictures in the bed, you open the bed and you find these pornographic magazines. Because they're paying too much money.
>
> U: They think they've got the right to humiliate people.
>
> N: Humiliate the people ... Macho people.

The legislation for family reunification required Nâlan to move out of informal employment in the ethnic economy into taxed work. Since bringing her son over was Nâlan's highest priority, she accepted unskilled work that she could get as soon as possible.[7] This work in the lowest ranks of the hotel industry again made her vulnerable to sexual harassment.

*Going into social work*
When her son arrived, she had to change her work hours (and therefore jobs) several times, finally working in a restaurant, where she got more practice and confidence speaking English.

> N: Once I had more confidence in myself, I started looking for other work. I started working as a sessional [kindergarden worker]. I also thought it had the

---

7    Chapter 6 discusses the difficulties of separation of migrant mothers and their children, including the dilemmas of economically caring for the children while being unable to provide face to face care for their children, in depth.

advantage of having childcare included. I got the job through the job centre, and then went on to work at a girls' project. During that time I thought, while I am doing this work I might as well get a qualification.

U: Was it easy for you to get into that kind of work – that girls' project?

N: Well, to tell the truth, I told them a lie to get the job. I told them I had worked in a kindergarten in Turkey; a friend of mine in Turkey (…) wrote me a reference. Because actually working with children is not that difficult. (…) Of course I had also started to get involved in (…) political movements here. Asylum, work … I had started to work as a community activist. Well you learn some things in the political movement. I had learned a bit of jargon, I saw a lot of my friends [doing social work] (…) When I went for the job interview I had asked a friend of mine what they are likely to ask, how are they likely to put the questions, what kind of questions I should expect. She gave me a general idea – they'll ask this and this, you should answer like this.

Nâlan's improved English might have been instrumental in enabling her to look for other work. However it is also crucial that she was freed from the pressures of having to earn a steady income in order to make possible her son's immigration. Moreover, at the time she was living with her partner on whose financial resources she could fall back in case the sessional work did not meet her and her son's economic needs. This points to the difficulties of single mothers: as re-skilling always involves risk-taking, single mothers face particular difficulties if they cannot rely on state or family support, as is the case for many migrant women. The economic security of migrant single mothers in a gender and ethnically segregated labour market is very unstable. Being in a heterosexual relationship and being able to rely on her partner's income during this crucial period was important in giving her the economic security to re-skill.

*Social and cultural capital*
Nâlan was active in migrants' and refugee groups as well as in feminist movements. She was involved in organizing Turkish-speaking women in campaigns against violence against women. Thus, in Gramsci's sense she was an 'organic intellectual'[8] (1971: 9) articulating feminist ideas in the intersection of ethnicity and migration experiences, trying to hegemonize a feminist consciousness in the context of migrant women from Turkey in Britain. These activities were outside of her work life, but she was able to use the skills acquired through her activism for professionalizing. Her political networks and her activism provided her with the

---

8 The 'organic intellectual' according to Gramsci is defined with relation to her participatory and mobilizing capacity of a social group or movement. Gutierrez Rodriguez (1999) discusses the role of migrant women in Germany as 'organic intellectuals' in-depth.

social and cultural capital to succeed in the job interview: the 'jargon' that she had acquired in her community activism enabled her to understand and reciprocate the interviewers' communication. Her social networks with other activists involved in professional social work enabled her to gain an inside view on the formal and informal mechanisms of access and closure. Apart from informal mechanisms of closure, such as knowledge of jargon, self-presentation and social networks, the need for a reference can be seen as an instance of formal professional closure. Here, again, Nâlan's social capital acquired in Turkey enabled her to surmount this difficulty.

Nâlan enjoyed her new job, and after four years applied for a job in a project for girls of Turkish background. This raises another important issue of social and cultural capital. While migrant women's educational or professional qualifications are often not recognized, their linguistic and cultural competencies are beginning to be valued in social work contexts, thus creating a new, ethnicized and gendered professional niche. The problematic positioning of migrant women in social care working for an ethnic clientele has been pointed out by Lutz (1991): often, their qualifications get underestimated and only their linguistic competences are recognized. Moreover, they find themselves in the problematic position of mediator *vis-à-vis* the ethnic community they are supposed to represent: they are confronted with differential expectations on the basis of their group membership both by the institutions they work for and the clients.

As Nâlan gained experience of working with young people, her interest in social work grew, and she started a university course in social work. She also felt that in this way she could make up for not having had the opportunity to study in Turkey. She enjoys her work and sees it as politically and socially important. However, she also finds it emotionally demanding and realizes that a lot of overtime is required. At the moment, Nâlan's main contact with people of Turkish background nowadays consists of her working life, as she stopped being an activist as the social movements she worked in declined. This has also led to a shift in her role from that of an organic intellectual and community activist to professional service provider, where she relates to the women she works with not as potential fellow activists but as clients.

Nâlan's story shows the difficult trajectory of moving from undocumented migration status into skilled work. This involved an initial de-skilling and a mobilization of her specific networks. Her re-skilling involved moving into a different employment sector as her qualifications acquired in Turkey were not recognized in Britain. The next life-story exemplifies how, despite the formal recognition of qualifications, institutional and interpersonal racism can pose obstacles to the realization of professional skills.

*How Universal are Professions?*

Birgül comes from a farmer's family. She is the youngest of six siblings, who all achieved higher education. Although the parents' financial position was 'not that good', they supported their daughters' education. In fact, older siblings helped the younger ones financially to obtain higher education. Birgül studied medicine, and during her studies became very involved in left wing student politics. After graduating, she worked as a company doctor for two years. In this job, she began researching occupational health, uncovering the companies' shortcomings. She entered the exams to do her professional specialization in gynaecology when the coup d'etat took place in 1980:

> B: And when I had just entered the examinations, I had gone to Istanbul, 12 September [1980 the military coup, U. E.] happened. I went abroad head over heels, me and my sister. During university life we had been much more political, we had worked in students' organizations, and I also worked in a political party. (…) Therefore, ah, well, I had to go abroad. There wasn't the threat of a trial or anything, but even to be democratic was a problem.

Birgül migrated as a language student, and did not apply for asylum,[9] initially she stayed with one of her sisters who was a labour migrant in Germany. In order to get independent as soon as possible, Birgül started to look for work after just four months of language classes. However, at her first job interview, she faced the problem of the residence permit, the work and special professional permit for doctors.

> B: The senior consultant (…) needed a junior doctor in that period, and they took me on. Only, and this is very important, the condition was – I didn't have a residence permit, or a work permit or professional permit, I had none of these. My residence permit was for one month. I told them about my position, and they said we can help you, but under these conditions, or you go back to Turkey and get this visa. I said, 'If I go to Turkey I cannot come back'. At the time I was wanted in Turkey with my sister. Then I thought about this issue. 'While there are all the state institutions here, why does it have to be the German consulate in Turkey? You can do it here, too'. [I said] 'Well, we can get your residence permit, work permit and professional permit under this condition that you work here for free until the holidays, that is two or three months'. (…) I thought I have to get my foot in, to be able to work in my profession and be independent, so I accepted it. That was a very difficult period for me. First of all, they had me

---

9   I did not ask Birgül why she did not apply for asylum, but there may be several reasons why she did not. Asylum applications are a very long procedure with an open-ended outcome, even if the persecution faced seems obvious to the applicant. During this procedure, the applicants have to undergo humiliating conditions, having to rely on welfare state provisions, and they are often forced to live in overcrowded hostels. Moreover, they are not allowed to do any political work. Finally, whether the application is granted or not, it is difficult to return to Turkey, since the Turkish state views the application for asylum itself as undermining the Turkish state.

work there as a regular [junior doctor] and didn't give me a penny during three
months. I was a slave there, they didn't even give me [lunch vouchers].

This first job was decisive for Birgül as it enabled her to secure a residence
permit, a work permit and a professional permit. Without the support of her boss
she would not have got them since employers are required to prove that there are
no suitable German or EU citizen candidates for the job before being allowed to
take on a third country national. Moreover, the entry into the medical profession
requires an additional professional permit. Thus, Birgül had to overcome several
institutional barriers. While her boss was supportive, the condition that she work
for free for three months exploited her dependence on this job.[10] To Birgül who
had been so active in struggling for rights in the workplace, this must have meant
a special humiliation.

*Struggling for the recognition of skills*
Birgül applied for a job at another hospital, where she could work in her
specialization as a gynecologist: 'Because they had a proportion of 25% foreigners
among the patients, they had a lot of foreign patients and therefore were thinking
of their own benefits. But it suited me well, too'. In Turkey, Birgül had already
gained experience as part of her professional training. However, her qualifications
and experience were not taken seriously, and she was not allowed to carry out
complex tasks:

> B: And then, despite this, when I got here, to be first of all a foreigner, then to be
> a woman, they really oppressed me terribly. After working there for one month
> during which they really sent me to the donkey's jobs ... I went to the senior
> consultant and asked, 'Have you not seen my catalogue of operations? I have
> done so and so many operations, you haven't even given me one operation',
> they were using me as second [class] junior doctor (…). He said to me, 'You are
> very impatient', etc. I said, 'I am working below my qualifications'. Then, well
> he talked to the senior physician and had me do an operation. And in the first
> operation the senior physician had to prove himself, not just whether I could do
> it, but he had to prove that he is the senior physician. He didn't leave me alone
> for a minute. 'No, you can't do the knot like this, you can't hold it like this'.
> Well, (…) I said 'Can I do it as I have learned it?' I said, 'The main thing is that
> everything goes well, the operation goes well, whether you make the knot like
> this or like that'. At first he let me do it ... but in the second operation ... he said

---

10   Similarly in Canada (Krahn et al. 2000) and the UK (Bloch 2004, Erel and
Tomlinson 2005) refugees and migrants are commonly encouraged to undertake unpaid
work as a way of gaining local work experience. However, some employers take 'advantage
of the newcomers by capitalizing on free full-time volunteers for months on end, with the
promise that eventually there could be an opening for a paying job' (Krahn et al. 2000:
80).

[shouting] *'Today you will operate like I want, not like you want'*. Then in the nightshift they didn't give me a caesarean, I struggled a lot for all this, much more than a normal German woman. (…) Because in order to be accepted, it was very difficult because I was a woman, and secondly because I was a foreign woman it was more difficult.

The conflict with the senior physician during the operation exemplifies the negotiation of authority. Although the apparent conflict is over styles of binding knots or holding scalpels, this stands in for a conflict over the authority of the senior physician: first, Birgül had challenged his judgment of her abilities and professional fairness by complaining to the senior consultant. Second, the fact that she employed a different style[11] implicitly challenged the professional knowledge of the senior physician. National curricula and training systems ensure that every discipline develops its own nationally specific styles and rules. The system of knowledge is held in place, by being able to fix the rules. If other rules are applied and prove viable, the authority of this system is shown to be temporally and geographically specific and thus, partial. The senior physician here articulates national difference not directly through rejecting a 'Turkish' surgical method, but indirectly as a conflict between a male senior representative of the German professional system and the female junior doctor having to adapt to his style of surgery, which is, however, endowed with a nationalized professionally institutionalized authority. The gender dimension here intersects with the other hierarchical relations to reify them.

### *'Your foreignness is put in the foreground'*

B: Then in the nightshifts, we were two [junior doctors]. When a dark-haired patient came they always woke me up. 'Your countrywoman has arrived' [in a derogatory tone] in this way. I went down and the woman was for example a Yugoslavian woman, she doesn't know a word of Turkish. They are fooling me, therefore I was woken up more during the nightshifts. There were a lot of foreign patients. Well, there were a lot of these racist things.

For a long time, a homogenized notion of 'Turkishness' symbolized foreignness in Germany, so that ethnic differences within the migrant population were eclipsed in favour of a dichotomy of 'Germanness' and 'Turkishness'. This quote shows how practices of homogenizing the racialized Other as 'Turkish' can work: in effect, delegating the foreign patients to Birgül means to select them according to Germanness and non-Germanness fixing the caring responsibility according to national criteria. Moreover, it increased her workload as she was the only doctor

---

11   Presumably Birgül's operating style was different, not wrong as she does not recount being taught about the deficiency of her method, but rather is told to operate 'like I want'.

of Turkish background. In addition to her medical work, Birgül was used as a translator all over the hospital.

Patients, on the other hand, identified her as a foreign woman, and challenged her to prove them that she was indeed qualified as a medical doctor. While Birgül feels that her working relationship with the nurses and midwives was good, she found it difficult to witness the ways in which they subjected migrant patients to racism:

> B: the nurses for one treated the foreign patients extremely badly, and continuously came to me to complain about the Turkish patients. The complaints about the foreign patients were that they had too many visitors. Second, they talk too loudly. '*You are too loud, can't you please talk more quietly*'. That's how they entered their room. A patient's morale is very low anyway because they are ill, and then they are constantly being reproved by the nurses. Well, by the doctors and the others – they treated them like dirt.

This treatment of the foreign patients has a double effect. First, it directly humiliates the patients. Second, the nurses treated Birgül as the point of reference to address their complaints about the foreign patients. Räthzel and Sarica (1994) point out foreign staff may experience this racism directed at patients as an indirect attack on themselves, as their collective identity as '*Ausländer*' is targeted. By addressing Birgül as a woman of Turkish background, responsible for the perceived 'misbehaviour' of her countrywomen, she is positioned ambiguously as a foreigner herself, and at the same time in her professional role as a member of the institution called upon to mediate in the interest of the institution. The multiple relations at the workplace, to senior doctors, junior doctors, nurses, midwives, patients, concurred – albeit in different ways – in determining Birgül's subject position in gendered and ethnicized terms.

Birgül characterizes her discrimination as both gendered and ethnicized, however she elaborates on racist discrimination rather than on sexist discrimination.[12] This may be due to the gender specific context of her work in a gynaecological ward, where the gendered and ethnicized hierarchies intersect and construct her commonalties with the patients as a 'foreign woman' as superseding the professional commonalties. Instead the social relationships reinforce the construction of difference to the German male superiors, so that foreignness comes to be a short hand for gendered Otherness, too. With reference to Black British women, Lewis points out that '"race" talk often acts as a metalanguage through which other axes of power, which organize social relations and construct positions, are at once spoken and masked' (1996:34). In the context of her work in the hospital, racist, sexist and professionally based hierarchies and power relations reinforce each other. On the other hand, her professional authority in relation to

---

12   This foregrounding of racist discrimination is not particular to skilled migrant women (cf. Morokvasic, 1987).

the German nurses and midwives and the German patients is not taken seriously because of her 'foreignness'.

Another example Birgül relates is the doctors' views about ethnically and culturally specific interpretations of health and illness. Thus, Turkish female patients were stereotyped as exaggerating pain, while their practices of giving birth were seen as primitive. The increasing interest in and adaptation of alternative birth practices by the hospitals on the other hand was regarded as a progress, disavowing the origin of these practices in the 'problematic' migrant patient group.[13] As a member of both the ethnic and the professional collectivities, Birgül experienced the devaluation of her professional role in favour of her gendered ethnic membership.

> B: However hardworking you are, however humane you are, your being a foreigner was always put in the foreground, in medical meetings, too. (…) Later I went to further qualification seminars, [e.g.] a small seminar of 12 people, even there I was always the only foreigner among them, and a foreign woman at that. And then, for example, I discuss on the same level with everyone else, but then the guy says to me referring to Turkish patients 'Is that not right, Mrs. S.?' That's when he turns to me. But I am also there to discuss the other topics, why don't you discuss those with me? He only refers to me about the foreign patients – that's how he sees it. It is not his problem how these patients imagine illness or what he can learn from them, or how one should approach this. Nobody thinks about this.

In this instance, she is turned into the representative of 'Turkish issues' while her perspective on other professional issues is not sought.

Another aspect of discrimination relates to competition among colleagues. Thus she recounts a conversation with a male colleague:

> B: (…) one day the senior consultant invited all the housemen for dinner. There was a colleague sitting next to me, and he said to me, (…): 'Don't you think of returning to your country once you finish?' And I said no. 'Why not?' he asked. 'Why?' said I. 'You may also wish to open a surgery once you finish your specialization, and I may want to do the same'. 'But we have a lot of unemployed doctors. You are taking away their place'. (…) I said, 'You know how long

---

13    Indeed, this alludes to a debate among German medical professionals during the 1960s and 70s, when studies measuring migrant women's pelvis were undertaken. These studies were based on a racist fixation of bodily difference to migrant women from different countries. This 'research' fizzled out in the late 1970s with the conclusion that both 'racial' characteristics and the 'lower degree of civilization' were causes for differential generative and birthing behaviour of women. Huth-Hildebrandt (2002) identifies this medical debate as one generator of the creation of gendered Otherness of migrant women in the German context.

our shifts are. We started at 8 o'clock in the morning and came back the next day in the afternoon. (…) We are all doing the work of two people. This is the reason for unemployment. I am not the reason for unemployment. Everywhere [you are used as, U.E.] a scapegoat, even my own colleague, who shares the profession sees me in this way (laughs) in the end. It was very exhausting for me to struggle against all this. Moreover, there was a great difference between this man and me in terms of the profession. I never had the same opportunities as a German doctor, I never had equal opportunities. (…) For example, when his specialization finished, he could make plans. He could immediately get the permission to open a surgery the very next day, there wasn't a problem. But because I didn't have a German approbation, because I was a foreigner, (…) I didn't have the right to open a surgery or anything.

U: Yes, of course.

Taking away place from Germans is a recurring topic in racist reasoning, and indeed the German 'foreigners' politics' or the plans for an 'immigration' policy, from the guest-worker policy to the present continue to be driven by the demands of the labour market. This premise of the priority of 'German interests' governs interpersonal relations as much as it does institutional racism, so that the individual Germans view themselves as incorporating a national interest which can justifiably be privileged over that of non-nationals. The presence of highly qualified non-Germans as colleagues thus challenges not only stereotypes about the appropriate social place and abilities of foreigners. It also challenges the self concept of Germans who unexpectedly find themselves on a par professionally with those whom they considered out of the race. This fear of being displaced from a position of privilege, legitimated through their national belonging activates verbal violence against migrants. Hage suggests that these acts of violence establish the non-migrants as spatial managers who posit themselves as potentially in control of who may and who may not be present in the national space. Hage terms as 'governmental belonging' a mode of belonging that 'involves the belief in one's possession of the right to contribute (even if only by having a *legitimate* opinion with regard to the internal and external politics of the nation) to its management such that it remains "one's home"' (1998: 46).[14]

*Institutional and legal racism*
Birgül's initial problems with the residence, work and professional permit continued to impact her working life for ten years as she had to renew these permits annually. This legal insecurity led to a dependence on her senior consultant, whose support was crucial for obtaining the permits. The bureaucratic organization of the procedures was also very complex and contributed to her distress. Three different

---

14    The politics of belonging and the legitimacy of migrant women's contributions are further discussed in Chapter 6.

offices were involved in obtaining the permits, and they threw the ball from one to the other. During her efforts to gain these permits, she 'got to know many people who were involved in anti-racist struggles. (…). And they were very helpful for me, really in order to get this type of permit etc'. Through these experiences, she participated in anti-racist struggles and helped set up other anti-racist groups and campaigns. Moreover, she did voluntary work for migrant centres, in particular for migrant women, on women's health. Three years into her specialization, she could not renew her professional permit:

> B: The senior consultant wrote maybe two pages for me, but despite all this, they did not renew my permit, although I had a right to four years. Then the senior consultant was very sad and came to tell me this, and I said, 'So what can I do now?' It is important for me, my specialization is important for me.

The senior consultant referred her to a friend of his in another city and *Bundesland* who agreed to take her on at his hospital to continue her specialization. However, here, too, she faced problems in obtaining the necessary permits. Birgül brought references from the advice centers where she had done voluntary work, who argued the importance of having a Turkish-speaking doctor in order to serve the needs of the migrant women. In the end, Birgül involved a lawyer and managed to obtain the necessary permits.

> B: However here it took me a full year. Thankfully I had started the efforts early, [while she was still employed at the previous hospital, U.E.] because otherwise I would have been unemployed, and because I was unemployed they would have sent me back.

This system of residence, work and professional permits jeopardized her possibilities of planning her career. Moreover, Birgül's fear of unemployment was aggravated by her fear that this could constitute a reason to deport her.

When she finished her specialization, Birgül wanted to open a surgical clinic and was faced with new obstacles. In order to do so she had to first obtain a registration with the Medical Association and the *Kassenärztliche Vereinigung*,[15] second, to do a registration period, i.e. to work for six months in a surgery, and third, to have German citizenship. Birgül fulfilled the requirement of the registration period by working for six months part-time in a surgery, while many of her colleagues did not work for a full six months en bloc.

> B: I applied for an approbation. After all this, the man at the Kassenärztliche Vereinigung said to me: 'Your approbationary period, these six months, is not valid'. 'Why?' asked I. 'I did it'. 'But,' he said 'You have done this without a German approbation'. 'I did it with my professional permit' I said. 'I was

---

15   Association of doctors registered with health insurers.

working for years on my professional permit. In this case you shouldn't accept my specialization, either'. 'I don't understand this' he said. 'What is it you don't understand' I asked. 'What is the aim, isn't it to gain experience? With or without a paper, I have experience. Moreover, I didn't work without papers, here is my professional permit. If you don't accept this professional permit, you cannot accept my specialization, either – which I did in Germany'. *'These foreigners' rules' he got up. I was standing anyway, you know. He called his secretary, as if I was a criminal, you know. He called his secretary like this: 'You can tell Mrs. S what is the matter. She doesn't understand. I have already suggested' he said, he was shouting so loudly. 'I have suggested, that the foreign doctors should go to a special training course or something, because they cannot understand all these many laws'.* I went out crying from there.

U: Ah, ay…

N: And then, I really had to do another six months.

*Challenging citizenship as privilege – Claiming rights*
The next problem she faced was the condition to be a German citizen for opening a surgery. At the time she could not fulfil the temporal requirement of residence to apply for German citizenship. Therefore, with the help of a lawyer she argued that 'on the paper of the professional permit it always says "provision for the population". (…) We benefited from this – there is no other doctor who speaks Turkish (…) as a gynecologist, as a woman'.

This argument to provide medical services for the population (*Bevölkerung*) is not just a resourceful use of the German regulations. It is at the same time a political intervention in the debate about whom state regulated provisions are for: the ethnic nation (*Volk*) or the multi-ethnic population, of whom ten per cent are not formally citizens. Birgül obtained her approbation as an exception, without being a German citizen. Her argument was strengthened by references from her employers and a number of migrants' and women's counseling centres whom she had done voluntary work for, who testified to the high demand for a Turkish-speaking female gynecologist. Thus, these instances of Birgül successfully claiming her right to continue her specialization and to open a surgery support Soysal's argument that even non-citizens can successfully invoke a universalist human rights discourse to supersede nationally bounded citizenship rights. Still, Birgül was granted these rights as an exception to the rule, so as not to create a precedent for others. This exceptional achievement of rights-claims of non-citizens alerts us that the human rights arguments may be invoked successfully only in singular cases. Such singular cases, however, contradict the postnational argument of universal validity of human rights over nationally bounded citizenship rights.[16]

---

16    The complex ways in which migrant women refer to both universalist and particularist discourses in elaborating their identity politics is discussed in more depth in Chapter 6.

Birgül's social and political activism constituted a resource for her professional development. This was instrumental in her argument of providing medical services to the migrant population. She mobilized her gender and ethnic identity in her voluntary work to bring her professional expertise to migrant women. This can be theorized as a mixture between the logic of a 'specific' and an 'organic' intellectual:[17] on the one hand, Birgül articulated her professional expertise in the service of migrant women,[18] which was at the same time enabled by identity politics that provided a commonality with the women she served. Her activism also served to show a lack in the medical service provision in terms of language and racist and sexist professional condescendence (as her experiences at the hospital showed). While her political and social activism cannot be reduced to a career strategy, it constituted an important resource of support for her application first for a professional permit, then for the approbation. It is argued that this reveals the interrelatedness of professionalism and social and political activism (cf. Chapter 6). On the one hand, the lack of adequate service provisions, including translators, makes it necessary for migrant women to access medical information and services through voluntary organizations. On the other hand, for lack of German citizenship, Birgül was excluded from offering medical services, sensitive to migrant women's needs, through the institutions of the state-regulated medical system. Radtke (1994) argues that the structure of social service provision for migrants in Germany is constitutive of ethnic groups, since it prescribes an ethnic identity logic. Rather than providing services through mainstream institutions, separate, ethnically specific social work organizations provide for them. This constitutes a paradox of universality and particularity: the mainstream institutions are presented as universal, and thus specific service providers for migrants, including translations, are being neglected in practice, as well as ignore structural and interpersonal racism within them. This makes migrants dependent on specific service providers outside the mainstream. On the other hand, Birgül's application for opening a surgery

---

17  Cf. footnote 10, I refer to Foucault's (1980) notion of the 'specific intellectual' as located though her professional position at a crucial point in the articulation of power relations and truth discourses to be used in a subversive or dominant way. Foucault argues that with growing professional responsibility, the specific intellectual's political role becomes more important, since she can use her knowledge 'in the service of the State or against it' (Foucault 1980: 129).

18  This formulation of 'in the service of migrant women' is ambiguous, in so far as it cannot be assumed that the women have a unitary interest base. However, her social position as a gynaecologist is also a nodal point articulating in medical and social terms ethnicity, gender, class and a nationalized and racialized politics of population. To my knowledge there is no research on this in the context of Germany. However, in the late 1980s feminist activists scandalized unofficial practices of encouraging women of Turkish background in particular to sterilize, and insufficiently inform them about the operation. Against this backdrop, a provision of gynaecological services that takes the individual woman seriously, rather than assuming that sterilization is best suited to this group of women, constitutes an effective intervention in this nodal point of social divisions.

was not treated as the universal right of any medical practitioner. The principle of universality was not applied to giving her access. She had to strengthen her argument with recourse to her skills to provide for a particular group of patients. This complex relation between universality and particularity is complemented by the relation between professional work and voluntary, social and political activism. While the professional role is conceptualized as a universal one, access to this is particularized through citizenship: Birgül had to argue that the particular needs of migrant women from Turkey should be taken into account in the universalized provision of medical services. This argument was crucial to enable her to provide these services in an institutionalized professional way rather than through voluntary work. In 1991, Birgül opened her surgery. Birgül feels that in her role as a gynaecologist she provides important services to migrant women. At the same time, she feels that her position as a female doctor of Turkish background, in the absence of other ethnically and gender sensitive doctors, requires her to provide more emotional and social advice to her migrant patients.

*Mobilizing Migration-specific Social and Cultural Capital*

In the following life-story, the processual, dynamic and at times contradictory processes of constructing, mobilizing and validating social and cultural capital in migration are explored, focusing on intra-ethnic dynamics of distinction.

Pakize is a 60 year old migrant from Istanbul. She has two grown up children who both live in Turkey. She migrated to Germany in 1969 where she did manual work in a factory for three years, then she moved on to become an employee at an insurance company and for ten years she has been working as a nursery nurse in a bi-lingual kindergarten.

Pakize grew up in Istanbul as the only child of a civil servant and a housewife. At the age of 15 she began courting with a man, whom she married soon after graduating from a girls' institute. She describes this institute as preparing girls for a middle class marriage, like a 'finishing school'.[19] Her husband was a pilot. Soon after the marriage, Pakize had two children. However she did not get along with her husband and they separated. Pakize was not prepared for this situation of having to look after herself and her children economically.

> P: Well, in Turkey at that time when you got married... First your parents take care of you, then you get married and your husband...well, I never lost a thought on money or worried about earning a living.

---

19   She graduated from a girls' institute, which Arat (1998) characterizes as finishing schools. The '(...) girls' institutes tended to attract students from the upper socio-economic strata. The education offered at these schools failed to offer employment opportunities and seemed "somewhat of a luxury" to low-income families'. (163)

*De-classing as a divorcee*

Her decision to separate from her husband led to a de-classing of Pakize, severe financial difficulties and debt. Moreover, it made her dependent on her mother-in-law for childcare. She remembers the attitude at the time towards women who lived alone:

> P: 'Are you going to be a bad person? What are you going to do on your own?. The men…' – that thought came to mind immediately. Now that has changed, women who divorce can live by themselves. When I separated, I lived with my mother-in-law. Everybody laughed at me, but what could I do?

The cultural capital she 'inherited' from her parents and her gender specific schooling prepared her for an appropriate marriage, not for conversion into privileged access to the labour market. When Pakize transgressed the specific gendered middle class norms of her family by divorcing, it undermined her class-specific, and urban status expectations.

Migration offered a possible way out of her financial problems. When a friend suggested migration to Germany, however, Pakize feared a loss of status:

> P: Going to work in Germany was seen as something very lowly at the time.

> U: What time was that?

> P: '69. They said, well only very simple people go there. So then I secretly went to the workers' recruitment office and got the formalities done.

Pakize raises the problem of having shared the economic position of other guest-worker migrants to Germany while feeling socially and culturally apart from them several times in her narrative. This is reflected in her description of the difficulties she experienced during the first period in Germany: the dirt and inconvenience of the long train journey are not described in terms of insufficient hygienic provisions and constrictions of physical space (cf. Jamin 1998a), but in terms of 'all kinds of people' she travelled with. This remark links the 'dirt' and 'smells' of the train journey to the 'kind of people' she travelled with, i.e. 'simple people'.

Pakize started working in a factory and was housed with co-workers in a woman's hostel. The de-classing process of becoming a migrant worker had contradictory effects: it enabled her economic independence from a husband while supporting her children. Socially, the migration meant a loss of status: in the workplace and the hostel it meant an association with working-class people from whom she dissociates herself culturally as people 'whose language I could not even understand'. Moreover, the ascribed status of a single woman guest-worker at first meant an increased gender vulnerability. Female hostel residents were stigmatized as 'prostitutes' by male migrant workers, laying them open to sexist abuse and harassment. She views this harassment as a class-specific behaviour of (rural origin) working class migrant men, with whom she would not have been in contact in Turkey. However, abroad, her class identity was ambiguous and did not constitute a barrier to their interference, since they presented themselves as the representatives and defenders of a national moral, bridging any class divisions.

*Building social capital in migration*
Pakize points out that she quickly made two very good friends. These friends' social status and habits as Istanbul middle-class women were closer to Pakize. She views her ability to make such good friends as an important asset, and also as luck, in this way she gives voice to Bourdieu's view of social capital as investment strategies, even if at times her agency is veiled by notions of 'luck'. One friend helped her find a job in the same insurance company as her husband. She also invited Pakize to live with her and her husband, to avoid the stigma of living in the hostel. Pakize had mobilized her cultural capital as an urban middle-class woman to access social networks of Turkish, middle-class skilled workers.

In 1974, the insurance company was taken over and relocated to A-city, taking the department in which Pakize worked with them. In the meantime, she had been supporting her children in Turkey financially. Her ex-husband refused to allow them to join her in Germany for a long time. Finally, when her daughter was 15 he consented that she join Pakize. Thus, when in 1984, the company re-organized and she was advised by the trade union to accept a settlement and leave, she was responsible for the two of them, making any attempts at re-skilling financially risky for Pakize. Pakize used her settlement to take time to enquire about possibilities of retraining, hoping a formal qualification would better protect her from unemployment.

When re-orienting occupationally, she was advised by the job centre to re-train as a travel agent. 'I thought alright. It would be … well, I have always wanted to do something mixing Turks and Germans'. While living in A-city, she had established a wide social network of friends of Turkish background. One of them, a social worker, informed her about a newly created vocational training for migrant women, to train as nursery nurses, that was supported by the job centre, too. This option seemed more attractive to Pakize. This instance underlines the importance of informal networks as a source of information.

*Capitalizing on 'good Turkish'*
When she was about to graduate from her course, an initiative of German and Turkish parents had secured funding for an intercultural and bi-lingual kindergarten.

> P: Some people from there came and looked around and asked us to enlist if we were interested. I said to myself, 'Will they take me? There are very good young Turkish and Kurdish women. And these are alternative people, they will rather work with Kurds, etc' But then I also wrote down my name.

U: Hmm.

P: And then, it was luck, quite some time passed and I got an invitation for an interview. They invited two people. (…) They were very happy with the other applicant. But they said we want you, because we want a person who speaks Turkish well.

U: Yes, hmm.

P: So that when our children learn Turkish they should learn a good Turkish. We liked the way you talk, you have experience, they said and then of course I was happy.

The fact that her Turkish was very good – in contrast with her co-applicants – was the decisive factor for offering her the job. This linguistic distinction is based on class, education, rural or urban origin, Turkish ethnicity and of course, generation of migration. At another point in the interview, Pakize states that the second generation lack a good knowledge of Turkish. Here, the implicit cultural capital is converted into an explicit person specification. While the parents' wish that their children should learn standard Turkish in kindergarten is entirely understandable, the racist effects of normalizing standard Turkish[20] deserve mentioning. Many second generation migrants have not received formal education in Turkish or if so, only partially. Moreover, those whose parents stem from rural areas and have low levels of education speak local dialects, which are considered low culture. Of course, there are also Kurdish and other ethnic minorities within Turkey for whom Turkish is the second language. Indeed, Pakize's expressed fear that 'alternative' people might prefer employing Kurds rather than Turks manifests a 'political correctness' discourse within the migrant population, where actual power relations are fantasized as inverted.

Language is a salient marker of distinction, and Pakize in her cultural activities produces and reproduces this (cf. below). The conversion of the cultural capital of speaking 'good Turkish' into economic capital is a relational process, based on the de-valuation of other forms of cultural and social capital, i.e. the vernacular mixed language of second generation migrants or rural dialects, deemed unworthy of transmission. This raises important issues, often missed out in discussions on cultural hybridity. Namely that there is differential societal value attached to everyday, or low cultural practices. If these practices are simultaneously ethnicized, as is the case with 'speaking mixed', the hierarchical devaluation of partial, ethnicized cultural practices and of working class, low cultural practices works to mutually reinforce each other. Often, the status of the 'cultural' is denied

---

20   Many migrants from Turkey in Germany do not speak standard Turkish but regional and class specific dialects, which has contributed to the devaluation of their and their children's cultural capital.

to these practices and instead, they are viewed as belonging to the realm of 'social problems'.

*Constructing intra-ethnic distinction*

Having pointed out how Pakize used her cultural and social capital in her professional life, I will now turn to examine her cultural activities outside of work. Bourdieu (1997) argues that the informally acquired cultural capital is an invisible, but therefore even more effective mechanism of professional closure that helps to reproduce the social status of professional groups despite the democratization of access to formal qualifications. I will examine how this works in the context of Pakize's professionalization.

In her leisure time she regularly participates in a choir that sings classical Turkish music and attends the training sessions of a Turkish theatre group. Although she does not act, she enjoys attending these sessions because 'they teach you how to speak nicely and the poetry too'. The choir and the theatre are focal points in her social life. Both classical Turkish music and theatre and poetry are high cultural forms that are a sign of 'distinction', as Pakize says: 'Not every one likes this music'. As opposed to cultural forms such as Arabesque or Pop music, Turkish classical music claims the status of being both, classical, high culture and Turkish, i.e. nationalized culture. Participating in these groups means both reproducing the cultural forms but also contains an identificatory moment of producing the self as a 'cultured' person. This self-production as a cultured person, competent in Turkish cultural practices is an important asset in Pakize's professional life. Through her own cultural activities, she sees herself as qualified to transmit 'Turkish culture' to the children.

*Making migration-specific cultural capital*

In her work with children Pakize can realize her professional aspirations and moreover contribute her social outlook. When asked about her social activities in Germany, Pakize talks about her work in the kindergarten, especially her commitment to fostering the adaptation of positive elements of 'Turkish' and 'German' culture. While she appreciates certain elements of German culture, she also wants to be recognized with her own cultural attributes. As an example of this, she gives her way of celebrating Turkish holidays in the kindergarten. Although these are religious holidays, Pakize emphasizes the cultural aspects and argues for a secular practice. In her function as educator, she realizes her views on legitimate Turkish culture. Within her social activities in Germany, she sees the construction of legitimate Turkishness as one of her achievements. While dialogue with Germans is important in so far as she expects to be granted recognition, the dialogue with other people from Turkey is an important site of her constructions of Turkishness, too.

There is an interesting tension between her activities in reproducing a high-cultured, secular version of Turkishness and her conviction that

P: The Turks aren't like Turks anymore. A new type of cultural person is developing in Germany, a mixture between Turk and German. If they can use this well, it will be a valuable thing. (...) (...) I say, a person should not be ashamed of themselves. Neither of their body, nor of their race or colour or age. They should be proud of themselves, also of their language of course. Let me talk my Turkish and educate myself as I wish, and let others think of me what they will.

Pakize's ideal of a culturally mixed identity relies on a particular version of Turkishness being used for the mixing. The issue of speaking Turkish and continuously educating oneself is an important part of Pakize's own biography. Although she had inherited the cultural capital that allowed her to appreciate high-cultural forms, her participation in the active (re-)production of these cultural forms in Germany means a 'work on the self' in terms of educating herself. This self-education, apart from other benefits has also played a crucial part in Pakize's life through building up the social capital that she could convert into her professionalization.

**Conclusion**

Gender specific reasons for migration, particularly as they pertain to single mothers and divorced women were highlighted in Nâlan's and Pakize's life-stories. The significance of transnational social capital for the initiation and support of migration become obvious in Nâlan's life-story. This social capital is not only determined by ethnicity, but also by her identification as part of oppositional, transnational social movements such as the women's movement and left-wing movements whose values she adopted. It is important here to point out the specificity of these social networks and the cultural capital attached to them as internally divided along lines of class, gender, sexuality and political positioning as well as other ethnic categories (cf. Vasta 2004). Nâlan's professional trajectory demonstrates a de-skilling and a re-skilling, for which her own resourcefulness and her social networks were as significant as the structural factors of immigration legislation, labour market segregation and the implicit normativity of a two parent family as demonstrated in her difficulty to earn a living in Turkey.

The categories of skilled or unskilled migrants are not simply descriptive. Instead, gendered constructions, migration regimes as well as racist stereotypes contribute to the social construction of these categories themselves. Thus at different times in their migration history, the same individual may be classified as an undocumented, unskilled, or skilled migrant. The categorization of a migrant often does not take account of their factual skills or professional experiences. Therefore categories used to control migration and migrants' access to the labour market should not be taken for granted, but deconstructed.

In the study of professional and highly skilled migration as opposed to labour migration, the relevance of social networks and the validation of cultural capital are rarely taken into account. It is assumed that for professionals these are neutral, rather than examining the class, gender and ethnic bases of constructing such neutrality. For migrants whose formal or informal skills and qualifications are not recognized in the country of immigration the de-skilling and re-skilling often takes place through ethnically specific networks. Migrant women participate in ethnically specific cultural projects and social networks, however as single or divorced women, the respondents build forms of social capital that offer alternatives to a unified, homogeneous notion of ethnic solidarity that is bounded by heteronormative family-centred forms of sociality and subjectivity. They use differentiated forms of cultural capital, be it through high cultural practices or through sub-cultural forms of party political or feminist movements, to construct social networks. These networks were important for their migratory and occupational projects, but they also created migration specific mechanisms for validating their cultural capital in migration. This pertained to aspects of building social status within the migrant community as well as *vis-à-vis* the receiving society. Thus, the authority to represent migrants, in an educational role, as in the case of Pakize, or through the role of cultural mediator, as in Nâlan's case, are instances in which this cultural and social capital was condensed into professional qualifications. An in-depth exploration of how migrant women made use of and gave meaning to their cultural capital in the context of migration has highlighted the role of internal differentiations within a migrant group. Furthermore, these explorations show the processual character of forming and – through giving new, migration specific meanings – transforming cultural capital.

Linking the analysis of the interviewees' experiences of work to debates of citizenship, some implications emerge. On the one hand, the institutional and informal obstacles to recognizing migrant women's skills and qualifications have been shown. Immigration legislation especially prevents undocumented migrants from accessing legal work, which only leaves the unskilled job market available to them. This type of undocumented work in the unskilled job market often requires long working hours and has no workers' protection, making migrant women vulnerable to economic and also sexual exploitation. It does not give them necessary resources of time and money to consider re-skilling. Once migrant women have been able to regularize their residence status, the necessity to prove a sufficient income can be an impediment to re-skilling and again force them into unskilled work. This can be particularly exacerbated, as in Nâlan's case, if the priority is to apply for family unification. It is not satisfactory to accept that migrants' access to social citizenship rights depends on their participation in the labour market. This should be contextualized with the unpaid caring activities of migrant women and its regulation through immigration control. Thus, the countries of residence put the onus of proving the economic capacity to care for their children on the migrants as a prerequisite for family reunification. In particular single mothers cannot rely on family or state support to alleviate the financial risks of re-skilling. This constitutes an important gendered and ethnicized legal and economic obstacle for them. As was shown in Birgül's case, even if migrant women's qualifications are formally recognized, in practice institutional professional protectionism can hinder the realization of their skills, as well as further qualification, or self-employment. These institutional barriers interrelate with interpersonal racism.

These obstacles reduce migrant women's access to citizenship rights. This reflects the contradictory effects of universal and particularistic practices of citizenship. Paradoxically, most debates on citizenship view migrant women as constituting a particularistic identity at odds with the universalistic image of an equal citizenry. However, here it has been argued that their particularity in the skilled labour market is as much a result of their exclusion from universal rights, than their self-identification. An exploration of the forms of the women's agency and the resources they can create and access needs to take this context of lesser rights into account.

An important resource women mobilized is their ethnically and gender specific social and political activism. As was argued above, Nâlan activated her social and cultural capital acquired in migrant community activism for her job networks that contributed to her access to skilled work. While this can be seen as a gender and ethnic specific particularistic resource we should be careful not to accept the institutionally enshrined practices of nationally structured credentialism and professional cultures as universalist. Instead, it is the exclusionary, but normalized elements of these that necessitated Nâlan's reliance on particularistic resources.

Birgül's anti-racist activism and voluntary work for migrant women complemented her professional work. Any claim to universality of her professional identity was constantly undermined through gendered and ethnicized discrimination. To be able to open a surgery and provide for the health needs of migrant women, Birgül had to make explicit the incongruence between the German nation and the population of Germany.

Current migration policy in both Britain and Germany clearly differentiates between skilled and unskilled migrants, stratifying their access to formal citizenship and substantive social citizenship rights. This needs to be challenged from a social justice point of view. However, in addition, the strict delineation of the categories of skilled and unskilled is not factually tenable, either: the experience of these migrant women reveals the instability of the category of professionality in a transnational context.

Paid work is one site for the realization of citizenship practices. Mostly this is reduced to a discussion of the conditionality of migrants access to social citizenship through the work-related social contributions they pay. While this is certainly important, this chapter has argued for a more in-depth and complex view, that looks at the culturally imbued notions of competence, professional and social recognition and the ethnicized and gendered role of unpaid care work as implicated in migrant women's negotiation of, and attempts to realize in practice, their participation in the host society through skilled paid work. The next chapter looks at how migrant women's practices of mothering interrupt and re-constitute notions of family, belonging and citizenship.

# Chapter 5
# Challenging Family Boundaries

This chapter engages with how migrant women live and narrate their sexual and personal identities and relations with a particular focus on mothering practices. The chapter begins by outlining the limitations of public discourses on migrant families from Turkey as they do not take account of the range of ways in which migrant women construct themselves as sexual subjects and the flexible and dynamic ways in which their mothering practices re-constitute notions of family. The concluding section discusses the implications of these issues for thinking about intimate citizenship and the role of the cultural aspects of care for children as constituting citizenship practices.

## Public Discourses on 'The Turkish Family'

Turkishness forms a highly salient ethnic and racialized category in Germany and while it does not occupy a central place in public discourses on ethnic minorities in Britain, some of the features of the discourses outlined here are applied to Muslim families in Britain, an identity ascription which tends to be applied to migrants from Turkey, too (cf. Küçükcan 1999). Ethnic minority families from so-called Muslim countries are often conceptualized as embodying a close-knit, traditional family. In this view, the main site of oppression of women is the family, which is backward and patriarchal (cf. Lutz n.d., Otyakmaz 1995, Waltz 1996). This view of the traditional family structure of migrants from Turkey can be interpreted in various ways. While in particular New Right ideologies may perceive a traditional family model as ideal for the dominant ethnic group, they may at the same time see the perceived strength of ethnic minority family ties as a threat to the apparently weaker, more vulnerable social structure of the country of immigration and of the majority population. Outspoken racists may see higher birth-rates of families of Turkish background as a threat to the national identity of Germany, in particular in conjunction with the decrease of the German birth rate. Such a notion was articulated during the German Green Card debate in 2000 by the slogan 'Kinder statt Inder' i.e. '[We need] Children instead of Indians', of course, the tacit assumptions is that the 'We'-group is nationally, ethnically and racially bounded. The *Zuwanderungskommission* commission for migration, in July 2001 put forward a contrasting, instrumentalist racist,[1] position in favour of controlled and

---

1 Leiprecht (1994: 37) defines instrumental racism as reducing migrants and other racialized people to their functionality for the needs of the dominant society. Instrumentalist

regulated immigration and integration of the existing ethnic minority population in order to safeguard the social security system and in particular the pension schemes which depend on the contributions of younger, working people. For this end, the relatively higher birth-rates of families of Turkish background can be seen as in the German national interest (as long as the children are happy to integrate). In recent debates the problem-discourse on higher birth-rates of immigrants is even reversed to lament that immigrants' birth rates soon adjust to those of the majority population. It remains questionable, how seriously such laments can be taken. The introduction of visa for children with a Turkish passport as young as six months in 1999, which applies to residents in Germany, legally establishes these children not as the saviours of the German pension scheme, but instead already casts infants as undesirable, potentially illegal aliens.

## Theorizing Intimate Relations

Thus, discourses on families of Turkish background in Germany are complex, multifaceted and contradictory. However they mostly converge around a general belief that the Turkish family is characterized by strong family ties and responsibilities as well as by a patriarchal structure. This view is based on a racialized dichotomy of modernity vs. tradition. Germany is seen as a modern society, characterized by individualization, fragmentation of stable relationships and forms of belonging, increasing speed of change and the pluralization of cultural options as well as a sharpening of social inequalities and a decline in economic opportunity (cf. Heitmeyer et al. 1997). The nuclear family is one of the central social institutions challenged by modernization (Beck and Beck-Gernsheim 1995). However, these challenges are also presented as having positive aspects such as an increasing realization of democratic and egalitarian family relations. Giddens' suggests that these changes in late modernity allow for the emergence of 'pure relationships' which are not based on economic or social necessity but instead freely entered and only maintained as long as they fulfil the partners' emotional and sexual needs for intimacy. In this sense, they are part of an increasing inter-subjective reflexivity, which is characteristic of late modernity (1992). Within such discussions of the modernization of family relations, migrant families' experiences are not considered and tacitly assumed as residues of tradition (cf. Klesse 2000). Families of Turkish background are contrasted to the German modern family as the embodiment of tradition in the sense of patriarchal gender relations, continuity,

---

racist discourses are often used to legitimize the presence of migrants, and thus appear to be 'friendly to foreigners' rather than openly racist. The arguments on migrant families are racist in that they reify the ethnic boundaries of the nation: The 'we' group to benefit from immigration is constructed as German. The assumption that the immigrant population is valuable and admissible only in so far as it benefits the interests of this 'we' group constructs the interests and motivations of the immigrants as secondary to those of the 'Germans'.

and stability.[2] In acculturation theories of migration, women, because of their familial role, are considered to be the bearers of 'the more originary type of the culture of origin' (Apitzsch 1996: 13). Yet, empirical work suggests that migrant women do not view family and paid work as mutually exclusive but instead in their self-representations reconcile both (Gültekin 2003, Gümen and Westphal 1996). The very notions of modernity and tradition are in themselves racialized (Bhatt 1997, Goldberg 1993).

Giddens' and Beck and Beck-Gernsheim's models focus on heterosexual relationships. Where reference to non-heterosexual relationships is made, this tends to idealize them as even more democratic, since gender inequalities do not have to be negotiated within these (cf. Klesse 2000). This is a problematic reduction of power relations to gender. Unfortunately, Weeks et al. (2001) who focus on intimate relations of non-heterosexuals seem to replicate this by downplaying the power differences within gay and lesbian relationships as well as communities. While they acknowledge power differentials of 'race', ability, class and educational status, they do not theorize them sufficiently in the framework of intimate relations or community building. Thus, they argue that Beck and Beck-Gernsheim's and Giddens' theories overemphasize the process of individualization and underplay the relevance of *relational* rights, not yet fully available to non-heterosexuals:

> The transformation of intimate life is about more than simply realizing *individual* potentialities. Ultimately, it is about the possibilities for new forms of *relationships* that can transcend the rigidities and inequalities of traditional forms of life (Weeks et al. 2001: 182).

They argue that these relational rights are beginning to be formulated and claimed through non-heterosexual 'community knowledges'.[3]

> Though access to community knowledges may be limited by such factors as gender, geography, ethnicity, socio-economic resources and physical access issues, their existence has been responsible for the growing confidence of non-heterosexuals (…) (ibid.).

---

2    The only instance of instability of the family structure is identified as originating from the so-called culture conflict between parents and children (for a critique cf. Auernheimer 1988, Otyakmaz 1995), with the parents upholding Turkish values, while the children may rebel against these and try to incorporate German values. This conflict may de-stabilize the second generation and lead to them entering criminal, drug and other 'deviant' subcultures.

3    By 'community knowledges' they mean knowledges developed and shared both formally and informally through non-heterosexual institutions, activists, social venues, etc.

I agree with their suggestion that community knowledges are relevant for articulating and realizing intimate relationships. This is particularly salient for non-heterosexual intimate relationships which have not been institutionalized but rather for a long time been marginalized and/or criminalized. However, the problem of inequality does not only start at the point of access to such community knowledges. Rather, the inequalities already emerge at the stage of production of community knowledges. Who contributes their experiences and epistemologies and whose stories are heard, institutionalized and multiplied as 'community knowledge?' Whose stories are marginalized as supplementary? Both the heterosexual and the non-heterosexual discussions of 'pure relationships', 'post-familial' (Beck and Beck-Gernsheim 1990) families or 'families of choice' (Weeks et al. 2001) use an analytical framework of modernity vs. tradition that is implicitly racialized even when it remains apparently silent on ethnicity and 'race'. Migrant and ethnic minority people's lives tend to be viewed either as 'traditional', in particular if they are of so-called Muslim background or as dysfunctional.[4]

The main concern here is to point out the inadequacies of a view of migrant family and intimate relations as the embodiment of stability and tradition. It is suggested we might view this representation as a stereotype. The stereotype is not problematic because it is false, but because it *fixes* a singular reality (Bhabha 1990). While stereotypes may contain empirically verifiable facts, the meaning attached to these facts exceeds them, producing ambivalent effects of love and desire as well as hatred and disgust. Viewed in this way the stereotype of families of Turkish background as stable embodiments of tradition exerts ambivalent responses of longing and envy for stability as well as disdain for a presumably archaic, sexist institution. The life-stories presented here put forward alternative views on families of Turkish background. For the migrant women, these accounts of family life also serve to construct a notion of Self that is in dialogue, negotiation and at times in open resistance to other, public German or Turkish accounts, such as the tradition-modernity dichotomy.

## Sexual Identities and Personal Status

One of the specificities of my sample is that most women are single or divorced. Another specificity is the inclusion of lesbian or bisexual migrant women. This is particularly important, since sexuality is rarely discussed in the literature on migrant women, thus contributing to the invisibility of lesbian and bisexual migrant women and reinforcing heterosexual normativity.

Few of the migrant women elaborated on the topic of partnership in their life-stories. This may be due to most interviewees being single at the time of interview, so that the topic may not have had high relevance. While one focus of this chapter

---

4    In Britain, dysfunctionality is particularly ascribed to female-headed households of African-Caribbean people.

are mothering practices, I do not want to advance a maternalist ideology that views motherhood as the primary route to migrant women's articulation of citizenship practices. It is argued below that mothering practices involve elements of citizenship practices, and should not be seen as merely reproducing ethnic particularity that remains external to an engagement with the society of residence. Thus, while I do suggest re-evaluating mothering practices as interventions into citizenship and spend some time making the case for this, it is not suggested that women who are not mothers are less actively involved in creating and participating in citizenship practices. Mothering should not be seen as a normative stage in the female life cycle. Instead, here the diversity of ways in which the migrant women formed their sexual and intimate identities and relationships are presented. This chapter points out how migrant women challenge regulations of their femininity both within ethnic minority and ethnic majority frameworks and elaborate alternative or oppositional sexual subject positions.

Single and divorced women of Turkish background, although increasing in number continue to be as the exception, and are ignored by the social science literature (for an exception, cf. Erdem 2000). In a recent study on Turkish migrants in Britain, Küçükcan (1999) theorizes the family as the core social organization of the ethnic community that continues to transmit ethnically specific values. There are no references to female headed households, or divorce in his study. While this can be seen as a consequence of the empirical male focus of the study, it is also a theoretically problematic omission of the increasing economic possibility of divorce or single status that migration enables. 'Motherhood, and in particular childbearing, continues to be defined as the supreme route to physical and emotional fulfilment and as essential for all women' (Phoenix and Woollett 1991a: 7). It is constructed as a key stage of the female life cycle. This is also true for childless women, who are defined as either potential mothers or as failed childbearers. In this sense, motherhood is a crucial normative aspect of femininity. Some of the migrant women challenge this link of motherhood and femininity and choose not to be mothers. Such choices need not be final, however what is interesting here is that they articulate particular forms of female subjectivity that rarely find a voice in accounts of migrant women from Turkey (for exceptions, cf. Lutz 1990, Gutierrez Rodriguez 1999).

Let us begin by discussing Dilek's self-presentation as a single, childless woman by choice. Then the chapter presents Nâlan's story of negotiating changing marital statuses from single 'sexual revolutionary' to a married mother with 'the appearance of a normal family' and then to divorced, single mother. This story articulates strategies of gaining agency through negotiating the statuses regulating female sexuality. It elucidates the argument that mothering is valued differently, according to the familial context. Thus, single mothers and lesbian mothers are often seen as second class mothers (Phoenix and Woollett 1991, Young 1994). Thirdly, this chapter discusses sexual orientation in the context of migration. Melahat's story of lack of articulation of lesbian identity in (rural) Turkey shows how migration can contribute to the (re-)formulation of sexual identities. Then the problematic equation of ethnic minority communities with 'tradition' in sexual minority communities is critiqued. With the example of Meryem's story on her 'multicultural' family of choice I argue for a more complex approach to the intersection of ethnicity, migration and sexuality that takes internal differentiations, overlapping and multiple identifications into account. Finally I discuss how the concept of intimate citizenship can be utilized to understand migrant women's sexual identifications.

*Dilek: 'Because I am Against this System I am also Against Marriage'*

Dilek's narrative emphasizes the normativity of heterosexual marriage and motherhood and the marginalization of other choices, particularly in Turkey. Dilek is a 40 year old researcher in Britain. In her life-story, she elaborates the theme of striving for individuation. This, to her means gaining the economic and social independence to be able to live alone. She worked for seven years as a researcher in Istanbul, where she was however unable to afford living by herself and had to share accommodation with her sister. Migration abroad for many years constituted 'a fantastic dream', that she hoped could enable her to try out a different gendered lifestyle. This has influenced her choice of a job, too, as her employer promised an opportunity to go abroad. In this sense, Dilek invested many years in her migration project.

Dilek presents her choice to be single as partly political resistant, and partly as articulating her radical notion of individuality:

> D: One thing, the marriage institution is one of the important institutions that helps the survival of the capitalist system, the nuclear family ... therefore I think the institution of marriage needs to be torn down. I think this system will not collapse unless marriage disappears. I believe that the capitalist system is based on this and will continue with it. Because I am against this system I am also against marriage. But moreover, I am against two people's long term relationship (laughs).

> U: (laughs)

> D: For example, I am not thinking of living with someone, either. People's personalities begin resembling each other when they start living together. They do not create separate ideas, but only one idea. You begin resembling each other after a while and also to pressure each other. I have experienced this even when living with my sister. (...) For example although I say these things, when I live with someone – probably it has to do with being an older sister – I am so responsible, like a mother I begin to think about what my sisters do, if they have eaten dinner even. (...) So it's not only the institution of marriage I reject, but also living with someone, and that seems very strange to people and therefore they do not accept you.

Dilek delineates her ideal of autonomy from notions of maternal care and views any cohabiting arrangement, not just in a couple relationship, as a restriction of her individuation. Gilligan (1982) theorized notions of care and autonomy as highly gender specific. According to her, girls' gender specific development and their identification with their mothers' gender identity leads to a stronger orientation towards relationality and care rather than autonomy. Women therefore develop a different form of subjectivity based on the ethics of care. Relatedness, dialogue, compromize and the ability to link justice and care are at the basis of Gilligan's notion of an ethics of care. Dilek's desire to develop a more autonomous self can be read as resistance to normative femininities. This contains contradictions, as Dilek ironically notes her own care about whether her sister has regular meals. The impediments to realizing Dilek's ideal of autonomy are however not only psychological or social, but, in this case, first and foremost economic. The dichotomization of femininity as caring and masculinity as autonomous is of course not Dilek's personal problem but a pervasive social construct, and possibilities of individually subverting this are limited. The tension between autonomy and responsibility and care cannot be fully resolved, as both aspects co-exist in constructions of subjectivity.

In Turkey she felt ostracized in many social contexts as a single woman. Thus she recounts about her relationship with her colleagues in Turkey:

> D: Because they look at you and think 'She's still not married, if only she found a husband and got married, then we could become closer friends'. This is the way they think. Whenever they start a friendship, it is always with family ties. No woman, even if she works, makes a move independently of her husband. Therefore, all friendships develop in this way. My relations with my married sister are also limited. Because she has children she makes friends with people with children, or with her husband's friends.

Dilek's experience indicates how deeply engrained an ideal of femininity she challenges by trying to shift the emphasis of her sense of subjectivity from care and responsibility towards autonomy. Thus, she criticizes that the hegemonic family-centred forms of sociality exclude single women.[5] How deeply Dilek's self-presentation challenges the hegemony of the heterosexual marriage and/or family ideal can be glimpsed from the incomprehension her views are met with:

> D: Anyway if you say [that you never thought of marriage], they don't talk to you. If you reject marriage, and if I say this, it seems very strange to them, and they annoy you and you annoy them.

The ideal of marriage and family is thus constructed as the horizon of what is thinkable and communicable. Dilek's formulation of her own ideal of autonomy

---

5   This is echoed by other interview partners.

that goes beyond this horizon leads to a break down of communication. If we take communication to be at the basis of community, Dilek's outspokenness in positioning herself outside of the hegemonic frame of communicability can be interpreted as a resistant subjectivity challenging the heterosexually normative modes of community in which female subjectivity is inscribed. When Dilek finally realized her 'fantastic dreams' of migrating to Britain, she could test out her ideal of living alone in practice.

*Nâlan : 'I Never Thought of Marriage as Inevitable'*

Nâlan relates a range of negotiations of female sexual subjectivity. As a young, financially independent woman she rejected marriage for personal and political reasons:

> N: I read another book. That is Wilhelm Reich's book called 'The sexual revolution'. (…) After that we made sexual revolutions in our life. Therefore, we always thought of marriage as myth, dependence. Therefore, actually I would have left home even earlier. But in Turkey if you are not yet 18 years old, the police can take you back home. That is why I stayed at home until I was 18.

When she began living with her boyfriend, she experienced strong social pressure both from her family and others. Thus, they were required to present a marriage certificate to rent a flat or when going on holidays: 'in these situations, women were humiliated very much' since it is the woman who is seen as without shame and honour and marked with the 'whore stigma' (Pheterson 1990). After a few years, she yielded to the pressure and got married 'as a formality'. However, she felt that the institutionalization of the relationship impacted on her subjectivity, through assimilating her into the hegemonic forms of love relationships. Although Nâlan's decision to marry was taken instrumentally, she was subjectified in the terms of these normalizing practices. Thus, the 'formality' of marriage is not independent of, but co-constitutes her subjectivity. The interplay of agency and subjectification is also expressed in Nâlan's account of becoming a mother. She bore her son during a period when she and her husband were politically persecuted after the military coup d'etat of 1980 and went into hiding. While Nâlan does not expand on the difficulties of mothering in such a situation, she points out the positive effects of having a child in this period. She felt very isolated, since contacts to their political friends were very limited.

> N: Of course, in this situation to have a child gave us something to do. Because the child takes up all your time (…) And (…) because of having a child we appeared more like a normal family, that is what made life a bit easier.

Although for Nâlan the identities of political activist and mother were both central to her notion of self, the role of mother supported an appearance of social and political inconspicuousness. When she decided to divorce her husband, this new status of divorcee, led to new forms of social control:

> N: But because I was alone, my brothers who hadn't been around until then started coming to my house. (...) On the other hand, [her husband's] parents (...) became all nervous. No one wanted us to separate. They were more afraid that as a single woman something could happen to me. And second, their honour... as a separated woman, a divorced woman on her own at home, your boyfriends will come. They were totally ... they didn't accept it. And I was a young woman, 29 years old when I separated from my husband. I realized this, when my brother threw a male friend of mine out, (...) He came and called me a prostitute and threw my friend out. That's when I realized that life is not going to be easy (laughs).

Her brothers' social control reveals a paradox: while the presumed reason for controlling her social and sexual life is to prevent her loss of reputation, it is precisely their own intervention that labels her a 'prostitute'. This social control was not only exercised by her family: Nâlan gives an example of walking late at night with a male friend. When a police man controlled their papers and saw that they were not married, he threatened to arrest them. Nâlan's narrative articulates the different forms of sexual subjectification she experienced through different life stages and marital statuses – as a single woman, as a married mother and as a divorced single mother. She developed new strategies of resistance against each of these forms of subjectification, one of these was her decision to migrate (cf. Chapter 4).

*Melahat: Conceptualizing Lesbian Love*

Through internal rural-urban migration and re-migration, Melahat experienced different gender roles. Thus, her own gender identity was questioned in the village: as she had grown up in the city and had not learned the female gendered skills of the village, she was seen to be working 'like a man'. In this sense, the villagers used not sexual desire or behaviour but her role in the gendered division of labour as a marker to ascribe her a (partial) gender identity. Her family tried to pressure Melahat into a marriage as a young woman and even planned this without consulting her. Melahat emphasizes that her reasons for not wanting to marry were purely emotional, not political. But she resisted so forcefully 'continuously in such a militant way' that her family gave up on the plan to marry her. Melahat recounts that one of the main reasons for her refusal to get married was that during this time, she had a love relationship with a woman in the small town. At the time she was not aware of the concept of lesbian love, and simply thought that she was 'experiencing something unique that no one else experienced'. She does not expand on this, except to point out that the separation from her lover caused her a lot of suffering. She could not share this experience with anyone. As she could not concentrate on her work, either, she got herself into debt and decided to leave the village to go to a big city. Although within a few years Melahat had established herself economically, her continuing suffering from this failed love relationship and her sense of being 'different' motivated her to migrate again, this time to the UK.

> U: What were your expectations when you came here (…)?
>
> M: Well, let me tell you this, I didn't have any expectations actually.
>
> U: Hmm.
>
> M: My expectation was first to gain some distance from that society because of my relationship.
>
> U: Hmm.
>
> M: My relationship or better, I couldn't even imagine that such a relationship could exist. I didn't know. I experienced it without knowing.
>
> U: Hmm.
>
> M: I came here and realized that this was a relationship.
>
> U: That it is relationship that can be called a relationship.
>
> M: Yeah.
>
> U: Before it seemed more like a close friendship …
>
> M: Something like that. I experienced it somehow differently but probably I was mad that I live like this and so on. I thought that only I live like this.
>
> U: Hmm.
>
> M: Ah, I don't know … (pause)
>
> U: You didn't have any expectations from here, it was more about getting out …
>
> M: Hmm. A liberation, liberation.

Melahat articulates how the lack of a concept of lesbian made it difficult to make sense of her relationship, so that the explanation of madness seemed the only alternative. Migration to a new society necessitates and enables a new positioning of the self, including in the area of sexuality. In this way, migration can trigger a process of coming out, even to oneself (Kuntsman 2000). During the interview Melahat did not talk about coming out or about sexuality explicitly. Instead, she talked about encountering open or covert homophobia in community organizations, at the workplace and in personal relations. Weeks et al. (2001) argue that ethnic minority people are faced with a particular constellation of risk at the interface of racism and homophobia:

> Members of minority ethnic communities frequently have to balance their loyalty to their communities of origin, which provide support against racism, however "traditional" their values, with attempts to explore their sexual desires and identities. … as such, black non-heterosexuals often experience further dimensions of risk in terms of navigating everyday life (Weeks et al.2001: 186).

While it is important that the authors address the intersectionality of racism and homophobia, the argument contains some problematic assumptions. First, there is an implicit dichotomization of ethnic minorities with 'traditional' values and 'non-heterosexuals' as predominantly 'white'. This is part of the modernity difference hypothesis that assumes a racialized geography of modernity. They furthermore essentialize the notion that black people have a loyalty to 'their' ethnic community. The problematic omission is that there are, of course, also ethnic minority 'non-heterosexual' communities. Moreover, ethnic minority people construct differentiated notions of community on the basis of ethnicity but also other commonalities and values. They view identification and belonging in the tension of homophobia and racism as more complex. Their families and friendships with ethnic minority people and groups are not only a support against racism, but some of them also support them in their sexual lifestyles. Moreover, they experience homophobia from both ethnic minorities and the ethnically dominant population. Their own strategies of building friendships and intimacy frequently cross ethnic boundaries, often as a conscious decision for diversity. Thus, homophobia should not be viewed as ethnically bounded. The experience of multiple forms of exclusion and domination requires and engenders partial identifications (Parker 1995) of ethnic minority lesbian, bisexual and transgendered people, requiring a higher degree of self-reflexivity and identity work than for ethnic majority people whose community knowledge and worldviews are normalized within gay, lesbian, bisexual and transgender subcultures.

*Meryem: Community, Family, Sexuality*

Furthermore, ethnic difference cannot be reduced to a black-white difference but involves complex relations of differential racialization. Thus, Meryem lives in a blended family with her son, her female partner and her daughter in London. Meryem characterizes their household as 'a very multicultural home' where different languages are spoken. Yet, she concedes that English language and cultural practices often prevail as it is 'something that both are familiar with'. This multi-ethnic family of choice may be specific but the issues they are faced with are not. The multiplicity of languages and identifications in this same sex family disrupts the narrative of 'traditional' ethnic minority families versus modern, 'white' families of choice. Meryem's story contradicts Weeks et al.'s (2001) assumption that for ethnic minority people, allegiance to family and to lesbian lifestyles are mutually exclusive. Meryem points out that at times the linguistic differences within her family can lead to conflicts. Their strategy of privileging English to avoid these conflicts takes up arguments about multicultural citizenship as the creation of a shared democratic ground, for communication is instrumental. Notions of multiculturalism differentiate between the public sphere regulated by shared principles of democracy on a universalist premise on the one hand and on the other hand the particularistic private sphere which contains ethnically specific values and resources. These are deemed mutually compatible as long as they converge in the acceptance of democratic values in the public sphere (cf. Kymlicka 1995, Rex 1993). However, Meryem's story challenges this neat distinction into private, particularistic and public, universalist principles. The relationship between private and public is therefore better conceptualized not as a divide but instead as aspects that co-exist in the same social spaces (Yuval-Davis 1997). This means that any public action contains private aspects and vice versa.

This section has highlighted the diverse range of sexual identities and the meanings and struggles around personal status elaborated by the migrant women. This diversity and complexity contradicts ethnicized notions of modernity versus tradition and raises questions of how to integrate sexual and intimate rights of migrant women into our understanding of citizenship. First I will look at mothering practices as another key aspect of intimate citizenship before discussing the implications of migrant women's practices for conceptualizing intimate and sexual citizenship in the conclusion.

**Transnational Mothering**

When migrant women cross borders of nation-states, they transform social and cultural practices of family and the meanings attached to these. One such transformation is that women experience separations from their children and/or partners. The practice of 'transnational mothering' (Hondagneu Sotelo and Avila 1997), or 'caring from a distance' (Parreñas 2001a) has recently attracted attention from researchers. In particular female dominated migration flows, such as those from the Philippines (Parreñas 2001, 2005) or, more generally female migration in sectors such as domestic work (Hondagneu Sotelo and Avila 1997, Lutz 2007) engendered cross-national practices of mothering. In earlier migration flows, practices of 'serial migration' (Phoenix 2007) have been particularly noted among Caribbean migrants, where migration has often been part of a trans-generational family project or even tradition. In this instance, grandparents or aunts have often enabled the migration of young women through caring for the children left behind (Olwig 1999), while adult siblings were key resources of help and information in the Diaspora (Chamberlain 1999). There have been concerns about the quality of care the children left behind receive. Indeed, in particular for those women migrants who provide care services through their jobs in migration, Hochschild (2000) has argued that they are implicated in global chains of care, which however, unevenly distribute the good of care. Thus, while they might be providing care to children in rich countries of immigration, producing a 'surplus' of care, their children in the countries of origin might be affected by a 'care drain', not receiving the care and love they ought to. This has been forcefully argued in the case of the Philippines (Parreñas 2001, 2005), where about 30% of children have one or both parents living abroad (Hochschild 2002: 22). On the other hand, some authors argue that children do not necessarily have to rely on their biological mother for care, and point to long established practices of 'child shifting' (Reynolds 2005) or 'non-singular motherhood' (Lutz 1998). Yet, the predominance of the Western notion that mothers are the preferred carers and that the mother-child relationships should be based on physical proximity has also affected families where non-singular mothering practices were normative before their migration. Thus, retrospectively and measured against the norms of the society of residence, mothers may critically evaluate their decision to leave children behind even if temporarily (Lutz 1998). Practices of transnational mothering vary and change with time. Thus, there is currently concern among some Caribbean scholars about the lack of emotional care for 'barrel children' who grow up without their parents and – unlike earlier generations – are not cared for by close family but distant relatives, as most of their immediate family is abroad (Reynolds 2006). Indeed, there, as in the Philippines, the replacement of face to face care with 'commodified motherhood' (Parreñas 2001a), i.e. mothers showing their love through sending, at times expensive, presents has been noted. While new communication technologies enable frequent communication for some families across the distance (Zontini 2007), allowing mothers to advise their children on emotional and educational issues, these separations are often very painful for family members. Indeed, whether or not long term separations of mothers and children are psychologically or developmentally damaging, both migrant mothers and children feel they need to justify and legitimate the practice of transnational mothering to integrate it into a narrative of 'liveable lives', acceptable in the country of residence (Phoenix 2007). Migration policy implicitly relies on an outsourcing of caring responsibilities to countries of emigration, yet the individual migrants are tasked with morally and emotionally negotiating these aspects of migration (cf. Ryan 2008).

Separations of mothers and children through migration have been a relatively common feature of migration from Turkey, for Germany, Nauck (1994: 141) found that 15% of migrant families from Turkey had their children raised by relatives in Turkey during their early childhood. Yet, research on migrant women from Turkey has paid scant attention to this, if it is mentioned at all, it is in passing (e.g. Potts and Krüger 1995, Franger 1984, Rosen 1993). Transnational mothering is 'one variation in the organizational arrangement, meanings, and priorities of motherhood' (Hondagneu-Sotelo and Avila 1997: 548), whereby migrant women, 'are in the process of actively, if not voluntarily, building alternative constructions of motherhood' (549). Yet, gender (Huth-Hildebrandt 2002) and family relations (Nauck 1994) among migrants from Turkey are seen as fixed markers for constructing ethnic difference. Dynamic aspects and change are not socially recognized, much less so are migrant women seen as agents of social change.

*Serial Migrations of Mothers and Children*

The process of migration may be a reaction to changing family relations, such as divorce and single motherhood, indeed even if the family composition remains the same, it changes family relations. Migration often does not take place for the whole family at once but is 'serial'. Yet, the question of who constitutes 'the whole family' is not unequivocal. Although the nuclear family is the only family type recognized for purposes of immigration, extended family networks frequently enable migration by providing support in terms of childcare and other resources (cf. Krüger and Potts 1995, Hochschild 2000). This points to the problematic logic of immigration legislation where the country of immigration's interests are paramount in defining who has a right to enter. Thus the reproductive labour of child-raising is 'outsourced' to Turkey. However this indirect, unpaid or under-paid, contribution to the smooth running of the economy of the country of immigration does not entitle these (mainly) women to any claims on that state.

The separation of mothers and children runs counter to Western hegemonic discourses on the mother as primary carer, and the emotional and physical closeness that is thus at once claimed and naturalized (cf. Tizard 1991, Phoenix and Woollett 1991). This is mainly debated with respect to the pros and cons of mothers' paid employment outside the house. The success of the initial mother-child attachment is seen as influencing the child's later social adaptation or delinquency, their educational success or failure, their ability to build a 'normal family life' and so on (cf. Tizard 1991, Young 1994). Other carers are seen only as substitutes. This effectively holds mothers singularly responsible for the child's' development, exonerating other persons, such as fathers, or social influences such as schooling, peer groups, media, poverty, etc. as factors significant for a child's development. In Turkish folk (Fritsche et al.1992) and official Kemalist (Delaney 1995) discourses, the role of mother is highly valued and idealized. While mothers' economic contribution to the household may be crucial, they are often overlooked; indeed breadwinning is rarely explicitly viewed as fulfilling mothering responsibilities, even less so women's migration. These discursive factors may contribute to the difficulties migrant women experience when leaving their children so that many women suffer from feelings of being (labelled) 'bad' mothers (Hondagneu-Sotelo and Avila 1997, Lutz 2007, Parreñas 2001).

In the case of migrants from Turkey, important factors the mothers considered were the availability of affordable childcare that suited their needs as single mothers, or mothers working in shifts, the price of childcare as well as the reliability and trust they put into the carers. Thus, it was often considered a better solution to separate from the children in order to have a trusted member of the family care for the child than relying on the care of strangers.[6] Moreover, many migrants initially lived with the 'myth of return' so that they wanted their children to be educated in Turkey where they should, according to the plan, eventually return. Of course, financial and legal reasons were crucial here. Thus, Nâlan was a single, shift-working mother of a young child, facing the challenge of legalizing her status as an undocumented migrant. Pakize who migrated as a single mother initially wanted to 'establish' herself before bringing her children over. When she was in a position to do so, her husband did not give his permission for them to join her: 'Neither did he care for them, nor did he give permission for them to go abroad and join me'. German migration legislation constitutes another obstacle: 'The residence permit of a working foreign mother is linked to the proof of having a recognized childcare place, crèche, kindergarten or after school club. Neighbourly help is not accepted' (Franger 1986: 101).

## The Mothers' Perspectives

The experience of separation can be very painful, not only for the children but certainly also for the mothers. One compounding factor is that the mothers may experience intense feelings of guilt. After Ayla separated from her husband, she migrated to other European countries and had to travel regularly because of her job. For this reason she sent him to her parents in Turkey and he only joined her after seven years at the age of 11.

> A: I missed him a lot and I was also thinking what am I doing – I felt very guilty. What am I doing to this guy? I took him away from his father and now I am sending him away from me. So that was a very bad feeling.

> U: Did you feel people were reproaching you or …

> A: No, it was never openly … nobody ever said anything but it was my own feeling, I didn't feel good about it.

---

6    Franger (1986) points out that institutional childcare is exceptional in Turkey, so that the migrant mothers are not used to it and prefer childcare through relatives and neighbours. 50% of children of German working mothers are cared for by grandparents, an option which is not available to migrants due to the restrictive family unification legislation.

Such feelings of guilt may be brought up much later during conflicts relating to different issues. Thus, Nilgün recounts that in the conflict that ensued when she and her sister left the parental home, her mother brought up these issues.

> N: Well, my mother could not cope at all [with our leaving home]. She felt betrayed because she worked hard for us all her life, and sacrificed all her life for the relationship because of her children.(…) She felt very frustrated, and she could not fulfil the role of a mother according to her own feelings. And the children were scattered, and at one point they came. And she had very big problems with this, she had huge complexes, actually. Everyone was alone in the family. Well, that is a whole issue in itself. She was very embittered.

Here, Nilgün expresses her mother's deep regrets about her experiences of mothering. She felt that Nilgün's leaving home was a betrayal of all her sacrifices. One aspect of Nilgün's leaving home is that it expresses her wish to lead a different life from that of her mother. This reinforced her mother's own doubts about her mothering role. Although Nilgün does not criticize her mother for any perceived lack of care, her mother interpreted her decision to leave the parental home thus. This indicates the strong normative hold of the argument that makes mothers responsible for their children's development (cf. Young 1994, Bhopal 1998).

Pakize's sole motivation for migration was to be able to provide for her children, after divorce:

> U: What were your expectations when you migrated?
>
> P: I didn't have any expectations. To be honest it was only and only to maybe live more comfortably. The mother-in-law had gone into debt and so on. Let us pay back the debt, and I didn't have any expectations from here, to be honest because …
>
> U: So was it in one way economic independence?
>
> P: Only that, only that. And then, I was planning to return to the children after a few years, but of course it didn't happen. Of course, it didn't happen as I had planned.

While Pakize did not return to Turkey, her ex-husband refused permission for the children to join her in Germany, either. Thus, for many years Pakize's mother-in-law cared for them, and Pakize saw them only once a year, during her summer holidays.

> P: Well, I went to Turkey every summer, every month I sent money. Of course, this is not good for the children … I was always a stranger for the children.

U: Yes, they must have missed you a lot …

P: Now, they would certainly have missed me. It is not about missing me, they expressed it by reacting badly to me. Because they were not staying with my mother, they were staying with the mother-in-law. And because the mother-in-law was not my mother, ah, well she didn't represent me very well to the children: 'Your mother is comfortable there, she is going out and enjoying herself'. And a child doesn't understand …

U: Of course.

P: All year [they don't see their mother], for one month they see the mother and the mother leaves. And then, well, they tried to get closer, well they were reluctant in front of their paternal grandmother, because she may get jealous. They already sensed it at that age. Because the paternal grandmother loved them a lot, she was very jealous of me.

This shows the ambiguity of the childcare arrangement: while Pakize depended on her mother-in-law's childcare, she also laid herself open to criticism about her mothering (cf. Bhopal 1998). As a teenager, her son turned 'very naughty', and his grandmother could not control him anymore. Pakize brought him over to Germany, however within a short time, he 'got into trouble' and she decided to send him back to Turkey. There, he began to pressure his sister and grandmother; however the grandmother could not assert her authority. The problems with her brother led to Pakize's daughter's wish to join her mother in Germany. At this point, finally her father gave his permission. Pakize's daughter was about to turn 16, after which age she would not have been eligible for family reunification. Therefore, Pakize was glad that her daughter took the decision to join her very quickly.

P: Well, she came within two months. If she hadn't come then, she wouldn't have been able to come anymore. I view this as luck. But of course, it was not that easy, two people who don't know each other.

U: Yes, of course it must be very difficult.

P: You are a mother, you love your child, but … maybe she loves you, too. However we were strangers to each other. She was a grown up girl, and well, me I am a person who has always lived on her own for years. Well, the difficulties started. (…) She was crying, only listening to music, she went and locked herself in. She often said 'I am leaving–.

Pakize and her daughter had to reconcile their expectations of mother-daughter relationships, characterized by love and understanding, with the diverging reality of being 'strangers to each other'. They had to work at getting to know each other and getting used to living together. Moreover, Pakize's daughter had to adapt to living in a new country. Pakize describes the first five years of their living together as very difficult. Her daughter reproached her 'why did you leave us behind?' which was very painful for Pakize. However, with time they 'got on better':

> P: From Turkey she thought (…) I have gone to a foreign country, I enjoy myself everyday and so on, that is what she thought. When she came here and saw my way of life, well she saw my friends. And then she realized her mother is only working here! That is, it isn't as she thought or as it was told her.

During this period, however Pakize 'got news [about her son] that were not good at all': 'I heard complaints from everybody'. After his marriage broke down, her son 'left and we don't know where he went to'. She did not have a chance to re-build a relationship with him. The slow and painful process of rapprochement with her daughter however was successful and they have a good relationship now. After working in Germany for some years, her daughter married and returned to Turkey with her husband, where Pakize regularly visits her.

Transnational mothers find different ways of caring over the temporal and spatial distance. They clearly delineate their form of mothering from abandonment, even if they have not seen their children for many years. Sending money, letters, photographs and phoning are ways of maintaining a relation with their children. Nonetheless, some experience that they loose the trust of and authority over their children through the distance (cf. Hondagneu-Sotela and Avila 1997, Lutz 2007). While some mothers think their children recognize and value their sacrifices, not all do. As some children grow up and articulate a critical view of transnational mothering, this can be an important source of mothers' self-doubt.

Mothers may also find it difficult to reconcile transnational motherhood with their own ideals of good mothering. Thus, they may feel regret and guilt for having had to separate from their children. Moreover, 'othermothers' (Hill-Collins 1991), that is women sharing mothering responsibilities with biological mothers, can have an ambiguous role. On the one hand, their childcare is indispensable for transnational mothers, and the children may see them as the primary carers. This can be a positive relationship, as Nilgun and Deniz argue. On the other hand, othermothers may also be in a position to undermine the relationship between the biological mother and her children through implicit or explicit criticism of her as a 'bad mother'. Yet, othermothers may be able to provide for the emotional needs of children, precisely because they do not have the burden of providing economically: As Reina Weems (1991) writes in an autobiographical essay, in her life emotionally attentive othermothers were 'women who did not have the onus of providing for me, and so had the luxury of talking to me' (1991: 126). Therefore, an acknowledgement of the mothers' role of breadwinning as a crucial part of their practices of 'good mothering' is an important step towards de-constructing ideals of mothering that contribute to the de-valuation of migrant women's mothering practices. Non-singular notions of motherhood allow for the differentiation of two aspects of care work, namely 'caring for' and 'caring about'. While Western normative notions of mothering unite both aspects in the person of the biological mother, where non-singular motherhood is seen as normative, these two aspects need not be fulfilled by the same person:

> The code of non-singular motherhood requires accepting the factual co-existence of these aspects in the migration project: leaving the 'care for' [children] to another 'mother' may be seen as the expression of the 'care about' [the children]. (Lutz 1998: 294–5, my translation from German).

Children may interpret their mothers' migration as showing a lack of love (e.g. Parreñas 2001), an interpretation commensurate with the normative Western 'cult of true womanhood' (Hill-Collins), yet

> it is impossible for observers – therapists, social workers, or others – to draw conclusions about a mother's love for her child based solely on her actions. It is necessary for observers to understand both what kind of power oppression her actions are related to, and what possibilities she has to realise her motherly love (Leira and Krips 1993: 87).

The life-stories of transnational mothering and daughtering are complex and contrast with the stereotypical public image of Turkish migrant women as over-determined by 'traditional' gender roles. The separations of mothers and children have created new problems and new ways of overcoming them. The argument on failed mother-child attachment a priori pathologizes transnational mothering. Instead, by making these experiences visible, I hope to validate them and show the agency of both mothers and children in constructing and maintaining relationships of mutual recognition, creating new ways of mothering and daughtering, even if this included difficult and conflictual experiences and feelings. It is not my intention to simply celebrate these transnational mothering practices as a challenge to normative mothering roles or ethnically specific stereotypes, since these experiences also generated a lot of pain that needs to be explored and addressed.

Regulations of 'good mothering' not only pertain to the closeness of mothers and children, but also construct women as the cultural reproducers of the national or ethnic collectivity (Anthias and Yuval-Davis 1989, 1992, Yuval-Davis 1997). Mothers are thus ascribed a crucial role in the transmission of ethnically specific values and resources.

*Transmitting and Transforming Ethnic Identities*

During the 1970s and 80s a key explanation for 'failed' integration of migrant young people was the so-called culture or generation clash. This assumed that parental attitudes and orientation towards a presumed culture of the homeland prevented young people from integrating. While this has been critiqued for relying on a reductionist view of culture and family dynamism, recent public debates on social cohesion and migration (in the UK) or on standards in education (in Germany) return to a responsibilization of parents and in particular mothers for what they perceive as failed integration of the young generation of migrants or ethnic minorities.

Women's role in ethnic and national projects is often conceptualized as passive and images of women are often used to symbolize a static, immutable essence of the national or ethnic group, while men are seen to symbolize the active and progressive elements in nationalism (Mosse 1985, Apitzsch 1996). Women's supposed greater truthfulness to tradition is seen as key in socializing children into the ethnic group and transmitting ethnically specific values. In the context of migration, where women are subjected to two sets of norms of femininity (Anthias and Yuval-Davis 1992) the pressure on women as mothers to transmit ethnically specific values and cultural resources to the children may even be greater.

This may at times lead to a more restrictive education of migrant children than even the parental generation themselves or peers in Turkey experience (Lutz 1991, Suaréz-Orozco 2000). On the other hand, the experience of migration can also open up new ways of living gender and family relations as the life-stories here testify. The migrant women negotiate and contest dominant ethnicized values and constructions of community in their own lives, an important instance of this is their decision to divorce from their husbands. Single and divorced migrant women of Turkish background, although increasing in number continue to be viewed as the exception, and are ignored by the social science literature (for an exception, cf. Erdem 2000). In his study on Turkish migrants in Britain, Küçükcan (1999) theorizes the family as the core social organization of the ethnic community transmitting ethnically specific values. There are no references to female headed households, or divorce in his study. While this can be seen as a consequence of the empirical male focus of the study, it is a problematic omission of the increasing economic possibility of divorce or single status that migration enables. In Turkey, living as a single or divorced woman is difficult both economically and socially and the percentage of single women is very low – Göbenli (1999: 29) states that among the female urban population only 1% is not married. Küçükcan's assumption of the normality of a heterosexual two-parent family theoretically reproduces the hegemonic conception of women's appropriate sexual behaviour, here intra-ethnic marriage and motherhood, as a marker of ethnicity. Moreover, by according the heterosexual two-parent family this centrality in the transmission of ethnic identity, it theoretically reifies women's role as cultural reproducers of the ethnic group, however only within the prescribed, ethnicized parameters of femininity.[7] Against this backdrop, it is argued that the interviewees' family forms of single motherhood can be seen as challenging rather than adhering to a fixed and unified notion of ethnically specific tradition.

---

7    These assumptions are not limited to Kucukcan's study (e.g., Rosen 1992).

The transmission of ethnically specific values entails a transformation of ethnicity (Inowlocki 1995, Fischer 1986, Lutz 1995, 1997, 1998). Thus, Inowlocki argues that the loss of inter-generationally constituted identity through migration can lead to a crisis. This crisis, can only be overcome by integrating changes into the shared intergenerational identity. She coins the term 'generation work' to refer to the negotiation and the reflection on change within the family. Generation work thus is the familial effort of making sense of experiences of crisis, rupture and discontinuity to integrate them into a liveable notion of self and family.

Thus, it is suggested we might view the stories about the mothers' transmission of ethnically specific values as a dynamic exchange in which the generations mutually constitute each others identities rather than a one-way process.

It is argued that mothers select specific cultural resources, practices and values they wish to transmit and engage in negotiations about the meanings of these ethnically specific resources with their children. Second, it is argued that these negotiations of ethnically specific resources between mothers and children also involve different, at times conflicting constructions of meaning of symbols and practices. Third, it is suggested we might view the construction of ethnic identity, both for the mothers and for the children as bound up with cross-ethnic relations and identifications beyond the dichotomy of culture of origin (Turkish) versus majority culture (German or English). People from other ethnic minorities can play an important part in the identity constructions of migrants of Turkish background, too. And this can lead to the elaboration of explicit, self conscious 'bi-national' or 'bi-cultural', hybrid or hyphenated or multiple ethnicities.

The following examples are taken from Pınar's, Birgül's and Nâlan's life-stories that gave mothering an important place. Pınar contends that since her divorce nine years ago 'My life revolved around my job and Derya [her ten year old daughter], and that continues to this day'. Mothering to her is a central part of her own subjectivity, which she heavily invests in. Like Pınar, Birgül presents her eight year old daughter as central to her life projects. She reflects that as a single mother she is particularly close to her daughter. While she sees this as a positive result of her own choices, she also strongly feels that the demands of being a single mother working full-time have an effect of isolating her, so that the relation to her daughter in terms of responsibility as well as enjoyment gains even more centrality in her life. These feelings were shared by other interviewees about their experience of being a single mother. Nâlan also gave her relation with her son and his problems in Britain a prominent place in her life-story. This is related to her concerns at the time of interview. Ugur, her seventeen year old son, had been living in Turkey for six months. Nâlan was happy that he had decided to spend some time in Turkey because she wanted him to get away from England, where he was part of a petty criminal friendship group, whose activities had brought him to court on one occasion. This crisis triggered a dialogue between Nâlan and her son about his choice of friends, and the values he embraced, as well as leading to Nâlan's self-reflections about her education.

*Pınar: 'A Priori Bi-cultural'*

Pınar views all second generation migrants like herself as 'a priori bi-cultural'. She is very active in feminist and migrants' political campaigns and in her personal life also values friendships and networks with other migrants. In this context, I asked, whether there were any values that Pınar regarded as specifically Turkish that she wanted to offer her daughter. Pınar emphasized the importance of teaching her the Turkish language, so that she exclusively spoke Turkish with Derya in her early childhood. She also encouraged Derya's father, who is Kurdish to speak Kurmanci[8] with Derya. Moreover, she sent Derya to a bi-lingual kindergarten and to mother-tongue classes at school. While the transmission of Turkish language to their children was an important issue for most of the mothers, not all of them had such clear educational strategies as Pınar. This may be linked to her awareness as a second generation migrant of the complexities of identification for migrant children. Moreover, Pınar views mothering also in the context of her professional and social-political networks and activities:

> P: The absolute priority is to educate Derya, according to my ideas what I think is right.
>
> U: Hmm, yes.
>
> P: Emancipatory work plays a very big role in this, consciously.

Thus, the project of educating her daughter is bound up with her professional expertise in terms of 'emancipatory work'. Pınar has a very high level of reflection, and of conscious decision-making, as well as being able to use her professional knowledges, such as familiarity with specific bi-cultural or migrants institutions in the education of her daughter.[9]

One element in this strategy is that Pınar takes Derya to certain activities and events such as folklore evenings, wedding parties, circumcision parties, or political events. Although Pınar herself is not that interested in these events, she wants to acquaint her daughter with these: 'I *consciously* took her there, she had contact with these people, she got to know the music but other things also and that was important to me'.

This quote shows Pınar's awareness that cultural competence and knowledge are important ethnic resources that are not naturally transmitted but acquired or accessed in a social way. Especially the participation in social events, such as life-

---

8   Kurmanci is the most widespread Kurdish dialect in Turkey.

9   The material and symbolic resources for mothering are also class-specific. Thus, for example Ayla's financial resources and her social networks enabled her to bring a live-in childminder from Turkey to look after her son. This helped to transmit the Turkish language to him, although Ayla was in paid employment and her husband was not Turkish.

cycle events, is a way of learning and getting to know cultural resources. Pınar says she herself is 'not that curious' about these events, probably because she participated in them before and may not identify fully with the sociality expressed in these events. This sociality is often centred around the nuclear or extended family and is part of elaborate gender-performances which clash with Pınar's ideas and practices as a divorced, independent, single mother. Thus, Pınar does not aim to provide Derya with an unproblematic, ready made ethnic identification. Instead, by participating in activities and events with which she herself does not fully identify, she also provides her daughter with a model for partial and contingent identification (Parker 1995).

Pınar's view of the legitimity of a 'bi-cultural' identity is borne out in the way she encourages Derya to use identity labels flexibly and situationally. Derya sometimes asks her mother whether she is Turkish, Kurdish or German. Pınar then tells her

> P: 'You are what you feel', you know. And that sometimes changes, she says 'You know what, mum, I think I am only German', and then I don't react by saying 'Oh my god, how can you do this to me!' as other people I know approach the issue. I say 'Well, than you are a German'.
>
> U: Hmm.
>
> P: And then some days she says 'I find it stupid how Germans deal with it' or something. And I don't force her to define herself. (...) But when she is asked by others, (...) 'Who do you love more, Germany or Turkey? 'Well, that happens often. And then she has said 'Both', you know, 'I love both (...) and the question is really stupid' she adds that, too.

Thus, in Pınar's view and in her educational practice, situational and partial identification with ethnically specific cultural practices and different ethnically based collectivities is both possible and legitimate. This certainly reflects her own ways of dealing with ethnic belonging.

In the above extract, the events she cites include folklore and political events. This reflects on the variety of practices laying claim to represent ethnic culture. While there is a tendency in multiculturalist discourses and practices to naturalize and de-politicize culture, political groups and parties use cultural performances as powerful tools of mobilization. Thus, folklore groups are often linked to political groups or parties. In particular the expression of Alevi or Kurdish culture in the context of racist Turkish state practices – dominant in the German migration context, also – is a political challenge to their marginalization and often a politicized re-invention of cultural resources (cf. Acik 2000). Many mass assemblies are centred on speeches, but importantly also on musical or dance performances.

Pınar's own priorities are reflected in her choice of taking Derya to political meetings in order to get to know politically and socially specific 'Turkish' cultural resources and values. This refers back to Pınar's own negotiation of her ethnic identity: As a young girl, Pınar experienced her parents' restrictions of her education and her movements as representative of Turkishness and as a teenager rejected Turkishness altogether. Only in the final years of high school did she get to know politically interested, socially progressive people which gave her access to versions of Turkishness (and Kurdishness) that were reconcilable with her own identification as an aspiring critical intellectual. Critically, this version of Turkishness encompassed a diversity of gender roles. This encounter with a different version of Turkishness was a turning point for Pınar's ethnic identification, motivating her to learn Turkish again and get 're-socialized into [Turkish] culture'. Pınar's notion of re-socialization is echoed by other second generation interviewees. It demonstrates a self reflexivity of the constructedness and also efforts of belonging. Pınar sees her own and her daughter's ability to partially identify with forms of Turkishness as an important marker of difference from Derya's German peers. In Pınar's narrative contact and access to German peers, institutions and cultural resources is tacitly self understood. What matters to Pınar is that her daughter knows that she can be more than only German.

*Conflicting meanings of ethnically specific resources*
Mothers are confronted with their children's appropriations and negotiations of ethnicity from diverse sources. Conflicting meanings are especially salient when they challenge values and attitudes central to the mothers' self-presentation, thus requiring a specific effort of generation work.

In contact with her grandparents, Derya experiences a very different version of Turkishness, and has to negotiate conflicting values of her mother and grandparents.

> P: And there she is confronted with religion for example. And she has a very different problem with religion, she *wants* to believe. She reproaches me because I don't believe.

> U: Yes.

> P: It's crazy! I have also discussed religion with Derya. I always try and keep it on a philosophical level. She is fascinated by her grandmother's praying and fasting. She finds that great.

> U: Yes, yes.

> P: (...) She is torn between the two, although I don't think she suffers from that but tries to reconcile it. Because they have faith and are so determined to hold onto it, while her mum decisively rejects it.

> U: Yes.

P: And she tries to find her own way. And sometimes she says 'I believe in God' and then again 'I don't believe in Him, otherwise [bad things] wouldn't be allowed to happen'. (…) She is very alert and observes and tries to make sense. But there she is part of the discussion [about religion] and as long as it is in a distance and reduced it's alright, it is also part of the culture.

U: Yes.

P: And I also try to simply see this religion only as culture.

Religion is a highly controversial, emotional and political subject in the context of migrants of Turkish background. Despite Pınar's effort to allow her daughter a choice of identification, Pınar's need to contain the differences between her daughter's and her own views on religion becomes clear when she emphasizes that she accepts these discussions as long as it is reduced to a cultural issue.

Pınar herself did not have such a plural picture of varying modalities of ethnicity when she was growing up, but in her own educational practice she does not impose her meanings of Turkishness on her daughter, and within certain contingencies allows for conflict.

*Fostering cross-ethnic identifications*

Pınar has put specific emphasis on enabling Derya to deal with being a migrant, she does not aim to educate Derya into Turkishness but rather to enable her to cross ethnic boundaries. Pınar tries to give her daughter opportunities to gain such a wider view. This happens through spending time with friends from different places. Thus, an important reference point for Derya when she was growing up was Pınar's best friend Alice who is Black South African. Derya grew up in close contact with Alice and her family.

P: Alice was here every day or we were at their place. We were a family (…) we celebrated holidays together. Whether they were Christian or Muslim or more cultural holidays. And for her it was a matter of course that there were Black people around her. Or for example we used to have picnics and barbecues with the children and other friends, Turkish friends, and I don't know, South American people, that is speaking Spanish, English, Turkish and the children played together, because we wanted it that way.

Pınar consciously gives her daughter an environment where she can interact with different migrant people as a matter of fact. Pınar helped Derya gain the language skills in English to be able to talk to some of her friends who do not speak German. Moreover, she tries to give her other opportunities of dealing with being a migrant by providing her with multicultural educational materials. As these are not readily available in Germany, she brings them from Britain or from South Africa. This shows on the one hand, the cultural and institutional limitations of her cross-ethnic educational project by the unavailability of educational material in Germany. On the other hand, it shows her agency and resourcefulness in using her transnational, cross-ethnic, cultural, social and economic capital (English language, ability to travel) in her educational project.

Pınar points out, that this cross-ethnic friendship network was a choice, she and her friends made. This is an oppositional strategy to the normalization and naturalization of ethnically homogeneous notions of community, closeness and intimacy. In particular her close relationship with Alice and her family, as Pınar points out was 'a substitute for what maybe lacked in terms of a conventional family, well father and mother together'. This can be viewed as a heterosexual, cross-ethnic 'family of choice' (Weeks et al.2001), transgressing normative assumptions of the naturalness of family-life based on a nuclear mother-father-child structure. After Alice's return to South Africa, Pınar is still in close contact with Alice, they write letters, send faxes and parcels and speak on the phone on birthdays. 'It is a part of family whose absence we feel. And for Derya – I find that important –it is something familiar, not something strange, you know. If anything, Germanness used to be strange to her'. If we take Pınar's description of Alice and her family as 'part of family whose absence we feel' seriously, this can be seen as an instance of transnationalization of a family of choice. She sums up her aim in educating her daughter as enabling her to deal with plurality. This goes beyond cultural or linguistic competence in Turkish and German but includes a capacity of understanding and relating to non-ethnically bounded cultural forms and to build inter-ethnic relations.

Pınar's practice puts into question a narrow view of mothering as the transmission of ethnic identity. On a very intimate and micro-level it can be seen as a case in point to critically assess current debates on belonging.

In these debates, the notion of the family is often used as an image of solidarity, closeness and cultural homogeneity. Indeed, some theorists assume family-like primordial ties to be the basis for national solidarities. This does not sufficiently take into account the complexity of processes of belonging and identification. Instead, we might take a cue from Pınar: her story of mothering calls particular attention to the fact that family-like solidarities are not necessarily ethnically bounded, but can transcend these boundaries. Pınar's mothering strategy constitutes a specific intervention into the normalized relation of gender, family, nation and ethnicity. Thus, rather than transmit a canon of specific Turkish or German cultural resources to her daughter, she wants to foster her ability to negotiate plurality and challenge ethnic hegemony.

*Birgül: Making Multilingual Education Normal*

Birgül put a lot of effort into educating her daughter bi-lingually. Thus, despite difficulties, she employed women from Turkey as childminders in Aysel's infancy. When Aysel was one and a half years old, she sent her to a 'progressive nursery' where one of the educators spoke Turkish. However, the children at the kindergarten were discouraged from speaking languages other than German:

> B: I went to pick up Aysel, everybody speaks German, and when she speaks to me she goes [whispering] in Turkish. I said 'Aysel, why do you whisper when you speak Turkish?' The language being suppressed made her insecure to speak Turkish, speaking Turkish came to be a source of insecurity.

When Birgül thematized this at a parents' evening, she was told that the kindergarten's language development policy aimed at fostering the German language only. Birgül initiated a debate among the parents and the workers about bi-lingual education. She joined the management committee, with particular responsibility for the migrant children and was instrumental in the adoption of a bi-lingual education policy. Although Birgül feels that this was not entirely implemented, it achieved the aim of children speaking more freely in their various languages at the kindergarten. Thus, Birgül's educational strategy does not remain in the private realm of the home but she reached out to institutionalize the acceptance of other languages in the kindergarten.

*Multiple identifications*

Like Pınar, Birgül supports her daughters' multiple identifications. Thus, she recounts that at her registration at school the headmistress asked about Aysel's mothertongue:

> 'What's the mothertongue of Aysel?' Mothertongue? I asked Aysel. 'My mothertongue is German Turkish' she said. 'I mean ...' the woman tried to explain herself. 'She is right, she speaks both of them perfectly' I said. 'Yes, I am born here and I speak both languages' Aysel said. 'What should I write here?' the woman asked. 'German Turkish' Aysel answered.

In recounting this dialogue, Birgül shows her pride about her daughter's creative and self-assured response. Moreover, re-enacting the dialogue, she performs her attitude of letting Aysel speak for herself: Thus, the head's question was initially addressed to Birgül who then encouraged her daughter to represent herself. The headmistress's hesitation and attempt to explain that the questionnaire required the identification with a single mothertongue shows how the institutionalized incitements and regulations of identification do not allow for multiple identifications. Aysel, nonetheless insisted on her dual identification and supported it with the argument that she was born in Germany. Although Aysel may not fully grasp the impact of the *ius soli* argument, nor be able to locate it in debates around citizenship, it is striking that she knows about this point of reference to validate her claims to a German 'mothertongue'. Birgül supported this by adding that Aysel's identification was borne out by her mastery of both languages. This is a claim to authority over a nationalized cultural resource, language, which functions as a boundary marker of belonging. This incitement to respond to categorizations as '*Ausländer*' is an everyday situation in the life worlds of migrants, as pointed out in Chapter 1. Birgül and Aysels's claim of a dual, hybrid or hyphenated identity challenges this normalization of exclusive national and ethnic ascriptions.

*Negotiating belonging relationally*
This strategy subverts an institutional context that reduces identification to a national or ethnic category. Yet, in other contexts, Aysel's identification is not limited to national or ethnic categories. Thus, when a friend of Birgül's asked Aysel for an identification, she responded:

> Birgül: 'I am a German-Turk, but my mother is a Turk-German' she said. I asked her 'What's that supposed to mean?' 'My mother is born in Turkey but lives in Germany, and I am born in Germany, but I am born from my mother. I love Turkey, and I love Germany. I have four countries, I belong to four countries'. 'Four?' I asked, 'Which ones?' She said to me 'I am born in Germany, I am German and I am Turkish, and I know Turkish very well, of course I am also a Turk. Moreover, I love Turkey a lot, and my mother is Turkish, too. I am both, *I am both*'. So she put it really very well and concretely, without even thinking. 'I have four countries. I love Turkey a lot'. We had been to Alanya last time. 'I love Alanya a lot (laughs), I love Germany, and I love Spain, and I have a fourth country that is fantasy country'. 'Oh,' I said. 'Where is that?'

> U: How nice!

> N: 'That is my country' she said. 'It isn't yours, you wouldn't know it. It belongs to me' she said. 'Well,' I said, 'can I come to your fantasy country?' I asked. 'No, you can't' she said. 'But can you show me around there?' I asked. 'How?' she asked, 'You could draw it for me' I said. 'But it would be a very big picture'. 'So we can put a few pages on the floor and you can draw' I said. That's what we did.

Since this story is related by her mother Birgül it reflects aspects of the relation between mother and daughter. Birgül appreciates Aysel's independent identifications and is proud of how well she represent its' complexity. Yet, alongside Aysels' assertion of independence, her identification with Turkishness is explicitly couched as an expression of belonging to her mother. While a parent might feel that the bond with the child is threatened if the child dis-identifies with the parents' ethnic or national identity (cf. Pınar's story above), Aysel's differentiated construction pre-empts such parental fears of divisiveness while at the same time taking difference into account: 'Continuity in the strengthening of family ties can be reached through an act of imagination as well' (Lutz 1995: 314).

Aysel's claim to four (or indeed five) countries presents us with the age-specific mixing of national and local identifications: thus she lists Alanya, a holiday resort in Turkey, with the countries (Germany, Turkey, Alanya, Spain and Fantasycountry) she claims belonging to.[10] It is striking, however, that despite her young age Aysel ably navigates the discursive terrain of (national) belonging situationally. Thus, her response to the headmistress and her initial statement of a German Turkish identity are commensurate with the hegemonic paradigms of national belonging. This co-exists with her claim for belonging to Spain and Alanya, legitimized by her love of these. Despite her affective claim for belonging, she does not claim an identity as someone from Alanya or Spanish. This can be interpreted as her ability to differentiate between affection for a place and the legitimized, institutionalized forms of claiming a national identity which are based on place of birth, residence or familial heritage.

Aysel's claim for a 'Fantasy country' and the spatial metaphor she uses to claim an idiosyncratic space for identification beyond the parameters of nation or even family is intriguing. I read this as resisting a totalizing of national identification. Birgül's request to share the space of 'Fantasy country' with her expresses an anxiety over an – albeit fantasy – separation from her daughter. Aysel's acceptance of the suggestion to draw a picture of fantasy country for her mother shows first, her willingness to share this space to a certain extent with her mother and second a complex insight into the working of representation: Drawing her fantasy country makes it visible to her mother, but does not divest Aysel's authority over it. This extract emphasizes that the process of transmitting ethnically specific identities and negotiating belonging is not uni-directional. Throughout the interview Birgül chooses different ethnic identity labels for herself, such as 'a person from Turkey', 'migrant woman', 'foreigner', '*Ausländer*' and does not identify as 'Turk-German'. Yet, her acceptance of her daughter's ascription as 'Turk German' signals how they mutual negotiate identity labels. These differences that could be potentially conflictive, are then transformed into shared meanings between mother

---

10    Research on national identification in children has similar findings: Following Piaget and Weil, Wacker (quoted in Marvakis 1995:73) differentiates three phases in the cognitive and affective development of children in relation to national identity: 1) unstable, spontaneous preferences based on individual fragments of memory. 2) Adaptation of familial orientations as an emergent group identity. In these phase, the differentiation between place, region and nation is not yet developed. 3) Adaptation of (dominant) national self-stereotypes. Marvakis argues that these phases should not be fixed to an age group nor viewed as finished. Instead, he suggests to view the cognitive and affective dimensions of national identification as processual, changing and developing during adulthood, too. Moreover, he argues that a merely psychological approach to these is not justified.

and daughter, to be related to me and possibly others as a story of – if not shared, then commonly negotiated belonging.

Mothering is context specific, and so are the stories told about it. Both Pınar and Birgül's stories about educating their daughters are temporally located in their evaluation of the present and projections of the future. At the time of interview Pınar's daughter Derya was ten years old and Birgül's daughter Aysel was eight years old. During adolescence or young adulthood where the mothers' control and influence are less far-reaching, differences between children and mothers might be more sharply articulated. In both Pınar's and Birgül's stories of mothering, the aspect of educating *daughters*, that is female children, is also crucial. The aspect of shared gender is important to understand the dynamics of mother-daughter relationships: this transmission of gender identity entails the tension between educating the daughter into a form of femininity embodied by the mother herself and enabling the daughter to embody different forms of femininity (Rosen 1993). Whichever elements may prevail, shared gender constitutes an important point of reference for negotiating similarity and difference in common and independent identity projects. In the following story of Nâlan about her relationship with her son, age and gender thus constitute important differences to the previous stories. Moreover, this story of mothering illuminates the specific context of England contrasting it with the experiences of mothering in Germany highlights the situated processes of differential racialization and ethnicization.

*Nâlan: Learning to Look at Life Differently*

Nâlan's son Ugur is 17 years old. He had joined Nâlan in England as a nine year old and had been living with her since. At the time of the interview Nâlan was preoccupied with the problems she had been experiencing with Ugur over the last three years. She made his involvement with a particular friendship group responsible for his involvement in petty criminal activities. These petty criminal activities on one occasion had brought him to court, where he was fined. Nâlan had had 'dreams' for her son that he would benefit from educational opportunities and become an academic. She felt 'disappointed' by his lack of academic interest, but more worried about his petty criminal activities. Therefore she urged Ugur to break his ties with this peer group; when he decided to join his father in Turkey for a year, she encouraged this. At the time of interview, he had been in Turkey for six months, but Nâlan felt it was too early to evaluate the impact of this. While migrant parents often send children 'back home', when they face these types of problems (cf. Hondagneu-Sotelo and Avila 1997), Nâlan's emphasis that this was Ugur's own decision exemplifies a pervasive aspect of Nâlan's story about mothering: she allows her son a lot of scope for his decision-making and accepts these, even when she does not entirely agree with them. For Ugur, going to Turkey also meant living with his father for an extended period of time (rather than only in the holidays). Nâlan hopes that Ugur will benefit from a closer same gender relationship. Maybe more than this, she also hopes that being in Turkey would allow Ugur to adapt different values from those in his British peer group:

> N: He gets into a different environment. In Turkey there are very different pressures. There, everybody is studying, everybody wants to go to university. Everybody wants to work in a good job. Well, people don't even look at you if you're not working in a good job. The career is very important. And therefore he will notice all these things and he will probably do something. Well, I want him to study at university, he will develop himself, and begin to look at life differently. (…) [It is less about academic achievements] more to learn to look at life differently.

Nâlan also hopes that being in Turkey would help him overcome his 'identity crisis' with relation to Turkishness.

*Belonging and use of ethnically specific cultural and social resources*
Unlike Pınar and Birgül, Nâlan had not actively engaged with her son's negotiation of ethnically specific cultural resources when he was growing up. Her story about mothering was informed by a concrete concern over his criminal activities. Therefore, she was concerned with retrospectively explaining to herself, what went wrong. This included self-critical reflections on her role as a mother, as well as seeking to identify other influences. She reflected about Ugur's ethnic identification as an aspect explaining his current problems:

> N: He said to me, the Turkish young people don't like me at all because I [hang out] with the black young people. But I can't be friends with [the Turkish youngsters] because all they listen to is Ibrahim Tatlises [a very popular Arabesque singer], he said to me. And Ugur did not grow up with this Arabesque culture. (…) At home we listened to Turkish music, but not to Arabesque music, (…) he doesn't know it. And for example most of these young people are from a Kurdish background and they live very closely with the politics of Kurdistan because their families are involved in it. Even if this is a national liberation movement, the people are very political. And Ugur doesn't have a political formation, he finds it strange. And those Turkish [speaking] friends he has are Cypriot Turks. Well, here he can only make friends with the Cypriot and the Black young people.

At his school and in his social circle, Ugur has access to a limited range of versions of 'Turkishness'. He perceives Turkishness – which is in fact a mis-recognition, since these young people are Turkish-speaking Kurds – as fixed to a culture symbolized by Arabesque music. Arabesque is a complex cultural form negotiating intersections of class, gender and ethnic identity in the Middle East and in the Diaspora. The subject positions which this cultural form enunciates are very different from Nâlan's as urban well-educated Turkish. This Arabesque culture is marginalized in Turkey (cf. Karakayali 1995, Tekelioglu 1995), that it appears as a central part of Turkishness to Ugur shows how much at variance locally specific expressions and ascriptions of ethnicity can be with hegemonic culture in Turkey. While Nâlan herself has access to other versions of Turkishness, she could not fully transmit this to Ugur. Although she used to be very active politically, she has not made Ugur part of her activities in the same way in which she describes Kurdish young people's political involvement through their families. One factor may be that her feminist political projects did not have the same family-based organizational structure and did not naturalize belonging and participation as is the case in the mobilization for a national liberation movement. Participation in feminist politics for boys or men requires complex negotiations of representation rather than providing an easily accessible collective resource of identification.

*Conflicting meanings*
While Ugur validates alternative forms of ethnic belonging that he develops with his Cypriot friends, Nâlan finds some aspects of this highly problematic.

> N: Recently […] it was again these *identity crisis.* One day he came home and told me 'I want to go to Turkish school, I want to improve my Turkish'. And I also want him to improve his Turkish, because he talks very well but his writing isn't good, he can't write Turkish (…) there was a Turkish school on Sundays, he said 'I want to go there', his friends went there, his Cypriot friends. But his Turkish is much better than theirs, some of them can't even talk. 'Well, then go there' I said. After three weeks he came home and on his neck he had a Crescent and Star necklace.[11] 'Look, mum!' I said: 'What's that?' His girlfriend gave it to him as a present for his birthday. And I thought, what can I do? I said [don't wear this]. 'Why, why shouldn't I? My friend gave it to me as a present'. All the Cypriots are very nationalist, you know. Crescent and Star, or Atatürk and so on, they claim these values much more than the people from Turkey. I tried to tell him what the Turkish flag means, what role it has and so on. 'Come on, who cares about this nowadays' [he said]. I said 'My son, at least think of me this once, even if you don't think of yourself' (laughs). 'When I take you to see my friends, they will think that you're a fascist'.

> U: Mmm.

> N: At the time he was working in a restaurant, and the manager was a Kurdish man. (…) I told [Ugur] all these things but he didn't take me seriously at all, of course. (…) [Ugur] says 'Mum, we were sitting together and [the manager] said "I'm Kurdish"'.. [Ugur] said 'So what?' (laughs).

---

11   Crescent and Star are the symbols of the Turkish flag. While the flag plays a central role in republican nationalism in general, Crescent and Star are also a symbol for fascist nationalist groups.

U: (laughs)

N: (…) The man thought he was a fascist. [Ugur] said 'All right, and I am from Istanbul' (laughs).

U: (laughs)

N: Then he said, 'So why do you wear this necklace?' [Ugur] said that's when he understood why [the manager] said 'I'm Kurdish'.

U: Mmm.

N: And [Ugur] said, (…) 'My friend gave this to me, don't be like this (…). I don't really have anything to do with politics. My mother and father are [Leftists]' to get the man off his back. (…) [The manager] told him everything, Kurdistan's history, the Kurds, Kurdistan and everything. That's when he took off the necklace. But the reason why he took it off isn't because he believed in this, but rather that this guy shouldn't get hold of him again and go on and on about this (laughs).

U: (laughs)

N: He doesn't have anything to do with politics.

This story exemplifies how dramatically different the meaning of the Turkish flag's symbols are for Nâlan and her son. Nâlan's reading of these symbols references the use of the symbol by fascist Turkish supremacist groups. Moreover, she takes into account the meaning the symbol takes on in the Cypriot context, as a marker of difference *vis-à-vis* Greek Cypriots. She also mentions the meaning the symbol has for Kurds and left-wing Turks. But Ugur discounts his mothers' multi-faceted reading of the symbol as outdated, insisting that the necklace is merely a symbol of his personal relationship with his girlfriend. He favours what he perceives to be a politically neutral interpretation of the symbol as showing his closeness with his Cypriot girlfriend and friends. The symbol may also be more relevant to Ugur as a marker of belonging and difference from his British environment, rather than locating it within a 'Turkish' or 'Kurdish' system of reference. In the same way, his attendance of a Turkish weekend school appears to be more informed by an endeavour to join in his Cypriot friends' activities than to enhance his access to ethnically specific cultural resources. He foregrounds the community building aspect, while his mother foregrounded the academic aspects of learning to write in Turkish. Nâlan's acceptance of his choice of school can be seen as a case in point for allowing him scope for decision-making and choice.

Although Nâlan tells this anecdote laughingly, she was clearly concerned. Ethnicity here is articulated through, and in turn articulates, other social

positionings, of political and social identity of mother and son, the identifications
of each being reflected in and used by the other: For Nâlan, her own identity as a
left-wing feminist activist risks being undermined by her son's appropriation of
the ambiguous symbol of Crescent and Star. Vice versa Ugur also uses his parents'
political identities to deter his Kurdish managers' accusation of ultra-nationalism.
While Nâlan chose not to socialize her son into her political identity, she finds his
avowed dis-identification from politics difficult to accept. What Ugur proclaims
as being politically neutral to her appears overly naïve. She fears that this naivety
renders him vulnerable to manipulation by right-wing groups, which may endanger
him and alienate him from her.

*Cross-ethnic identifications as 'identity crisis'*
Ugur's cross-ethnic or partial identifications for Nâlan are problematic indications
of an identity crisis:

> N: The identity problem is probably the most important issue that Ugur has
> faced in the last few years. He couldn't see himself as a Turk. We spoke Turkish
> at home and so on, but (...) when he went to school and for example met a girl
> he always introduced himself [by an English/Christian name]. If the phone rings,
> they ask for [this name].

> U: Mmm.

> N: Ugur says they don't understand his name and take the Mickey, that's how he
> tried to explain but ... I understood it like this, he dressed like the black boys,
> wearing big trousers and wearing his belt very low.

> U: (laughs) Funny fashion.

> N: These very funny fashions, he tried to speak like them. He could change his
> accent and speak with a Caribbean accent because ... But this was problematic.
> He went to a boys' school where bullying is very widespread. ... In the past
> years Ugur became involved in many well, things, umm. He became part of sort
> of groups that I didn't approve of. They were doing petty criminal activities.
> And because I was very much against this, he explained it to me like this 'I had
> no choice but – to be friends with them. If you have a friend with the stronger
> people in the school then you won't get bullied, you know'.

Nâlan links Ugur's 'identity crisis' with this petty criminal peer group. As she
remarked he could not identify with his peers from Turkey but rather with the
African-Caribbean and Cypriot young people.

> N: Well and many of the black boys, maybe I am saying something very racist
> here, well ... but many of the black youth, well of the young people get involved

in criminal activities. What do I know? Credit card fraud and so on and so on. Well, and Ugur used to be very successful at school until two years ago. In the past two years he began to make sexual experiences ... he didn't care about school anymore and started to go out with girls, I mean usual stuff. But one day they start to get involved with the other stuff, criminal stuff.

In Nâlan's view Ugur's identification with his Caribbean classmates was linked to his wish to assimilate. It is worth noting, that this integration is not into an undifferentiated white British society, but instead into a differentially racialized and gendered 'Diaspora space' (Brah 1996), where ethnically and racially minoritized people relate to each other as much as to an assumed white centre. The concept of 'Diaspora space' acknowledges the dynamic relations between individuals and groups through which ethnicity is lived and articulated. This is a complex, polyvalent process. Take Ugur's (situational) adaptation of an English/ Christian name: although a name signals ethnic and national belonging, it also contains other meanings beyond the national and ethnic: Ugur's explanation that his friends take the Mickey points to his experiences of ethnic discrimination but can also be read as a justification to his mother, downplaying his own agency. The use of a name, 'hailing' is a crucial site of subjectification. Ugur's use of a name different from that given by his mother, can also be seen as an assertion of independence.

It is important to keep in mind Nâlan's narrative is articulated in the relational dynamic between mother and son. In Nâlan's view, Ugur's identification with this particular form of Caribbean masculinity expressed in his local school and peer environment entails gaining sexual experiences, dismissing academic achievement in favouring instead involvement in petty criminal activities. These elements of enhanced sexuality, sensuality eclipsing intellectuality and rationality and delinquency are salient in both mainstream racist discourses on youthful black masculinity as well as in the desire to positively identify with Black masculinity (Blauner 1989, Jones 1988, Frosch et al. 2002, Fanon 1986, Sewell 1995). The effectivity of this stereotype lies in its ambiguity of generating both strong negative and positive feelings. Nâlan is insecure about how to formulate her 'maybe very racist' views. Her afterthought that involvement in criminal activities is not indeed specific to *black* young men but rather to *young* men is an attempt to de-racialize the discourse of crime in favour of an age-specific explanation. The difficulty of escaping the hegemonic racialized and gendered discursive repertoire is however apparent since she remains within the parameters it sets. Nâlan argues that in the local context of Ugur's school black young men are seen to be 'the strong people' (cf. Sewell 1995). Ugur's justification for choosing his friendship group resonates with the stereotype of the young black male criminal. In this explanation Nâlan constructs Ugur's choice of his friendship group as an attempt to escape victimization rather than foregrounding his positive identification. Despite her explicit anti-racist identification Nâlan's narrative on Ugur's cross-ethnic identification oscillates between the rejection of and the allusion to racist stereotypes.

The discussion of Nâlan's view of Ugur's cross-ethnic identifications reveals complex processes of differential racialization. The intergenerational differences in their ethnic identifications may be related to the different conditions of socialization in Turkey or Britain. Moreover, Nâlan views her son's multiple and flexible identifications as the expression of an identity crisis. The concept and terminology of identity crisis is a common sense notion,[12] and Nâlan's use of it to explain the problems of her adolescent son is not surprising. The notion of identity crisis has been used in many different contexts, however has gained particular currency in the context of migrant or ethnic minority young people. It is problematically based on essentialist notions of ethnic identity, fixing the content and expression of 'ethnic identity', mis-recognizing inter-generational change and conflict for ethnic identity confusion (Auernheimer 1988, Otyakmaz 1995). Moreover, the focus on ethnic identity eclipses other identificatory moments such as gender, sexuality, class and education. Nâlan's use of this notion of ethnic identity crisis, articulates Ugur's academic problems and his involvement in petty criminal activities. Lutz (1997, 1998) argues that in migrant families the topic of identity (crisis) constitutes a legitimate topic of family talk. She interprets this as compensating in intergenerational dialogue for migration-related topics that are silenced. The salience of the topic of identity talk within the family, according to Lutz, is a consequence of its centrality in public discourses on migration and ethnicity. In Ugur's positioning, the aspects of a search for an institutionally validated 'Turkish' essentialist identity (as exemplified with reference to his Cypriot friends) as well as a cross-ethnic, hybrid identification with his Black Caribbean friends co-exist. While Nâlan views both moments as part of an identity crisis, she articulates her concerns relating to his academic and social position with respect to ethnicized and racialized fears over identity.

## Conclusion

The life-stories presented in this chapter challenge the ethnicization of notions of (late) modern versus traditional intimate and sexual identities and family relations. In the first section a range of ways in which migrant women negotiate

---

12    The idea of identity crisis emerged from Erikson's developmental identity model and has been widely used in the social sciences and psychology, as well as social work, trickling down to everyday discourses. Nâlan's professional knowledges as a social worker may contribute to her use of this explanation for her son.

and challenge hetero-normative and family-centred female subjectivities through articulating alternative or resistant modes of femininity as single by choice 'sexual revolutionary', divorcee, single mother or lesbian was presented. The second section explored how migrant women elaborate liveable notions of self against the devaluation of their transnational mothering practices, combining 'caring for' and 'caring about' their children in the tension of singular and non-singular notions of motherhood. The lack of positive conceptualizations of transnational mothering compelled them to create their own notions of 'good mothering'. These implicate othermothers, as both, supporting or potentially undermining their transnational mothering. The complex transnational relationships of mothering clearly contradict a stereotypical fixing of migrant families as stable, traditional and oppressive. They show how important the resource of (transnational) familial ties is in providing childcare to enable mothers' migration. Yet, the mothers did not only stretch their relationship with their children geographically, they also changed the meaning of motherhood to encompass providing economically and, despite emotional and relational difficulties attempted to reconcile their mothering identities with changes in their gendered lifestyle. Finally we turned to de-construct the notion of mothering as a simple transmission of ethnic identities and showed the complex inter-generational negotiations of ethnically specific resources and how these are employed flexibly in a dynamic of re-interpreting ethnic identifications of mothers and their children. Mothers do not only involve themselves with the intra-familial expression of identities: Birgül's strategy of becoming active in the management committee of the kindergarten to initiate a debate about bi-linguality is an instance of mothers' educational agency extending to the public sphere, to challenge and transform institutions. Thus, mothers' transmission of ethnicity should not be viewed as limited to the private sphere. Pınar's educational practice is a case in point to critically assess theories of Diaspora (e.g. Cohen 1997) or transnationalism (e.g. Faist 1998) that view transnational, intra-ethnic networks, based on primordial family-like solidarities, as the main sites of identity construction. This does not take into account sufficiently the significance of local (cf. Ryan 2007) and transnational inter-ethnic relations for processes of personal and collective identification. Pınar's story calls particular attention to the fact that familial solidarities are not ethnically bounded, but can transcend these boundaries. While I am not claiming representativity for any of these cases, it is worth underlining that all migrants are faced with negotiating ethnic difference and this includes elements of cross-ethnic identifications.

*Intimate Citizenship*

Some of the issues around personal status and transnational mothering can be explored with the concept of 'intimate citizenship' which Plummer (2003: 13) puts forward as a 'sensitizing concept, one that is not meant to be tight and operational but open and suggestive'. It refers to:

the *control (or not) over* one's body, feelings, relationships: *access (or not) to* representations, relationships, public spaces etc.; and *socially grounded choices (or not) about* identities, gender experiences (Plummer 1995: 151, emphasis in original).

While this is a potentially useful concept, in discussing the globalization of intimate citizenship, Plummer re-inscribes a racialized dichotomy between tradition and (late) modernity into his argument. He portrays the Third World as at the receiving end of the negative aspects of changing articulations of intimacy. With respect to migrant women's experiences of transnational mothering, he points out the aspects of victimization but does not consider that practices of transnational mothering, while inscribed in global and local power relations, are also ways in which migrant women actively negotiate these very power relations and create meaningful forms of transnational intimacies despite their constraints. Yet, to overcome these constraints the importance of realizing transnational intimate citizenship rights might be invoked. Transnational intimate citizenship rights should enable migrant women to make substantial choices about how to organize their intimate lives. As it stands, immigration legislation regulates and constrains partnership choices (which has implications for sexual identity and personal status) often taking the most restrictive gendered and sexual norms as their basis. British and German immigration legislation only recently acknowledged same sex partnerships, and gender and sexually specific grounds for asylum are not fully institutionalized or realized. For migrant women from Turkey, socially grounded choices about sexual identity, or personal status, such as being single, or being a divorcee, are constrained and stratified according to class, education, and the rural-urban divide. Furthermore, ethnic minority people are marginalized within the social, political and cultural representation of sexual minorities. Similarly, heterosexual migrant women who are single by choice, divorced or single mothers are bracketed out of the representation of migrant communities, as well as that of the ethnically dominant group. Weeks et al. (2001: 198) suggest 'The creation of grass-roots realities, and the circulation of stories about them to audiences ready to hear them, is re-shaping the meaning of what it is to be a full citizen'. Yet, in claiming such a new status as full intimate citizens, lesbian, gay, transgendered and other sexually minoritized communities need to be vigilant not to reproduce ethnicized exclusions in the community knowledges they produce. For this purpose, it is important to contextualize intimate citizenship rights as multi-layered and intersecting with other power relations such as those of class, ethnicity, gender and migration status.

Richardson (2000) suggests that citizenship studies, while increasingly concerned with everyday practices, lacks a clear understanding of sexual rights. She identifies three substreams of sexual rights: 'conduct-based rights claims, identity-based rights claims and claims that are relationship based' (2000: 107). The discussion of the migrant women's life-stories has touched upon the latter two categories of rights. Richardson argues that the right to recognition of sexual identities entails viewing sexual identities as part of the public sphere. Since, if lesbian, gay or transgender people cannot publicly express their identities they are effectively marginalized from partaking in public fora where the substance and form of citizenship is debated. 'The ability to be "out" and publicly visible is therefore crucial to the ability to claim rights' (2000: 120). Another aspect of sexual rights, Richardson suggests, should be the ability to develop diverse sexual identities in an unhindered way. Both these aspects need to be further developed to take account of migrant women's experiences. The differential, geographically and culturally specific understanding of sexual identities and the ability to live them without fear of ostracization was shown in the life-stories. One condition for realizing rights to a range of sexual identities, is a restructuring of heterosexist institutions and public, popular culture. The active cultivation of marginalized sexual identities would mean 'rights to enable the realization of sexual diversity; for access to the cultural, social and economic conditions that will enable previously marginalized and stigmatized identities to develop and flourish as a legitimate and equal part of the "cultural landscape"' (2000: 122). As migration is one way of realizing choice in sexual identities, our understanding of sexual rights should take account of this, revoking heterosexist assumptions of migration and integration policy. Many citizenship rights are grounded in notions of heterosexual coupledom, which is taken as normative. For migrants, the regulatory potential of these hetero-normative notions are often exacerbated explicitly or implicitly as they become conditions for attaining residence rights or formal citizenship (such as family unification regulations).

Mothering is an important intimate relationship, which is constrained for migrant women, particularly single mothers. Transnational mothering practices form one way in which migrant women try to combine their economic and emotional care for their children. These practices are often a consequence of the combined constraints of poor working conditions, poor, inadequate and/ or inaccessible childcare facilities and migration regulation. Thus, to realize migrant women's intimate and sexual citizenship rights, legal obstacles such as age restrictions on the immigration of children should be revoked; moreover, improvement in the provision and quality of realistically affordable childcare facilities is needed that takes account of the widespread full time employment and unsocial hours of migrant women's work. This is particularly important for single mothers, who cannot or do not want to rely on familial help with childcare. While this chapter has examined past practices of transnational mothering and daughtering, the practice of transnational mothering is highly relevant for women migrating today, not only those who are domestic workers, but also particularly asylum seekers and undocumented women. Therefore, concepts, demands and policies of intimate citizenship need to take into account that migrant women's mothering practices also rely on social mothers, often in transnational contexts and thus our thinking about citizenship responsibilities and rights needs to evolve to validate their practices of care, too.

*Migrant Mothers as 'Cultural Workers'*

Caring responsibilities for children and others are often viewed as preventing women from fully participating in the labour market or in political citizenship. Yet, for migrant women, the ways in which they raise their children to integrate into the society of residence is under particular scrutiny. Thus how well they are able to teach them the language or other cultural values of the society of residence are seen as indicative of their own competence for social participation. Kershaw argues that ethnic minority women (his focus is particularly on African American women) have had limited access to domestic time. As economic conditions, migration legislation and social policy target ethnic minority women as 'welfare mothers' or reduce their capacity to choose their family forms and economically support their families. 'The interaction of discriminatory public policy and the unequal distribution of socioeconomic resources (both intra- and internationally) produce obstacles to domestic participation that disproportionately impede some social groups more than others' (Kershaw 2005: 111). Many migrant mothers do not have the time resources to enjoy their families. One reason why family and personal networks play an important role for migrants is because they can potentially provide the positive recognition that is lacking in the public sphere, as well as a refuge from racism. In this sense, giving and receiving care can constitute a site in which positive cultural and emotional resources for self-presentation are transmitted. While I agree with Kershaw's argument about the relevance of the right to a family and the family's important role in helping to cope with racism, it is important to be analytically nuanced. Thus, his argument presents 'ethnic and faith-based' communities' identity as resistant, without exploring the regulatory and conflictual aspects of these communities. The argument also risks essentializing the family as the central site of caring and producing a positive identity. Yet, as we have seen, e.g. in Pınar's account of growing up (Chapter 3), the family can also be a key site where migrant women's projects of identification are undermined. Furthermore, other caring relationships that do not conform to hetero-normative or normative notions of family within ethnic minority communities need to be validated. With these critical caveats in mind, I would like to engage the notion of mothers as 'cultural workers' that he bases on Hill Collins' (1990) work. Kershaw argues that caring for children and instilling in them a positive cultural identification against the backdrop of the devaluation of their selves and culture they experience in racialized societies is a cultural achievement of ethnic minority women and should properly be recognized as an aspect of political citizenship: '*Qua* cultural workers, mothers contribute significantly to the project of "group survival" by transmitting an ethnocentric worldview to the next generation' (Kershaw 2005: 117). This essentializing view of mothering as transmitting a bounded ethno-cultural identity to children then leads Kershaw to caution against the development of ethno-cultural identities that compete with loyalties, attachments and commitment to the broader citizenship community and may end up being socially divisive. Yet, the problem of social divisiveness Kershaw thus warns against, is part and parcel of the way in which he conceptualizes ethnic minority cultures as hermetically sealed off from each other.

Instead, I would like to further develop the idea of migrant mothers as 'cultural workers' by emphasizing that mothers are also active participants in creating new cultural forms, using different ethnically specific resources and in the process crossing ethnic boundaries. This engagement and re-working of ethnically specific cultural resources takes place both within the home and in more public settings, such as kindergardens or schools. Indeed the institutionalization of new cultural forms, such as the setting up of bi-lingual or intercultural educational institutions, constitute active citizenship practices. Thus, we can re-interpret the notion of mothers as 'cultural workers' to emphasize that migrant mothers actively negotiate what count as 'ethnically specific' resources and re-constitute the relation between cultural resources, ethnicity, identity and claims to belonging to the society of residence. Mothering in this sense not only relates to intimate citizenship rights, but the cultural aspects of care for children also constitute active elements of citizenship practices that build and transform identities and resources for social participation. It is in this sense, that mothering can be seen as a transformative citizenship practice.

Migrant women claim belonging in many different ways. The previous chapters have explored how they find new ways of being a mother by imagining and doing family in ways that challenge national and ethnic boundaries. They elaborate new forms of cultural capital and forms of validation in the site of work and struggle for a place in educational institutions against their marginalization. The following chapter explores these processes with a focus on social and political participation. How do the migrant women introduced in this book do and think about their social activism? How do they give meaning to their political and social participation and how does this relate to their sense of belonging? What are their trajectories of becoming active, and the fields of activism they develop? Which issues do they choose to politicize and how do they articulate them?

# Chapter 6
# Longing and Belonging

This chapter explores the active dimension of migrant women's citizenship in terms of their social and political activism. This is explored through the lens of a politics of belonging, emphasizing that belonging is actively negotiated. For many of the migrant women whose life-stories are presented here, their social activism is an important instantiation of claiming belonging, despite not being recognized as legitimate participants shaping the societies they live in. The notion of belonging is often used as a criterion to 'restrict access to goods, rights or entitlements, to the "true" nationals or citizens said to really "belong" to the country in question' (Favell and Geddes 1999: 10). Yet, an exploration of migrants' belonging can sidestep the binary focus on either integration or exclusion of migrants. Instead the issue of belonging to the nation should be explored as a question of degrees rather than an either-or (Hage 1998). The boundaries of belonging are negotiated and struggled over, as are the criteria for inclusion, in this sense migration poses epistemological challenges of defining boundaries (Crowley 1999: 30) which is one reason for the violent reactions it yields.

Current debates on citizenship and migration are about who can be included into the political community. However, the 'test of people's capacity to be fellow citizens is implicitly formulated as their ability to "live together" – in some supposedly relevant non-political sense' (Crowley 1999: 31). That is, cultural and social constructions of belonging are used as conditions for access to political participation. This view is gaining strength politically; in particular with the introduction of citizenship tests about national culture, customs and the political system in both the UK and Germany, a notion of national values to which migrants must adapt is instated. In the German case, this has culminated in debates about the relevance of a German 'Leitkultur', i.e. the need for migrants to adapt to a German dominant culture in the early 2000s. Recent debates about Britishness have similarly tried to identify social and cultural elements to create a sense of 'shared futures' (CIC 2007). While this emphasizes assumed cultural particularities to which migrants are expected to adapt, in both Britain and Germany another discursive strand claims universalist values such as upholding of human rights and democracy as distinctive attributes of the national culture. As Yuval-Davis observes: 'Emancipatory ethical and political values can be transformed, under certain conditions, into inherent personal attributes of members of particular national and regional collectivities (Britain, the West) and, thus, in practice, become exclusionary rather than permeable signifiers of boundaries' (2006: 212–213, cf. Solomos 2001).

Migrants are expected to perform belonging not only to acquire formal citizenship. Instead, the extent to which (citizen and non-citizen) migrants belong is constantly negotiated and re-negotiated in everyday encounters with majority citizens and institutions. For those who hold valid residence permits or even formal citizenship, thus the requirement to produce residence or citizenship documents constitutes in itself a way of marking their difference from those who have citizenship by birth (cf. Hage 1998: 50).

Hage differentiates the 'passive belonging', where one feels part of the society from 'governmental belonging' where one feels entitled to take part in decisions, in particular about policing who should be allowed to enter, live there and claim particular rights. In Hage's study on constructions of whiteness in Australia, he found that some migrants feel 'passive homely belonging but not governmental belonging' (1998: 49). For him, the extent of governmental belonging is a question of cultural entitlement in the sense that migrants and new citizens strive to accumulate as much 'national capital', i.e. cultural capital that is validated as properly part of the national culture, (e.g. good English with an Australian accent, educational credentials, fluency in vernacular culture) as possible. This will then legitimate their belonging to the political community (cf. Chapter 4 for a discussion of the significance of cultural capital). While the question of (non-) recognition of cultural competence is important in understanding how migrant women as political and social activists are positioned in particular contexts, their stories jar with this neat account of belonging to the nation in important ways, to which I will turn shortly.

First, I introduce the framework that will be put forward to distinguish between different levels of belonging. Yuval-Davis (2006) argues that an analytical framework for studying belonging should differentiate between three levels: The first is concerned with social locations, i.e. individuals' and groups' positioning in terms of class, gender, ethnicity or race, ability, age and others. The second level is about individuals' identifications with collectivities and groupings and the third level 'relates to ethical and political value systems with which people judge their own and others' belonging/s' (2006: 199). While these different levels are interrelated, they cannot be reduced to each other. The differentiation of these levels is important to theoretically untangle belonging and further to be able to politically deconstruct particular politics of belonging. It is not just important where we belong but also how this belonging is evaluated and closely related to this, where the boundaries of inclusion and exclusion are drawn. The politics of belonging is thus about 'the contestations around these ethical and ideological issues and the ways they utilize social locations and narratives of identities' (Yuval-Davis 2006: 203–4). In this sense, the question of where the boundaries of belonging to the nation should be drawn and on what basis partly depends on the social locations and experiences of people, but more so on their values.

While constructions of identity can be forced on people and therefore become important dimensions of their social locations, such as was shown with the category of '*Ausländer*' in Chapter 2, people are able to activate their social imagination to create new ways of seeing themselves and making meaning. Thus, social locations and identities are not simply objectively given but are articulated by political subjects. This chapter looks at how the migrant women made sense of their identities, and how they made meaningful and politicized social positions.

Going beyond Hage's idea (see above) that migrants strive to validate their cultural capital as national capital to achieve inclusion and belonging, in the following life-stories I ask how the women challenge visions of the national and what alternative, emergent or oppositional visions they put forward. Favell suggests that belonging to the society of residence for migrants is not an unquestionable good or a precondition for meaningful political action: 'there might be resources of power and cultural action, to be found by refusing (or, better, playing with) the logic of belonging; by rejecting, countering or evading social norms that are imposed and enforced on newcomers and outsiders when they are integrated (or "tolerated"; or "welcomed") into a national political and social culture' (1999: 220). While he suggests that these alternatives ways of belonging are articulated primarily in transnational social and political spaces, the migrant women's life-stories suggest that there are multiple levels of belonging that can be articulated as meaningful, rather than viewing the transnational as the privileged site of activism. Indeed, they might be able to articulate the levels of activism and belonging only fleetingly, as an imaginary space of 'elsewhere', a place that has not (yet) come into being but is – at least for them – 'thinkable'.

In Chapter 2 it was suggested that we view citizenship as a multi-layered and multi-dimensional concept. In this chapter I look at the ways in which the women locate themselves *vis-à-vis* local, national and transnational communities. The migrant women's stories testify to their contributions to the countries of residence through their professional, social, cultural and political activism. The notion of the private/public divide posits women's activities of child bearing, and caring as merely reproductive and ignores its social and political aspects. The women's stories contradict this. Thus, mothering is an important aspect of articulating, transmitting and negotiating belonging, also *vis-à-vis* institutions of the society of residence (cf. Kershaw 2005), as has been argued in the previous chapter. Women's continuing responsibility for caring can however limit their access to the exercise of political rights (Sales 2000). While citizenship entails passive aspects of access to rights, this chapter focuses on the active and participatory aspects.

Migrant women's contributions to the societies they live in are rarely recognized, and most often their 'citizenship practices' are presented as merely being passive recipients of social rights. Here an alternative view is substantiated that migrant women instead actively re-articulate the notion of the political.

In Pınar's story of politicization, the question of how identity feeds into participation is thrown into relief with regard to national belonging and the articulation of homeland vs. migrant politics. Gender articulates a critical stance *vis-à-vis* both 'homeland' and the society of residence's national identity. By elaborating a non-ethnically bounded political identity position, Pınar conceptualizes a field of politics that encompasses her paid work and her social activism. These issues are refracted differentially in Birgül's story of political activism which relates to both explicit and implicit forms of identity politics, critiquing a hidden form of identity politics within majority citizens' forms of political organizing. While both Pınar and Birgül articulate an enabling link between gendered and ethnicized identification and political activism, Selin's story critiques this from the point of view of someone who, through lack of validated cultural capital is marginalized. It articulates the difficulties of creating political community across divisions of gender, sexuality, educational and class hierarchies, when one's experiences do not fit the frames of validated discursive forms.

## Pınar

### *The Beginning of a Process of Politicization*

When I asked Pınar to describe her motivations and the factors contributing to her politicization, she presented the seeds of her politicization already in her reading. In order to evade her parents' suspiciousness towards reading, Pınar and her sister secretly read with torches underneath the bedcovers. When, as a twelve year old her father found her reading a trade union newspaper, he asked:

> 'Where did you find this' and then he took the paper away from me and kept saying 'Soon you're going to turn into communists' and that used to be a curse, as you know.

Since Pınar did not know what 'communist' meant she looked it up in a dictionary and liked the concept. She started to investigate the meaning of communism at school and with teachers, and was fascinated by the wide variation of responses it elicited. In her adolescence, she loved to discuss social issues with her peers. As discussed in Chapter 3, Pınar's fashioning herself as a passionate intellectual was part of her strategy to assert her resistance to the emotionally and physically violent and difficult situation in the home. Pınar's circle of friends of Turkish background from Gymnasium was active in left-wing organizations. Though they were important in her politicization, she emphasizes that even at the time, she viewed some aspects of these organizations critically.

> These were all left wing organizations and they had the aim of building communism in Turkey, so to speak. To make a revolution. (…) [I got to know different organizations], I found all of them (…) too dogmatic. Many things bothered me, I have to say, because I found it too much directed towards Turkey.

For Pınar the experience of being a migrant was a central political issue, already at the time, although there was little collective articulation of a migrants' political position. This led to conflicts with the members of the left-wing organizations, both about determining the privileged field of politics and about authority. They denied the second generation any political competence 'You haven't got a clue, you're the second generation, you are mostly socialized here and you aren't even refugees, your parents are not even politicized', 'you look at these issues too much like a European' were the arguments put forward to disqualify Pınar's interventions.

This is a typical conflict where the generation of migration is used to construct a privileged, authentic knowledge position to claim superior authority. Such a strategy constructs an ethnic authenticity as a necessary basis for gaining knowledge and political authority. The field of politics – 'revolution in Turkey' – is pre-given, as well as its conceptualization. The argument of a necessary experiential basis for doing politics or for participating in strategic decision-making is highly problematic (cf. Anthias and Yuval-Davis 1992, Yuval-Davis 2006a). It constructs politics as statically expressing a pre-given social position and identity, where any re-conceptualization of the process or political aims amounts to deviation. Moreover, it assumes a set of fixed characteristics and opinions as a pre-condition for participation at the level of decision-making, not allowing for differentially positioned people to articulate any political differences. Such differences are seen as a deviation, threatening the aim or unity of an organization. The gender and age based hierarchies within this type of political organization also contributed to Pınar's standpoints and opinions as a young woman being marginalized.

Despite this, Pınar insists that her contributions were important: These organizations needed the second generation people for 'translating leaflets or fly-posting them etc. And I do think that we allowed ourselves to be instrumentalized'. Pınar was not a member in one organization, but got involved in organizing a platform of left-wing women activists across party political divides, which she sees as an important achievement (cf. Avrupa Kadin Bülteni, 1991). This was the first time that migrant women got together to discuss the role and position of women in left-wing organizations critically and to develop women-centred or feminist left-wing political projects. However in this forum also, Pınar recalls conflicts on issues of authority between the generations.

Through her marriage, Pınar unselfconsciously became part of her husband's organization. Retrospectively, Pınar is self-critical about this. This is a common mechanism, whereby women get subsumed under their male partner's political attitude and status. One of Pınar's criticisms of her husband during their marriage was that he used his political ideals to postpone his actual responsibilities, to which Pınar responded: 'The revolution starts here at home, not outside in the big world'. Thus, she debated also with her husband about the status of politics in everyday life. While she presents her husband as expecting communism to bring the solution to the problems in Turkey, Pınar characterizes her own approach as taking small steps to achieve concrete change. A turning point in her political work was the death of a close friend who was accidentally shot in an argument with another political group. While Pınar had opposed political violence all along, seeing her friend die prompted her decision: 'After this it was clear that I would quit. This finally convinced me'.

*Politics of Experience and Place*

After her separation from her husband, Pınar got involved with a woman's NGO where she started doing 'grassroots work ... with women in situations of separation, counselling, everything on a voluntary basis'. This constituted a change in her field and conception of politics. Pınar was soon elected into the management committee of the NGO and became involved in its international projects. She participated in planning, evaluating and setting up women's projects, such as refuges or health projects in developing countries. At first the new responsibilities put a great strain on her. Gradually, as she trained and familiarized herself with the work she enjoyed it a lot since she 'saw the direct benefits' of her work. She worked in this NGO for four years, until its dissolution. At the same time she began paid part-time employment at a migrant women's centre. This job gradually developed into a full time job and recently Pınar has entered a managerial position. After her involvement with the NGO, she continued to work politically on women's issues:

> P: My interest to work on women's issues developed very quickly.

> U: Hmm.

> P: Through the personal but also through the political.

> U: Do you mean your experience of the pregnancy and your marriage?

> P: But also through the experiences at home with my parents, you know. And it was very important to reflect on all this. We founded a group for migrant girls and women and we had an exchange about things we had experienced ourselves.

Pınar participated in the foundation of a women's group for migrant and Black women, where they had 'a lot of space to work through' their own experiences, such as her experiences of violence in her childhood and youth, as well as the problems of her marriage and learned to be open about experiences of violence. The shame of being victimized that Pınar had felt as an adolescent and that made it difficult to speak about her experience of violence gave way to a political articulation of her experiences defined by actively and collectively 'struggling' rather than being victimized. The group offered seminars and workshops for migrant women and girls in various cities on issues of racism and violence against women. The group thus formed part of an emergent vocal and visible movement of migrant and black women articulating a specific political position.

P: There were the first books where migrant women started to … we really *fought* for this, against the white structures here, to say that we do not want to be researched about … by white Germans. Instead we want migrants to research about us, you know.

U: Hmm.

P: And we do not want to be seen as objects … on whose back … others make a name for themselves, but we want to be involved creatively and actively and we want to participate more, also in political events and legally and everything.

They organized a series of workshops and conferences, inviting international speakers, to develop strategies in the areas of political, cultural, legal and social representation. During this phase of the early 1990s, a political subject of migrant women was formed in delineation to white German feminism which was the 'direct milieu'. In this story of her political work Pınar articulates two related issues. She had previously articulated a subject position of an independent fighter for herself which was resistant to her parents' projects of femininity, as well as in contrast to the passive and merely supportive role that she rejected in her marriage. In the left-wing organizations directed towards Turkey, she had contested the relegation of her standpoints to a secondary position as inauthentic. Pınar's participation in the creation of a migrant and black women's movement articulates her strategies for creating a subject position as a collective political subject. The fight for recognition as a subject with agency pervades her life-story and informs her conception of the political collective and its strategies.

Pınar presents this period as very significant on a personal level as a 're-socialization into the culture of origin', a process which she suggests had already started during her relationship with her husband. How does Pınar conceptualize 'the culture of origin?' In this context, by re-socialization she means an increased interest in learning and speaking Turkish, engaging with the political situation in Turkey and its left-wing Diaspora politics. This engagement with a culture of origin however need not signify a nostalgic yearning for ethnically bounded wholeness. Instead, Pınar's notion of engagement with a culture of origin is ethnically differentiated and contains elements of cross-ethnic dialogue, such as her engagement with her husband who was a Kurdish political refugee from Turkey. The meaning of 'culture of origin' in the context of her engagement with migrant and black women on the other hand is consciously cross-ethnic and relates different trajectories of migration and processes of racialization. The engagement with differentially racialized women and the construction of shared political projects contains a process of cross-ethnic community building, as Pınar engaged in in her 'family of choice' (cf. Chapter 5), too. When she presents this community building as a 're-socialization into the culture of origin', she uses the metaphor of a shared origin, subverting the myth of common origin that is often employed to naturalize national and ethnic cohesion (Anthias and Yuval-Davis 1992, Bhabha

1990). As Parekh (2008) notes, the myths and stories a nation tells about itself are important in creating a notion of national identity. One way in which migrants can gain recognition is by making visible the historical presence of multi-ethnic populations and indeed re-imagining a historiography which creates new forms of collectivities, across the boundaries of migrant – non-migrant. Yet, such projects of creating new forms of relating and belonging to the nation challenge hitherto dominant national narratives, be they related to history, present or future and can be contested violently (cf. Modood 2007). Pınar's strategy of projecting a commonalty of migrant and black women in Germany into the past contains elements of fantasy in the sense of myth-making. Pınar's presentation of 'origins' appears more constructed than naturalized national historiographies, however this is due to the marginality of such a cross-ethnic project of doing and representing history, rather than its lacking coherence. Thus, Ohliger (2000) argues for a de-nationalization of historiography, to engage more adequately with the present and future concerns of globalization instead of reifying national paradigms and narratives.

> In such a view, marginal populations such as immigrants and minorities could become central. They would offer the possibility of researching history from the periphery, narrating it from the margins, partly against the *telos* of the centre and thus opening up historical imagination for much larger, more open but also more conflictual interpretations (Ohliger 2000: 2).

Pınar's representation of history is part of her project of constructing a cross-ethnic political subject of migrant and black women, and thus part of a construction of belonging based on shared political projects of a gendered and racialized subject position.

In Pınar's story of her political work, not only the subject and field of politics, but also its location has changed. During her involvement in Turkish left-wing organizations, their efforts were directed at the long-term goal of building communism in Turkey. Retrospectively, she criticizes this approach for neglecting practical political work that takes one's own life and living environment as a starting point. When she worked in the women's NGO, she worked internationally co-operating with local partners. The women's projects she helped set up worked for tangible changes locally. In this context Pınar refers to a shared experiential basis of the identification as woman that constitutes a link to her own life, which she presents as more concrete than the 'homeland' orientated politics. The meta-discourse of a shared gender position and its underlying experiential basis allows her to construct her international field of political activism as related to her own living environment. In this context, an essentialized notion of womanhood serves to de-essentialize a national identity basis for politics in order to delineate this type of activism from her previous Diaspora politics. Currently Pınar's political work focuses on the living conditions of migrant and black women in Germany, where she tries to achieve practical changes. She emphasizes the importance of this shift for her own identification, since to her it signifies that the centre of her life is in Germany, not Turkey. She concedes that her visions have changed, also, and are now based on her life in Germany. She sees her political connection to Turkey as one of supporting individual feminist projects, e.g. through funding from German NGOs, contrasting this with her in-depth knowledge of the German political process that enables her to intervene effectively on different political levels.

*Germanness?*

Pınar presents her decision to take on German citizenship as an ambivalent processes. For a long time she had thought of taking on German citizenship as a form of 'treason', having been caught in the logic of either belonging to Germany or to Turkey. However she now thinks that the second generation of migrants have a 'bi-cultural' identity by virtue of growing up in Germany. Her decision to take on German citizenship was triggered by the increasing racist violence at the beginning of the 1990s following German unification. At the time, Pınar felt frightened and feared 'that with underlying economic developments it would not improve but get more difficult'. She argues that taking on German citizenship enabled her to get more actively involved in the political process in Germany. However, she evaluates the taking on of German citizenship as a

> detour. ... Why should people who have decided they want to stay here, why should they not be able to be elected or to participate in elections. For me ... this totally contradicts the universality of human rights.

Pınar delineates her strategy of taking up German citizenship from assimilation or one-sided integration. Instead, she views it as enhancing her possibilities of articulating political dissent and furthering the impact of her advocacy of migrant and black women's rights.

Throughout the narrative Pınar emphasized the political salience of her paid employment. Working in a migrant women's centre to Pınar is one way of intervening politically. Thus, through her job she is part of a number of local and regional governmental committees in which she enjoys participating and making her presence felt. She is often criticized for 'complicating everything' when she intervenes against the normalizations of dominant identities. 'It is always in situations like this that one is uncomfortable for people'. Pınar views her job as a field of political activism, where she offers services to migrant women but at the same time is able to 'give voice' to their concerns. In this sense, the professional field is a central area in which Pınar articulates her citizenship as social participation. This includes the levels of community building, providing services but also initiating and sustaining campaigns. This political activism also initiates legal change, Pınar gives the example of a campaign to end the dependent residence status of married migrant women to the marriage, broadening the basis for citizenship, of which residence rights are a crucial component (cf Yuval-Davis 2006).

Pınar's story of activism has highlighted the political aspects of constructing the political subject of 'migrant woman', as an individual and collective identity. The evolving and shifting fields of her activism and conceptions of the political emphasize that the ways in which identities are mobilized for political projects are articulated in conjunction with both personal and wider histories.

Pınar's construction of a political community is shared by other interviewees, mainly second generation migrants. In this politics of belonging gaining a voice both in terms of gender and as (second generation) migrants are the key themes. The theme of locating oneself *vis-à-vis* claims or denial of belonging to national communities (both of the society of residence and that of origin) is a further commonalty in these narratives. While not all of them share Pınar's internationalist outlook, none of them identified primarily in national terms. Instead, the idea that the position of in-betweenness gives privileged access to questioning social relations and their power basis was commonly shared. Others shared Pınar's view, that their professional work or paid employment, relating to migrants or migrant women, formed part of their social or political activism (cf. Chapter 4). While these themes are not limited to the second generation, they are elaborated differentially in the first generation migrants' stories. Among the first generation migrants the politics of belonging and the relation to place are articulated differentially. The first generation interviewees do not present the process of ethnic identification as an articulation of political subjectivity. However they share with the second generation women a claim to a 'double consciousness' (Gilroy 1993) of being both from Turkey and from Germany or Britain (cf. Gültekin 2003). In contrast to the second generation, they present their experiences of power relations and inequalities and their own responses to these in Turkey as a constitutive part of their political positioning. This is most articulate in the life-stories of those who were politically active in Turkey. Nâlan and Birgül elaborate on their politicization through the 1970s in Turkey. This was a highly politicized period of students' and workers' protests, where left and right wing activists clashed with each other and the state (Landau 1974). In this sense, their generation plays a role not only as a generation of migration but because their age cohort was the most active in the political conflicts of the period (ibid.). As Nâlan puts it: 'But I think at that time you had to be something because the political environment was so hot. At that time everybody was political ... you had to take sides, everything was very political, everybody was talking politics'.

## Birgül

*'The Times were Very Lively'*

While Birgül was in the last year of high school the coup d'etat of 1971 took place. Through the theatre group at her school she found contact to 'progressive and politicized' teachers and pupils.

> B: (…) they had founded a theatre group, like a people's theatre. In the theatre group there weren't any girls. The boys participated but they couldn't find any girls. Because nobody – it was a bit like, girls shouldn't play theatre, it could be a measure of respectability. Therefore no one [of the other female pupil's parents] gave their permission. I said, I will play in the theatre! And then, I will never forget this, I got the role of the servant (laughs).

> U: (laughs)

> B: It wasn't important to me at all, whatever role it was. The important thing was to safeguard the continuity of this theatre. And then I participated in the play and through this theatre group I got into politicized circles. (…) And then I participated in all the discussions among them and I started to read different books and so on.

Birgül here describes her politicization as influenced by the national political upheaval of the coup d'etat. By joining the theatre group Birgül not only entered a progressive social circle, but also transgressed gendered norms of respectability. Her exclamation 'I will play in the theatre!' thus courageously asserts her disregard for her (sexual) reputation. In tension with this individually taken, gender-specific risk of the loss of her reputation is her next statement that her stake was not in expressing herself personally, but in safeguarding the collective project. The relation between individual responsibility and commitment to a collective project is a key theme in Birgül's story about her political work that I will return to below. I read this sequence as expressing the gendered dilemmas of individuality and collectivity that were characteristic of the left-wing groups at the time, where women were in general accorded supportive roles in the background (Tekeli 1991). This is somewhat ironically reflected in Birgül's acceptance of taking on the theatrical role of servant. While left-wing groups of the 1970s had gender transformative projects, these focused on challenging both traditional and bourgeois constructions of femininity, in contrast, the positive, revolutionary femininity envisaged a validation of women as de-sexualized sisters ('baci') of their male comrades. Yet, women were regarded as inherently more at risk of moral corruption through 'bourgeois values', thus required to prove their adherence to revolutionary values, including that of sacrificing individual ambitions for the collective struggle. Otherwise, however, gender specific issues such as sexuality were regarded as secondary to the workers' revolution (Göbenli 1999). Birgül herself does not reflect on this during the interview.

*Stories that Can(not) be Shared: 'I Diverted'*

When she started university the next year, the politicization of the universities was at its height, with left-wing activists, police and right-wing activists clashing on the campuses:

> And then my university life started with, on my first day at university, there were stones flying, doors that were broken, somebody was shot, and so on. That was just the period of 1972, I started university in 1972 (…) And then, in this way, my political life began to be more established. Of course university life was very lively. But at the same time it was very difficult. (…) there was always pressure, there were constantly demonstrations, and constantly the university was closed down. Constantly there were attacks, that's the way my university life passed.

While this period was clearly important for Birgül's life-story, especially as her activism resulted in her to eventually fleeing Turkey in the wake of the 1980 coup d'etat, she preferred to elaborate on her political activism in Germany. Indeed, she cut her story on her political life in Turkey short, 'I diverted, better for you to ask the questions' and even when I suggested she continue describing what her activism in Turkey meant for her, she continued to talk about her life in Germany. This indicates a biographical strategy of locating herself firmly within the German context in which she lives, rather than in a retrospective or future 'homeland' orientation as is typical for many Turkish left-wing groups and organizations (cf. above Pınar's criticism).

Birgül emphasizes that she fled Turkey head over heels and had not considered migration before the coup d'etat of 1980 (cf. Chapter 4). One possible interpretation of this is as a justification for leaving. There is a recognition in the literature that refugees can have feelings of guilt for leaving, and, especially if they were politically active, may face reproaches and feelings of having abandoned the most difficult cause by leaving the country (Abakay 1988, Sales 2001).

*Identity Politics: 'As if There's a Different Politics for the
Germans and the Turks'*

Birgül underlines her interest and involvement in the political and social life in Germany. When she was living in the small town, where she had started her professional specialization and experienced difficulties in obtaining the necessary permits (cf. Chapter 4), Birgül set up different anti-racist campaigns. In this way, her own experiences of racism and her personal struggle motivated her. As she points out throughout the interview, the experiential dimension of racism has been formative for her self-representation and how she views her part in German society.

In this sense, Birgül's activism involved some central elements of identity politics. Thus, Birgül's formulation of an anti-racist politics that politicized experiences of racialization rather than submitting to the role of client of 'foreigner-friendly' German activists and mediators (cf. Radtke 1994) challenged not just the hegemonic analyses of racism as 'enmity to foreigners'. It also challenged the reified relation between migrants as victims or as merely recipients of support and protection of 'foreigner-friendly' Germans. The pitfalls of identity politics as essentializing and homogenizing personal and collective identities are well-known. Still, they carved out a space for gaining political agency for migrants disenfranchized and excluded from party politics and marginalized in other forms of political organization (e.g. about trade unions: cf. Toksöz 1991, about feminist politics: cf. Arbeitsgruppe Frauenkongress 1985 etc.).

Birgül was also active in traditional left-wing organizations, dominated by Germans:

> Birgül: I was involved in political activities here. However in the political groups I also experienced that they treated us as if we didn't know Marxism: 'Have you ever read anything of Lenin?' they asked me. 'Have you read this book of Karl Marx?' 'Of course' we said, 'we have read it'.

> U: (Laughs) As if they had written it themselves.

> B: No, there wasn't a bit of difference to those experiences in the hospital, there was no difference to that in the political groups, either.

> U: Yes.

> B: There, as well, as I said earlier as if there is a different type of medicine, you know, for the Turks and the Germans. As if there's a different politics for the Germans and the Turks, as if there were different books that we read and different books that they read. If you have read the classics, we have read them, too. That was the approach, you know. And then we made anti-racist politics, but we are the only ones responsible for this. We were not included in the general politics, the decision making and discussion and so on. Only when the issue of racism came to the agenda they asked us for our ideas.

> U: Yes.

> B: Well, there as well we experienced racism.

Birgül emphasizes the similarity of the devaluation of her knowledge and capacities in both her workplace and in the political group. This group was not based on identity politics. Yet, it is argued that some of the epistemological and organizational elements that Birgül recounts follow the logic of invisible identity politics. By 'invisible identity' politics, I mean an identity politics that is taken for granted, both constituted by and constitutive of the normalization of dominant identities, their legitimated standpoints, epistemologies and decision making processes. The term identity politics is usually ascribed to the organizational and epistemological forms developed by marginalized groups to articulate their interests and organize around these (Alice Echols quoted in Rowbotham 1992: 274). Thus, women, migrants, disabled people, gays and lesbians' organizations are seen as doing identity politics. When men, members of the ethnically dominant group, heterosexuals or able bodied people organize, they claim to do so on the basis of their political views which they present as based on generalizable knowledges, rather than on specific experiences or interests (Harding 1991).

Members of dominant identity groups have privileged access to the state, media, economic and other resources to present their view of the world as valid and neutral (Anthias and Yuval-Davis 1992) and their entitlements as justified (Parekh 2008: 52). This is also true for politically oppositional groups and the resources of their institutions and networks, albeit that the resources and the reach of their knowledges is more restricted. These representational resources can strengthen their claim to define what counts as generalizable knowledge in the interest of all and what counts as specific knowledge based on specific identities. This power of representation and definition is so generalized that the normalization of dominant identities appears as neutral.

*Politics of Belonging*

Birgül delineates her political activism in Germany from the lack of involvement of many other migrants from Turkey. However, she feels that the German members of the left-wing group, and later on of feminist groups did not allow for such an internal differentiation of the category of migrant:

> The workers here, or the Turkish families here, Turkish or Kurdish, they live here in a rather isolated way, they are ghettoized, because they are not at all *recognized*. If you try to do the opposite then you get put into a different position, too. You are discriminated against, although you are not that way. As I said, you are constantly struggling.

Birgül has an acute sense of not being recognized as a legitimate participant in social and political groups. Birgül identifies cultural differences in (political) socialization as another difference between her and her German fellow activists:

> B: Well, the people from Turkey, me as a person, too, we come from a different socialization, we have a mania for social life. Well, our political struggles before 1980, there was no individual, everything was collective. When I came

to Germany I realized that the individual had more importance. That was very exhausting and difficult for many people, for me, too, because all of a sudden you can see how important the individual is. Still however the collective or community is very relevant for the people from Turkey and I see this as very positive, too. In the German groups, be they political or personal or other, everybody lives very much for themselves, they are very individualized. That disturbs me, it still disturbs me.

While Birgül finds it valuable to recognize the importance of the individual, she does not want to give up her value of collectivity or community. To her these are 'Turkish' values, however she specifies that they are values relating to her own political socialization into a historically specific political movement. This can be seen as an instance where nationally specific forms of sociality articulate other political identities (cf. Johnson 1993). While Birgül perceived her political identity as a socialist or Marxist as non-national, and viewed her political socialization as compatible with that of her German comrades, her authority over the knowledges of socialist texts was questioned on the basis of her ethnicity. Moreover, the forms of sociality within the group in Germany where very different from those she had experienced and practised in Turkey:

B: [I find it important] to be interested and put efforts in other people and their problems. Of course (…) it is important to see your own values too, because you are an individual in the collective. If you cannot stand in for yourself as an individual under the conditions of life in Germany you suffer from all types of psychosomatic illness, ranging from depression to I don't know what (laughs). But I am speaking of political life even. Even there in a group discussion, where we had extremely intense discussions, with *comrades* when you met them on the street they didn't even greet you, they didn't even recognize you. And one expects of them 'Oh, hello, how are you' and so on. Well, outside of the meetings there was no communication.

U: Hmm. Hmm.

N: And that disturbed me a lot. Or [in Germany] the political life is organized like the working life. The weekend was the time when we struggled the most in Turkey, [but here] after work, at the weekend the political life, everything stood still. Of course, the individual has an importance, too, here in Germany, that was bad in Turkey. Of course, to understand both, which one is right which one is wrong one needs a lot of time.

In the earlier extract about the theatre group, Birgül stated that she gladly put the continuity of the group before her individual wish for recognition; however she finds that her experiences in Germany have made her reconsider the importance of the individual *vis-à-vis* collectivities. This is reflected in her valorization of the social location of 'foreigner' as affording reflexivity on national belonging:

> because to be able to get to know two different ways of life, cultures, can enable you to see many things more from outside and observe them. (…) But on the other hand, the negative side of being a foreigner is that after a while you loose the roots anyway. You don't feel *at home* [original in German, U.E.] anywhere.

She juxtaposes this to her daughter's claim for belonging to and being both German and Turkish (cf. Chapter 5). Instead of claims to Germanness, she finds that other migrants are the people with whom she most easily feels she belongs on the basis of their common experiences of racism. The experience of non-recognition and marginalization is central to how Birgül views her social and political participation in Germany. She gives examples of this experience in other areas of life, such as her participation in creative writing groups, where German participants question her status as a writer on the basis of her ethnicity and the fact that she is writing in German, her second language (cf. Adelson 1997). This is an example of how her linguistic and cultural competence is de-legitimated because she is seen as not belonging.

Yet, there is no unilinear relation between feelings of recognition or belonging and participation. Thus, while Birgül has become active in social and political groups relating to Germany soon after she arrived in Germany, until very recently she emotionally evaluated her stay as 'temporary'. At the time of interview, Birgül still felt that she was not recognized as a legitimate part of the society she lived in. Nonetheless, she had projects relating to this society, such as doing research into migrant women's sexual health issues, as well as a creative writing project. Birgül's story of her political and cultural activism calls into question any *a priori* assumptions about the relation between social location, identification and the political values and views she holds and realizes through her social participation. She points out that her feeling of 'belonging is reduced', both towards Turkey and Germany. However, she follows political events and developments in both countries. After her migration she has participated in social and political campaigns in both countries, e.g. in feminist transnational and diasporic networks. However, she critically evaluates the groups that she has participated in, in terms of their hidden identity politics. Birgül does not construct belonging as a given, but rather as negotiated and struggled over.

Birgül's story of her political and cultural activism articulates her experiences as a refugee who had been a political activist in Turkey. She discusses these experiences as a background story to frame her activism in Germany. The experiences that she gained in Turkey such as organizing, as well as her political outlook as a socialist, influenced her activism in Germany. I examined two interrelated forms of politics she was engaged in: on the one hand her anti-racist activism in the early 1980s was a challenge to pre-existing forms of foreigner's politics because it formulated a critique of German institutions' racist practices on the basis of her own experience as a '*Ausländer*'. This constituted a subject position for herself as an active and agentic participant in anti-racist struggles, rather than being merely the object of these struggles as formulated by Germans. In this form of politics, Birgül articulated a link between experience, identity and resistance yet re-formulated the link between experiences of racist victimization and an ascribed identity of *Ausländer* as passively enduring this. Closely linked to this were her political values which led her to analyse as racism what was otherwise commonly viewed as 'enmity to foreigners'. As a participant in a German dominated socialist group, she experienced marginalization and the ascription of compulsory difference, which has been termed a hidden identity politics of dominance.

## Selin

In their stories of activism, Birgül and Pınar construct the collective subject position of migrant women as a political resource to counter their marginalization and the de-valuation of their knowledges in political groups and processes. Yet, in the following story of political activism I would like to highlight that even these projects of building a political subject of 'migrant woman' did indeed marginalize some people and construct internal hierarchies. Particular forms of cultural capital enabled some migrant women to play a more central role in decision making and processes of representation. A lack of the 'right' cultural capital meant Selin felt dis-abled to express her particular experiences of gendered ethnicization and, more to the point, felt that this marginalization was structurally reified even within feminist migrant political groups. Thus, this story sheds a critical light on the tensions within migrant community and feminist activism. At the time of interview Selin was questioning herself and her biographical choices, triggered by recent personal crises. This is important to contextualize her narrative which focused on a critical re-evaluation of the gains and losses.

*Migration and Community Activism*

Selin's story of her political activism is closely bound up with her story of migration. She experienced a number of internal migrations within Turkey and views this experience as central to her self-representation as characterized by a 'double consciousness' (cf. Chapter 3). As a young woman she left the village again to join her older sister in a small town and help bring up her children. During this time, she attended vocational courses and soon began to manage her brother-in-law's business. This economic independence enhanced her status within the family as well as her self esteem. During this time, she also gained a reputation in the small town and neighbouring villages:

> I was someone who helped everybody out, who was good natured and willing to help, I had such a very good communication with the people. The old people, the

miserable came from the villages, they brought some eggs [and said] 'Come on, let's go. We have some problems at the registry office regarding our children'. Well anything to do with I don't know what, old age pensions, and that kind of thing, I was always busy doing this kind of thing. And out of these 46 villages, maybe (…) 70% of the villagers knew me'.

Selin refers to this period as formative to her self-representation as respected, competent and caring for others, a theme she elaborates in the context of the UK where she got involved in a community centre. Selin presents this as a continuation of her role in the small town in Turkey as she did not identify as 'a political person'. As a member of the management committee and in several other functions, she did unpaid, voluntary work in the community centre for three years.

While Pınar experienced conflicts between different political groups in the form of violent clashes which led her to give up left-wing homeland politics. In Selin's case, these conflicts were carried out in power struggles within the management committee of the community centre. Like Pınar, as someone without party-political affiliations she got marginalized and caught up in these conflicts:

S: I had a bad experience with this, because you need to be a member of group A or group B. And because I was not a member I experienced a lot of pressure because of being independent.

U: They wanted you to join their group …

S: They wanted that, but when it didn't happen, they treated you differently. Then they treat you as if you don't exist. Because group A takes this side, group B takes that side, group C takes the other side, and you're left in the middle because you are independent.

U: Hmm

S: (…) When they realize that you don't belong to any group, all the three of them start to put pressure on you at once. Now, there was no one questioning the machismo, the sexism, the hierarchies there. The only thing they do is to say 'women's health' and put up one announcement, and that was me because I was [one of the, U. E.] only women on the management committee.

While sidelining her as a person in the decision making process, the issues Selin prioritized, such as gender politics were neglected and the centre's women's politics remained tokenistic.

Cultural and linguistic competence were used as ways to de-legitimize Selin's work. Thus, while Selin was made head of the women's branch, the secretary did not inform her about council meetings concerning women's issues but attended them in her place. When Selin challenged her, the secretary argued that Selin could not attend because of her lack of English. However, Selin insisted on going to the council meetings herself with a translator. Selin interprets this as a conflict over who is recognized as representative of the community centre by the council, which was also the grant-giving body. This points to the problematic status of representation *vis-à-vis* the local state. As feminist writers have pointed out, British multiculturalist policies often lead to a legitimation of 'community leaders' whose basis for representing the community is not democratic and moreover, often partakes in strengthening sexist practices and structures (Brah 1997, Patel 1997, Sahgal and Yuval-Davis 1992). Selin critiques the practices of the community centre as 'the opposite of equal opportunities'. This is an important case in point for the paradoxical dynamics of multiculturalist local authority policies. Equal opportunities are a core principle of local multiculturalism. However, while Selin learned this concept in her community activism, she also realized that it was not sufficiently put into practice in the community centre. Instead, even, or especially, in the dealings with the council, hierarchies of education, gender, and corporatist party affiliations worked to exclude those like herself who have adapted this core value.

When Selin began co-operating with feminist migrant groups from Turkey she experienced hostilities by her colleagues in the community centre. 'They call you a feminist, a lesbian, all of a sudden they call you a pimp, you sell women (…) I was attacked in many ways'. While men may support women's community activism, they may at the same time fear a loss of patriarchal control through the women's increased scope for agency: 'Women involved in these activities are under scrutiny not for their politics or their activities for the group, but as women. Criticism of a woman's [alleged, U. E.] sexual behaviour can be used by men as means of maintaining control of women's political activities' (Kofman et al. 2000: 184–5). Such patriarchal control is also exercised by other women, not only men. For Selin, this culminated when her first term of office in the management committee ended. There were attempts to intimidate her not to stand for re-election:

> S: A couple of the women literally said to me 'Look if you don't get out of this management committee these men are going to take you and fuck you in some place, they are going to rape you and bring you back and drop you in front of the community centre'. That is how they threatened me.

> U: Oooh. who…?

> S: Well, people from group A or B who did not want me to go into that management committee. Because you are independent, there is no protection behind you.

> U: Yes.

> S: Because all of this, as I say, are power relations.

Selin did not heed this attempt to intimidate her and was re-elected into the management committee. Not being affiliated to a party contributed to her critical stance in the management committee, but it also made her particularly vulnerable since she did not have a pre-existing group to protect her. These threats, although meant to prevent her from pursuing her politics, were directed at her sexuality: the threat of rape was directed at her physical, psychological and social integrity. Rape or, in this case, the threat of rape, as a means of political intimidation is used not only to attack the person, but also to ostracize her from a community whose dominant values may still view it as tarnishing the victim rather than the perpetrator: the threat of leaving Selin in front of the community centre contains the aspect of making the rape public. This is a crucial aspect of the way in which rape is used in political repression as a means of setting an example, scaring others off and tarnishing the 'honour' of those associated or related to the victim (cf. Nordstrom 1997: 124–132). Having defied these pressures once, Selin decided to leave the community centre at the next election period.

*Acculturation into 'Turkish' Feminist Groups*

Selin invoked feminist principles throughout her life-story, yet, also developed a critical view of her involvement with feminist migrant groups from Turkey in the UK, a period which she portrays as formative. While in Chapter 4 I examined the uses of cultural capital for developing intra-ethnic strategies of validation and distinction in the site of work, this section highlights the meaning of a lack of recognized cultural capital for validating migrant women's political and social participation.

While Selin politically sympathized with migrant feminist groups from Turkey, she also felt culturally very different from them, prompting both feelings of curiosity and of inadequacy:

> S: I came to this country for the first time, I looked around at some women around me, some groups. I admired their freedom, their independence. Look, I had no idea about any of these things, you know. Neither the theatre, nor the music, whatever, [all of this was] *Turkish, Turkish! Let alone [English culture], this was Turkish [culture that was unknown to me]!* And I wanted to catch up with all of this, you know.

This feminist, 'Turkish' culture was at once strange and attractive to her; it held the promise of change of gender specific life-styles that she had been looking for through her migration. Selin not only wanted to emulate these cultural forms but the type of feminity associated with these. The assumption that, coming from the same country, she would be closer to the cultural forms of other migrants from Turkey at once denies her difference as Kurdish and emphasizes this difference as a lack of cultural capital. Selin's initial response was an attempt to 'catch up with' these cultural knowledges and forms. Her eagerness to learn was felt and expressed acutely:

> S: During this time I went to meetings, from here to there, always on the go in order to learn these things, that was very important for me.
>
> U: Hmm.
>
> S: I am a person who has never in her life been to the theatre, never to the cinema. I went as a child a few times, but they all know best about it. Bless them, all my friends – who knows where I found them – they are all intellectuals.
>
> U: (Laughing) Where have you found them?
>
> S: (Laughing) Well, where have I found them, I am talking of that period, I always looked for those circles. I always chose to live through such an oppressedness and feeling of inferiority because they know and I don't. *Oh, they know and I don't, I was constantly looking for something, why don't I know these things!*

The high-cultural practices of theatre or cinema going in which a disposition and an ability to appreciate is produced and expressed, were alien to her. Selin, like Bourdieu's 'old-style autodidact' (1996: 84) wanted to learn about these cultural practices as much as she could in a short space of time. And, she wanted to learn about the entirety of these practices. According to Bourdieu it is this high standard one sets for oneself that shows up the autodidact as opposed to those with 'inherited' and 'always having been there' cultural capital who are able to admit or mask ignorance (ibid.).

Selin conceptualizes the issue of cultural competence as relational. She recognizes that this particular cultural capital is specific to 'intellectuals' and that she actively participated in the validation of this particular cultural practices by according them the status of authority. Selin ironically speaks of her complicity in (re-)producing their authority since she 'chose' to feel inferior. This relational dynamic created for her the inferior subject position of a 'learner' and made her question herself as inadequate.[1] These dynamics were crucial in the political conflicts she experienced in the 'Turkish' feminist groups.

*The Boundaries of Feminist Politics of Experience and Representation*

A core principle of feminist thought and politics is the validation of women's experiences as a starting point for challenging dominant knowledges. This has been elaborated in particular by Black feminists who emphasize the significance of validating different class, race and ethnic identies of women (cf. Hill-Collins 1990, hooks 1983).

> U: But did you not value your own experiences?

> S: But they don't know about my experiences. Sometimes they talk in such a way, that they express the things I know much better. (...) they start talking about the village (...) as if they have always lived in the village. Yes, they can put things into words so beautifully.

> U: Hmm.

> S: And they make such good sense of it, I could not make sense of what I lived through with such beautiful words like them.

> U: Hmm.

> S: And therefore, they are much better villagers then me, they are much more educated...

> U: (laughs)

> S: They are much more political, much cleverer than me. How could these people be so lucky. Because I feel this pressure on myself, I always want to learn

---

1    This extract exemplifies an inter-subjective dynamic at play between Selin and me. I partake in the educational privilege she critiqued. This privilege need not necessarily be used as a practice of distinction and appropriation, but it holds the potential to be used thus. My uneasy laughter can be read as a defence of those 'intellectual' friends with whom I thus unwittingly constructed a commonality and solidarity. Selin, in turn tries to calm my self-doubt by projecting and fixing her statements to 'that period' and thus relieving me of any role and responsibility in this conflict. My identification with her intellectual friends is problematic. Reflection on my role in this conflict is legitimate, but should not have pre-occupied me to the extent that it prompted her to 'protect' me from her criticism of 'intellectuals' and its possible implications for my self-image in our research relation.

something, I looked at them *like an idiot. I didn't say to myself, just sit back and forget about all this, you cannot cope with all this pressure.*

Selin points out that it was not experience, but the ability to participate in validated discursive forms that conveyed the authority to represent. By being able to give meaning to such experiences in 'beautiful words' her educated feminist friends gained the authority over the subjectivities formed through these experiences. In this feminist story telling community (Plummer 1995; 2000 cf. Chapter 1), the construction of authoritative discourses replaced the authorizing strategy of first person experience. Thus, Selin's role became that of a listener rather than narrator in this story telling community. This exclusion from an articulating and theorizing subject position reified her status of inferiority. It is ironic that a feminist public created to validate hitherto unspeakable experiences and elaborate politicized identities on their basis made Selin's experiences unspeakable.

Selin criticizes that the reification of hierarchies between women based on feminist or educational credentials is dis-empowering for those women deemed not 'conscious' enough. She found that women who were seen as uneducated, rural or working class were only viewed as passive recipients of the services, instead of involving them as (potential) political activists. Moreover, she felt that the group's structure was based on an implicit ethnic hierarchy, where she was given the status of token Kurdish woman among the Turkish feminists:

S: They took me everywhere with them as a Kurdish woman, but there weren't any other Kurdish women around them. And then, the microphone is constantly in their hands (…)

U: Why [weren't there any other Kurdish women]?

S: *Because they [Kurdish women] can't approach them. There is no dialogue, no communication, no understanding.*

U: They are excluded?

S: *Of course, they are excluded. (…) This is where my differences with these [Turkish feminist] women started.* (…) They only helped them [Kurdish women] but it is a different thing whether you just help or whether you give them a consciousness and bring them to leadership.

…

S: Then, that night we were discussing these things. (…) 'Look, as your friend I feel like this among you. And I like you a lot, you are my friends. But this disturbs me. Why don't you let others [take leadership positions]? Why do you always have to be the head of the women's centre? (…) Why, is this your tribe?' (…) At this point … because they do it professionally. Because they are paid by the council's women's unit, they are paid £22 000, £25 000. (…) Would they ever leave this position?

Selin argues that the feminist group reified intermeshing hierarchies of class, ethnicity and education by reducing 'other' women to service recipients and clients. Moreover, she argues that the unwillingness of some feminist women to share leadership and educate others to partake in decision-making and leadership was based on their vested interests as professional representatives of the community. This highlights the ambiguity of professional work as political activism. The conflation of professional and political authority can lead to rigid hierarchies that exclude non-professionals from decision-making since those in leadership position may not only see their political authority at stake, but also their livelihood. Those who do voluntary, unpaid work, like Selin, may feel that their own contributions are not adequately valued.

Selin's wording: 'Why, is this your tribe?' is significant here. Tribal organizational forms rely on inheritance of social functions, as well as patron-client relations. Tribe as a social organizational form plays a role in Kurdish political and social life, and is often viewed as a backward, 'primitive' and undemocratic institution. Referring to tribal relations, Selin ironizes the self-presentation of this group as modern and democratic.[2] This highlights the tension between avowedly democratic processes of legitimation and the underlying undemocratic hierarchies based on gender, class, ethnic and educational inequalities.

There is of course another side to this conflict. As migrant women who are professionally engaged in and for migrant women's projects point out, they value the political relevance of their professional work. However, the blurred boundaries between their own identity and the demands for loyalty on them as parts of institutions at the same time as 'the community' they are supposed to represent and serve are problematic. These factors mean they are prone to stress, overwork, exhaustion and may neglect caring for themselves. The importance of the services

---

2    Wallerstein (1991) de-constructs the paradox of particularism and universalism. He argues that so-called pre-modern, pre-capitalist forms of social organization were explicitly based on gender and ethnic differences and self-consciously maintained hierarchies through birthrights in estate-like systems. Modern democratic legitimity, on the other hand, he argues is based on the claim of the universal equality of humans. The avowed principle of hierarchy is merit, rather than birth-right. However, in practice this principle of achievement continues to create and reify gendered and ethnicized hierarchies. Instead, he argues that universalism and particularism mutually constitute each other and are both necessary for stabilizing existing hierarchies, in practice as well as ideologically.

provided by such 'mediators' (Lutz 1991) is undoubted. They often enable access to welfare state provisions and are instrumental in creating new services adapted to the specific needs of migrants and specifically migrant women, thus forming an important enabling factor in the realization of social citizenship rights (cf. Brah 1997, Lewis 1996, Sales 2000). Moreover, as groups or individuals they are often key in campaigning for legislative change to improve the lives of migrants and migrant women (cf. Brah 1997, Kofman et al. 2000; Sales 2000). However, from Selin's standpoint other problematic aspects of the role of 'mediators' are articulated. Drawing on her research with Turkish and Somali health advocates, Sales cautions that 'some women become over dependent on the advocates. Many lead isolated lives and do not learn English even after many years in London, so that their interaction with the welfare services is always through someone else' (2000: 18). Increasing integration of community groups as service providers who are closely regulated and often underfunded is an ambivalent process. On one hand the professionalism of the services provided by community organizations is valued, on the other, control is taken away from the community. In conjunction with perennial underfunding, in particular of core functions, this limits the ability of community organizations to campaign as they are focused on maintaining or attracting funding to provide services responding to the urgent needs of migrants (Erel and Tomlinson 2005). This leads to a re-casting of migrants as 'clients' rather than as (potential) fellow community activists (Zetter et al. 2005). While these tensions are common in the process of institutionalization of the voluntary sector, they become particularly salient against the backdrop of social exclusion from the mainstream society, as well as divisions within the group of migrants from Turkey and their representation as Turkish-speaking community (Sales 2000: 19–20, cf. also Uguris 2001: 11, cf. Zetter et al. 2005; cf. Chapter 2 for a discussion of the construct of 'Turkish-speaking community').[3]

Selin's critique that the construction of Kurdish and/or working class and rural women as 'ignorant' reifies their subjection is echoed in Sales' (2000) findings. It is important to recognize the different conditions for becoming active and developing skills based on the intersecting differences between Turkish and Kurdish women and how these articulate with education, rural-urban and other factors. However, differential cultural capital should not simply be accepted as a justification for continuing exclusion from positions of leadership or professional service provision. Instead, projects of empowerment need to go hand in hand with a de-construction of privileged subject positions and those elements that reproduce dominance *vis-à-vis* rural, working class and Kurdish women.

---

3    Sales' analysis is very important, since it calls attention to the differential dynamics of representation, institutionalization and professionalization. In this respect it constitutes a much-needed exception, as Uguris points out '(…) existing studies [on the Kurdish and Turkish Diaspora, U.E.] and subsequently the state policies do not question these divisions, tend to homogenise these communities and overlook the different experiences of men and women, of different social classes and ethnicities' (Uguris 1999: 1–2).

*Longing and Belonging*

Selin stated that she is 'looking for something else', however without knowing where this could be found. At the same time, when questionned how she saw her position in Britain, she claimed 'all the rights the English have, I want to have them, too'. Thus making a strong claim to belonging, emphasizing that she saw herself as part of this society, 'as if I was born here'. Yet, for Selin the fantasy of a new migration elsewhere or the longing for Turkey co-exist with a strong commitment to participating in and being part of British society. This underlines the importance of differentiating between a fantastic form of longing, that Selin expresses for Turkey or for 'elsewhere' as opposed to her concrete 'integration work' (Lutz 1998) into British society. By 'integration work' Lutz means those efforts, usually overlooked both by researchers and migrants alike, to 'maintain an everyday order, restructure or reorganize it under changed everyday conditions' (1998: 286, my translation from German).

Selin's story of her activism is bound up with her quest for change, learning and widening her horizon, for which she uses migration as a metaphor. Despite shared values, differential social positioning and cultural capital can mean that some members of groups, such as Selin's critique articulates, can be marginalized in decision making and representation.

**Conclusion**

The neglect of the active dimension of migrant women's citizenship in the literature suggests that, as they are often marginalized from political and cultural representation in the nation-states they live in, they do not participate in the society, either. The migrant women's stories contradict this. Instead, I argue for a more differentiated examination of political activism, including women's work in community groups, voluntary work, as well as informal activism (cf. Kofman et al.2000). The fields of politics the women chose are diverse, ranging from 'homeland politics', internationalist or transnational feminist or socialist activism, to the voluntary work in community organizations, and local women's groups. One commonality in the women's activism is that they view their gendered and ethnicized experiences as one important element of their identities which triggered their interest in articulating political positions and campaigns about the living conditions of migrant women. However, this use of experience as a basis for developing critical knowledges is complemented by other principles of knowledge and organizational forms. Thus, Pınar's work with and for migrant women importantly constructs common epistemologies, strategies and interests across ethnic differences. She self-consciously articulates a common history of experiences of subjection but also of struggles and resistance with migrant and Black women in Germany.[4] Birgül's experiences of marginalization within a German dominated socialist group highlight that the exclusionary aspects of identity politics are also at work in groups that explicitly organize around universalist principles. This was analysed as a form of hidden identity politics of dominance. Selin's experiences of community activism and of feminist activism raised similar issues about the reification of hierarchies of gender, ethnicity, education, class and sexuality. Her story of community activism exemplifies how women's position in these groups can be ambiguous and tenuous. While this activism enhanced her agency and widened her scope for social participation, it made her vulnerable to attacks on her gendered identity. She challenged the social divisions of gender and education that she was faced with in the management committee and in her voluntary work. These criticisms, together with her vulnerable position as an independent member laid her open to increased pressures by her fellow activists, specifically using patriarchal instruments of control. In the migrant feminist groups from Turkey, Selin experienced the marginalization of her voice, in sharing her experience, and in participating in decision-making and representation. This was due to another hidden identity politics on the basis of intermeshing identities of (Turkish or Kurdish) ethnicity, class, education and rural-urban origin. Selin's critique of such internal divisions is particularly salient since the homogeneity of migrant communities is often reified in social policy, too. Therefore, it has been an important concern to allow this dissenting voice to be heard. It has been argued that the problematic politics of representation is not just an internal or personal problem of migrant (women's) community groups, but bound up with the problematic status of representation that multiculturalist policies endow 'community leaders' with. Thus, community activism can have contradictory, empowering and dis-empowering effects:

Given (...) migrant women's limited access to policy-making bodies, women have used other forums and other forms of representation to present their interests.

---

4   The notion of political Blackness as articulated in the late 1970s in Britain has been adapted for the context of migrants in Germany in the late 1980s. Although some of the literature claims that this concept has been overcome during the 1990s, others (e.g. Brah 1996, Sudbury 2001) argue that it should not be simply discarded. They argue that political Blackness has never been unequivocally accepted to start with, however that it continues to be an important notion to highlight the commonalties of experience, outlook and activism. For a discussion of multiracial Blackness in British Black feminist groups and its articulation of difference and commonalty (cf. Sudbury 2001).

Some people argue that these new forms of associations and networking provide better means of accommodating the new pluralism and multiplicity of identities among migrants in Western society. However, at least some of these forums reinstate gendered and racist hierarchies. Besides, these networks can only be one strategy within the multipronged approach necessary to improve public provision and representation of migrant women in Europe (Kofman et al.2001: 191).

This points to the continuing importance of achieving both formal and substantial citizenship rights for migrant women. I have further examined the notions of belonging the interviewee's put forward. Avtar Brah's concept of diaspora space distinguishes between 'homing desire' and the desire for a 'homeland' (1996: 180).

> When does a location *become* home? What is the difference between 'feeling at home' and staking a claim to a place as one's own? It is quite possible to feel at home in a place and, yet, the experience of social exclusions may inhibit public proclamations of the place as home (Brah 1996: 193).

These contradictions are born out in the interviewees' narratives of belonging. Thus, Pınar who locates herself firmly in the space of German society and on different levels struggles for changes in this society, claims a bi-cultural identity in which she wants to protect an allegiance to what she views as 'Turkishness'. Birgül, while having participated actively in the professional, social, political and cultural life of German society claims an affective identification as outsider, and non-belonging, both *vis-à-vis* Germany and Turkey. Her refusal to proclaim national belonging does not prevent her from her activism, however. Selin uses the metaphor of migration for broadening her horizon and her quest for recognition. This includes a search and attempts at creating belonging on different levels. The ambiguous effects of ethnic belonging in her community activism have been to lay her open to attacks on her gendered and sexual integrity. In her activism with Turkish feminist groups in London, on the other hand, she encountered cultural difference, articulated through the marginalization of her ethnic identity and the highlighting of her educational lack. This reveals that 'home' can be sought on the basis of different commonalties, not only nationality. However, even in such non-national constructions of 'home' or belonging, conflicts, hierarchies and differences are at work. 'Home' need not be, indeed never is, a place of pure harmony (cf. Räthzel 1994). Selin's homing desire is maybe best expressed in her fantasy of a new migration, which articulates 'home' as 'somewhere else'. This fantasy however co-exists with her concrete efforts of 'integration work' into British society and her claim to belonging and rights in it.

This leads on to another important point, thus, all these interviewees construct community and commonality across ethnic differences. They either feel they most easily relate to other migrants, like Birgül, consciously construct a political and emotional community of migrants and Black people in Germany, like Pınar, or overcome linguistic difficulties to reach out and learn new things about themselves and others in cross-ethnic friendships, like Selin. There are, of course, also interviewees, who do not give such centrality to cross-ethnic social and political relations, however they also incorporate cross-ethnic relations in their life-stories. This finding is stressed because often the experiences of migrants are examined only within a binary frame of reference of 'Turkishness' versus the ethnically majoritarian society of residence. This does not take account of the multilayered, complex process of locating and positioning themselves in a multi-ethnic, differentially racialized social space.

Yuval-Davis (2001) argues for a politics of belonging that

> would transcend the older dichotomous choices of the universal and particular, equality and difference. Such a politics of belonging would take into account people's emotions, fears and hopes, but would not construct ethnic and other primordial identities as the only available havens in a fast changing and globalizing world. Such a politics of belonging would add, rather than substitute, identity politics to the participatory politics of citizenship (2001: 13).

The interviewees' stories of activism have highlighted some of the ways in which migrant women's agency can inform such a new politics of belonging. Thus, to return to the discussion of belonging in the introduction of this chapter, the migrant women's stories show that there is no unilinear and necessary link between identification, passive belonging and socio-political participation of migrant women. Thus, even though they lay claim to passive belonging in the sense of having and claiming rights, they problematize an identification with their nation-states of residence. This, however does not prevent them from belonging to the places they live in by by intervening politically and socially, even when they do not feel recognized as citizens. Finally, it is suggested we should refine the notion that migrants strive to accumulate 'national' cultural capital to seek recognition mainly by majority citizens. The migrant women presented here do not always seek validation through inclusion into the symbolic national capital. Instead, they try and construct alternatives. There is variation to how these are articulated. Thus, Pınar constructs a form of belonging with Black and Migrant Germans, Birgül affirms an affinity with other migrants, while Selin articulates a vaguer notion of a fantastic 'somewhere else' as the place of belonging.

# Chapter 7
# Conclusion: Transforming Citizenship

There is a disjuncture between academic debates on inclusive citizenship attempting to mobilize 'citizenship' as a momentum concept to democratize an ever widening range of social relations on one hand and current governmental attempts in both the UK and in Germany where citizenship is increasingly constructed as a privilege. Governmental policy suggests that the privilege of formal citizenship must be achieved through citizenship tests, integration classes (Germany) or volunteering for the community (UK). This goes hand in hand with governmental attempts to revitalize and revalue citizenship through building social cohesion. Current governmental discourse, both in the UK and Germany contrasts the notion of social cohesion built around common values to multiculturalist ideas of celebrating difference. Multiculturalism in this sense, and indeed implicitly the notion of multi-ethnicity, is presented as undermining social cohesion. Of course this is contested, and in the practice of institutions it may be difficult to discern how social cohesion policy and multiculturalist policy are realized. There is also considerable contestation of this dichotomization of multiculturalism and social cohesion (e.g. Bourne 2007, Modood 2007, Parekh 2008). One problem with the professed shift from multiculturalism to a social cohesion (UK) or integration agenda (Germany) is that many of the egalitarian impulses of multiculturalism are abandoned, too. Whether multiculturalism has been an institutionalized policy (as it has been for decades in the UK) or a frame of reference for alternative social projects (as in the German context since the 1980s), after 11 September 2001, it has increasingly been blamed for ethnic minorities supposedly leading 'parallel lives' in many European countries. This in turn has been seen as a prime reason for the radicalization of some Muslim young men. Ethnic minorities and migrants, especially Muslims in Europe have come under increasing pressure to prove they are willing and able to integrate. One of the key discursive strands in the de-legitimization of multiculturalism has been the argument that multiculturalism is too tolerant of ethnic minority groups' cultural practices that are assumed to be oppressive of women. Black and ethnic minority feminists have long critiqued such articulations of multiculturalism that empower the authoritarian, patriarchal – supposedly most culturally distant – social forces as representative of ethnic minority cultures. They argue that this disregards internal divisions, and importantly leaves intact a claim of ethnic minority leaders, lacking any democratic legitimacy, to control 'their' women (Patel 1997, Sahgal and Yuval-Davis 1992). Yet, the current mainstream critique of multiculturalism as detrimental to ethnic minority women does not build on this critical, anti-racist feminist tradition. Instead this 'peril of multiculturalism for women' (Bilge 2008) discourse reproduces elements of the version of multiculturalism it supposedly critiques. First, it is based on a cultural determinism that views ethnic minorities, and in particular women, as overdetermined by 'their' culture. Second, it essentializes ethnic minority groups' cultures as homogeneous and always based on women's oppression. Third, it dichotomizes this with a construct of 'western' liberal culture on the other hand. Lastly, it presents ethnic minorities, and in particular ethnic minority women as victims without agency who cannot either interpret 'their' culture differentially or act differently from its assumed tenets. Indeed, a narrow notion of social cohesion as currently promoted in Europe attacks not only anti-racist struggles, but also Black feminist struggles. In a recent case, the London council of Ealing decided to withdraw funding from Southall Black Sisters, the only local specialist provider of advice and advocacy to ethnic minority women suffering from domestic violence. The council argued that this provision excluded white women and therefore contravened race equality legislation and undermined social cohesion. Southall Black Sisters successfully challenged this in court on 18th July 2008. Yet, this signals a troubling wider political issue. The cohesion agenda views organizing around ethnicity and 'race' as encouraging segregation, yet reaches out to 'a male religious (largely Muslim) leadership, and it thereby encourages a "faith" based approach to social relations and social issues. This approach rejects the need for grassroots self organization on the basis of race and gender inequality but institutionalizes the undemocratic power of so called "moderate" (authoritarian if not fundamentalist) religious leaders at all levels of society' (Patel 2008). In this way, a shift from multicultural to multifaith society is institutionalized that marginalizes secular groups or those who do not organize around religion. This case is also a remarkable, though not unique, instance of how the rhetoric of race and gender equality is turned on its head and used to undermine anti-racist and anti-sexist practices, portraying antiracist and anti-sexist groups as responsible for or even creating racism and sexism. In this sense, indeed, ethnic minority and migrant women's scope for agency is reduced and further limited by this backlash against multiculturalism. Indeed, rather than shifting from multiculturalism to multifaithism or a renewed assimilationism (Back et al. 2002), it is important to hold on to both difference and equality as key elements of a differentiated citizenship (Bilge 2008).

One way in which academic debates on inclusive citizenship can connect effectively with political debates on citizenship practices is by taking seriously and making relevant migrant women's experiences of citizenship across different social sites and relations, pointing out where migrant women's practices already challenge our understandings of citizenship. Migrant women's citizenship practices can serve as evidence that alternatives to exclusionary practices of citizenship are possible and exist, though they might not be readily recognized as such.

In this conclusion I will begin by proposing a notion of citizenship that pays attention to three moments: 1) becoming subjects with agency, 2) substantiating capacities as political, cultural, working etc. subjects, 3) becoming rights-claiming subjects. Then I will draw out implications for extending rights, in particular for the areas of work and family and finally turn to propose an epistemological shift in our study of citizenship.

## Three Moments for Conceptualizing Citizenship

Becoming subjects with agency is the first moment in migrant women's citizenship practices. This has been conceptualized in two ways: on the one hand the migrant women become subjects with agency in constructing knowledge about themselves and the world they live in from their standpoint, in the process negotiating and contesting representations of themselves as culturally overdetermined, passively oppressed by patriarchal practices and values of their ethnic background and incompetent and unentitled to participate in and shape the societies of residence. On the other hand, the things they do to negotiate their ethnic and gendered positioning, be it in the sites of education, work, gender, sexuality, family or political activism constitute ways of making themselves. Becoming a subject with agency is not a once and for all achievement but an ongoing process. Indeed, it has been argued that the migrant women continuously make themselves through the things they do and the things they say. Sharing their life-stories in the interview situation is one instance where they constructed their subjectivities.

Secondly, the women also substantiate their capacities of political, caring, ethical working and cultural subjectivity in relation to others (citizens). Whether the form of subjectivity they articulate is 'political' or 'cultural', 'working' or 'caring', 'ethical', 'sexual' etc. depends on the circumstances and sites. These are not neatly delineated from each other and indeed, the women have articulated political subjectivities in the settings of education or work and vice versa also articulate aspects of cultural subjectivities or caring subjectivities in their political activities. Thus, the 'etc.' points to the multiplicity and open-endedness of articulating particular subjectivities. The conception of citizenship I hold views aspects of these relationships as citizenship practices: in all of these sites and relations, questions pertaining to citizenship such as belonging, legitimacy of entitlements and participation are negotiated.

A third moment is the constitution of the women as rights-claiming subjects. It is this latter moment which is most usually associated with citizenship. This view posits citizenship primarily as a status: rights-bearing subjects claim their rights *vis-à-vis* the state and it is this relationship which bestows the identity of citizen. Status matters, of course. As has been argued in previous chapters, stratified statuses of residence or citizenship have far-reaching implications for the ways in which migrant women have access to education, work, choices about their sexual identities and family life and opportunities to social and political activism. Yet, this book has argued that we must consider the process of 1) becoming subjects with agency, which includes developing knowledges about themselves and the world in which they live which are often, though not necessarily, critical of dominant forms of knowledge and 2) becoming political/ cultural/ working/ caring/ sexual subjects in conjunction with 3) the status of rights-claiming subjects. I have argued that formal citizenship remains an empty promise if it does not take into account and enable migrant women's capacity for becoming political subjects. All these three moments feed into and articulate each other.

To clarify the interrelatedness of these aspects through an example: Birgül, who did not hold formal German citizenship was repeatedly faced with the undermining of her ability to work as a doctor because of the difficulties of obtaining and renewing work, professional and residence permits. It is this experience of *lack of status* which propelled her into becoming a political subject through establishing anti-racist campaigns. When as a non-citizen she was refused permission to open a surgery, she took the matter to court. She successfully argued that the law foresees health provision for the population (Bevölkerung), not just the nation (Volk). This population encompasses migrant women from Turkey, and Birgül argued that access to a female, Turkish-speaking gynaecologist should form part of their entitlement to healthcare. This can, of course, be read as an instance of Birgül's *rights-claiming*, in the sense that she claimed her right to open a surgery while she was a denizen rather than a formal citizen. Yet, such a reading would be limited. It misses out on the way in which she becomes a political subject. As a *political subject* she does more than gain the right to practice her profession in a setting of her choice. She questions the nationally bounded provision of healthcare. This challenges the supposed neutrality of the provision, as she points out that gender, ethnic, linguistic and cultural sensitivity matter to migrant women's health. In this instance, Birgül's act went beyond rights-claiming to re-evaluating the substance (culturally and gender-sensitive provision of local health provision) and subject (the ethnically heterogeneous population rather than the ethnically homogeneous nation) of rights. Birgül's act took place although – indeed because – she did not hold formal citizenship, yet, it constitutes a transformative citizenship practice.

I do not suggest that formal rights of migrants, be they formally citizens of the countries of residence or not, are not important. They clearly are. What I am suggesting is that for a fuller understanding, we need to explore citizenship practices as bound up in all three moments of becoming subjects with agency, substantiating their capacities and becoming rights-claiming subjects, and these three moments are in turn interrelated.

Indeed, citizenship practices of becoming subjects with agency and substantiating their capacities as political, cultural, caring etc. subjects enable migrant women to make rights claims. By demanding respect for their practices of education, constructing skills, sexual identities, family relations and political activism, they create a social consciousness that the exclusions they experience are unjust, thus transforming our notions of justice and extended or creating new notions of rights. By accepting or even fostering multiple, hybrid and cross-ethnic identifications of their children the women practically challenge the idea that mothers are simply transmitting an ethnically bounded culture. They transform notions of mothering from one that is mainly defined as recipient of (integration) services into one where mothers are actively creating resources for multiple and cross-ethnic identification, enabling themselves and their children to develop resistant perspectives to the homogenization of national and ethnic groups. This does not only take place within the home but also transforms institutions such as nurseries or schools. Thus, shifting such educational institutions' position from viewing multi-linguality or multiple ethnic identifications as problems to be remedied to acknowledging these as resources is another instance where migrant women's citizenship practices are transformative. Thus, the women's capacities as caring and political subjects are central for the right to education in the mother tongue to be substantiated. In this sense, our analytical tools need to link political and caring subjectivities as they intersect. Thus, our thinking about citizenship needs to link the moments of becoming a subject with agency, substantiating capacities (as political/ cultural/ caring/ working subjects) and becoming rights-claiming subjects. These three moments are mutually constitutive.

*Becoming Subjects with Agency*

The structural reading of the life-stories has brought out the restrictions the interviewees face in making choices. However, the women have also taken initiatives to widen their scope for choice. Gender was an important aspect in constructing these restrictions and choices. Thus, it has been argued that migration for some of the women constituted a conscious choice to escape particular forms of gendered control and stigmatization. Migration constituted a means of escaping the stigmatization as a divorcee or single woman, enhancing their possibilities of economically supporting themselves and their children and of exploring sexual identities. The women have developed self-conscious strategies for different aspects of their lives. An important strategy was the construction of self-knowledges and self-presentations outside of the parameters of regulating practices and knowledges. In this way the women were viewed as agentic in naming and locating situations of domination and re-interpreting or refusing stereotyped identity ascriptions on the basis of their gendered ethnicity and/or class identity. These were important for constructing subjectivities that negotiated and at times transgressed and resisted fixed ethnicized gender norms. They questioned and went beyond dominant racist and Orientalist representations (cf. Chapters 2 and 3).

Migrant women's agency in realizing their migration, education and professionalization had important effects in changing their everyday lives. The transformation of their everyday lives meant they experienced new situations that required them to re-conceptualize their social position and relations. At times this enhanced the women's vulnerabilities. I have argued that agency and victimization should not be seen as opposites, but rather as dynamically related so that victimization at times propelled women to action and at other times, their agency led to their victimization.

*Substantiating Capacities*

*Working subjects*
The migration of women, even if motivated by a search for greater choice of gendered lifestyles and a wish to escape gendered social control for some women led to greater gendered vulnerability. This was specifically true for undocumented migrants or those with irregular residence and work permits. However, they can mobilize even limited resources to counter their victimization. The role of ethnically specific networks was ambiguous; even if they may provide a counter structure to migration regimes' restrictions of mobility, they can exploit sexual vulnerability of women, in particular if these migrant women have little other social capital. Therefore, establishing non-sexist or women's networks to provide access to jobs, information and housing were important strategies. It should be pointed out, however, that such networks themselves may also be structured hierarchically along social divisions of ethnicity, class, cultural capital and the rural-urban divide. Moreover, such non-sexist networks, like other migrants' specific networks, have a limited scope, often occupying marginal spaces within the society of residence. I have furthermore argued for inscribing agency into the notion of cultural and social capital, taking into account multiple boundaries, power relations and markers of distinction of ethnicity, nation, class and gender. Recognizing women as actors in their own right, rather than as markers of distinction or resources shows that gender is a differentiating factor in the constitution of cultural capital through formal and informal education. Moreover, access to social capital is gender differentiated, and transgressions of ethnicized gender roles can marginalize women from ethnically specific networks, necessitating the construction of alternative networks.

Examining social and cultural capital as dynamic and differentiated resources has shown that migrant women invest differentially into the diverse subject positions available to them. These subject positions are also materially constructed and access to them is restricted through structural factors. Nonetheless, it is important to point out the agency that migrant women exercise through constructing diverse subject positions and identities for themselves.

*Caring subjects*
The ways in which women imagine and make new forms of family relationships, gives a more complex picture of their experiences and subjectivities than Orientalist representations allow for. By developing ways of caring from a distance, they challenge stereotypes of migrant families as solely 'traditional' and re-conceptualizing mothering and daughtering practices to encompass multiple social relations of othermothers. They also challenge normative notions of 'good mothering' based on physical proximity. Re-building the relationship between family members, once they were re-united meant negotiating linguistic and cultural difference and diversity among family members. These findings clearly contradict stereotypical representations of migrant families of Turkish background, and in

particular mothers' role in these as embodying stability and tradition in gender oppressive ways.

The elaboration of inter-generationally shared meanings is a key element in the transmission of ethnically specific identities. This process involves a transformation, not only of the childrens' identifications, but also the mothers'. Mothering can entail a conscious project of constructing alternative 'families of choice', and elaborating new ethnic identities. Whether part of a deliberate project of re-constructing ethnic identifications or not, cross-ethnic relations with co-parents, peers, or cross-ethnic identifications through media and sub-cultures form an important part of elaborating the mothers' and childrens' ethnic identities. These cross-ethnic relations and identifications are not limited to the binary opposition of Germanness – Turkishness or Britishness – Turkishness, but implicate other ethnic minority identities also. Whether mothers view cross-ethnic identifications or alliances with suspicion or foster them, they form an important part of the transmission and transformation of ethnic identities.

These findings counter essentialist notions of mothering and daughtering in two important ways: first, the social-psychological arguments positing the centrality of the mother-child dyad for the psychological and social development of children should be qualified. The diversity of mothering practices, and the possibility of 'good mothering' provided by different persons should be recognized. As the daughters' accounts show, they recognize that their mothers' 'care about' them motivated their migration and separation, so that other social mothers 'cared for' them (cf. Lutz 1998). Second, mothers' role in ethnic and national projects is often presented as central for transmitting ethnic identities to safeguard the continuity of the ethnic group. The exploration of the projects and practices of transmitting ethnic identities has shown that these are complex, transformative processes that can elaborate also new, hyphenated, hybrid ethnic identities.

### Cultural subjects

Cultural production is often viewed as the prime site for subverting essentialized links of nation and culture. However, as argued above, the site of mothering is also key in transforming ethnic identities, as well as challenging fixed notions of ethnically specific cultural practices and forms. As the cross-national comparison between Germany and Britain has shown, such cross-ethnic identifications take place within different dynamics of differential racialization. Thus, identities of 'Cypriot', 'Kurdish', 'Turkish', 'Black', 'African-Caribbean', 'Irish' or 'Greek', 'Yugoslav', 'Italian' take on different salience in Germany and Britain as aspects of identification. Moreover, the meaning and openness to interpretation attached to these identities differs across the national contexts. The formation of identities and alliances across ethnic boundaries is a complex process, involving both resistance against (some) social divisions and the consolidation of others. Therefore, I suggest to further contextualize nationally and ethnically hybridizing strategies with the identities, boundaries and social divisions they produce in terms of class, gender and education.

It has been suggested that notions of hybridity and transnationality need to be used in a way that is more attentive to class divisions and intra-ethnic differential cultural capital. Bhabha's (1996) view emphasizes the subversive potential of hybridizing strategies *vis-à-vis* the nationalization of cultural forms and identities. However, the intra-ethnic differentiation of cultural forms into high and low cultural forms is an important marker of differences of class, rural-urban origin, and education. Migrant women who master high cultural forms, endowed with the authority of national culture, are more likely to succeed in establishing their versions of cultural mixing. An instance of this is the consolidation of educational, cultural and political authority into professional positions or community leadership positions of the ethnic minority group. For example the education of migrant children or the representation of migrant women can include ethnically hybridizing strategies yet may at once reify class, educational and other ethnic hierarchies. Thus, hybridity may come to be a more refined marker of cultural hierarchy.

Likewise, the validation and application of transnational cultural and social capital is differentiated. The ability to transform cultural and social capital into access to occupational mobility was shown to be differentiated along lines of gender, marital status, class, education, rural-urban origin and ethnic differences within the migrant population.

*Political subjects*

While mainstream citizenship studies privilege national and ethnic forms of belonging, it has been argued that the migrant women are located in various communities, based on gender, ethnic, class, cultural, educational or political commonalties, sometimes across national borders. These communities may be cross cutting each other, and are never ready made, but negotiated and changing. Moreover, the women, also participate in constructing new communities and new political subjects. The women play an active role in organizing and articulating their subject positions and political views, sometimes as women of Turkish background, and sometimes as migrant women; or they may choose a universalized, gender- or ethnic neutral epistemological and political stance. While the migrant women's political projects and identifications vary, the countries of residence are a central site for articulating these political projects. They experience multiple practices of exclusion from the state and society of residence. Some of them articulate their belonging as bi-cultural, hybrid, or outside of national parameters. Others claim a right to belong and contest the national logic of legitimacy. Moreover, there are strategies of creating cross-ethnic communities of belonging, such as the identities of migrant, Black, or women of colour. A further important element of belonging is the construction of 'elsewhere' in the imaginary space, a utopian space that promises recognition of the multiply subjected facets of their subjectivity. All of these practices of belonging however co-exist with an engagement with the society of residence. This 'integration work' (Lutz 1998) takes place on the personal level of friendships, love relationships, as well as more public levels such as that of work, political activism, cultural and social activities. The migrant women position themselves towards ethnically, socially and politically diverse groups in the country of residence. While Germanness and Britishness are central instances of contention and sources of recognition, their meaning and articulation varies.

One important site of constructing belonging is the family. The family often serves as an emotionally charged metaphor for national solidarity and homogeneity, and a cornerstone of nation-building. As has been argued, the experiences and constructions of family also contain important elements of cultural diversity and differential access and mastery of ethnically specific cultural resources. Therefore, in practice, the family cannot only function as a model for ethnic homogeneity and solidarity, but indeed as a model for negotiating diverse identifications. Between parents and children and different siblings, identifications and access to ethnically specific resources vary, still they achieve a sense of belonging. This sense of belonging does not exclude conflicting interpretations and identifications. Concepts and practices of constructing belonging should therefore be examined on various levels, as complex, cross-cutting, contradictory and flexible. Instead of viewing the articulation of belonging as an indicator for migrant women's engagement with their society of residence, I have found that experiences of exclusion can indeed form a powerful motor for participatory aspects of citizenship.

This book focused on the migrant women's agency and brought out the participatory element of citizenship as central. Contrary to the national logic of citizenship laws and hegemonic common sense notions of belonging, that view migrant women as outside of or marginal to their societies of residence, their sites of participation were multiple. This should be seen as extending the theorization of citizenship practices also to the crucial sites of mothering practices, and also include the area of work lives, which the migrant women viewed as an important area of their social participation. They also participate, however, in elaborating old and constructing new sites and subjects of political activism.

The analysis of the migrant women's stories led me to contest the normalization of dominant identities on various levels and around various social divisions. The legal and institutional normalization of national-ethnic identities posits migrants as marginal to society, although they contribute to it through their paid and unpaid labour, their social, cultural and political activities. Multicultural policies tend to reify the male ethnic minority subject as the representative of the community, thereby strengthening and reproducing gendered hierarchies and sexist power relations within ethnic community organizations. Migrant or ethnic minority women's organizations and interests are not homogeneous, either. Class, sexuality, ethnic hierarchies, as well as educational hierarchies create internal hierarchies that affect the capacity of individual women to participate in decision-making and representation. A further reification of hierarchies can take place when functions of community representatives become professionalized, so that the split between voluntary and paid work strengthens social divisions of class, ethnicity and education and institutionalizes the differential power in decision making and representation.

While the professionalization of migrant women as mediators, social or educational workers can have empowering effects on the individual women and moreover, allow them to represent certain interests and voices of migrant women that find no other advocates, it may at the same time dis-empower and marginalize others, such as women with less cultural and social capital, working class women and Kurdish women. This dilemma of representation cannot be solved within a framework of group representation that neglects intra-group differentiation. To further the potential of theoretical debates of citizenship it is suggested therefore that we examine multiply marginalized identities as analytically central to evaluate the impact of democratizing policies, which I will turn to below.

### Rights-claiming Subjects

The socially constituted sites of power relations are multiple and should all be included into a project of theorizing and realizing citizenship as progressively democratizing. Migration and residence rights are central for such a democratization, as they have implications, among others, for migrant women's legal status and access to social services and provisions and the ability of migrants to participate in formal politics and thereby intervene into the formulation of the boundaries and substance of citizenship at the formal level. As these issues have been discussed by other authors (e.g. Carens 1995, Bauböck 1995, Bosniak 2008, Hayter 2004, Rigo 2008) I want to point out two other aspects where we need to extend our notion of rights to do justice to migrant women's transformative practices.

### Work and skills recognition

Migrant women create new practices that call for new or extended rights of citizenship. One site for this is that of work. Skill is not simply an attribute of a person but is socially constructed. As argued in Chapter 4, the social construction of skill includes gendered and ethnicized aspects. Current migration policy in Europe, which dichotomizes skilled migrants as desirable and easily integrated and unskilled migrants as only temporarily undesirable and threats to social cohesion, is problematic. It neglects the ways in which migrants who do not fit into the strict criteria of what it means to be 'skilled' are effectively de-skilled, thus rendering them less 'competent' citizens, both through misrecognizing their cultural capital and limiting their opportunities for economic participation. It is important to create opportunities for recognizing migrants' skills or re-skilling. This is particularly relevant for migrant women who may be marginalized from male-centered social capital that could provide an alternative source of validating their skills. Furthermore, such opportunities for recognizing skills or re-skilling need to take account of migrant women's caring responsibilities, both for children who are co-resident and for transnational family members. Current policy emphasis on migrants' proving their economic self-reliance makes it more difficult for migrant women, in particular those with caring responsibilities, to realize their skills. Yet, this would require a radical change in current policies of migration as well as recognition of skills. The recognition and realization of skills and qualifications of migrant women is hindered by the categorizations of entry and residence rights, so that undocumented migrant women have no access to labour markets where they can realize their skills but are instead employed in the informal economy. In Britain, the 'ethnic economy' is an important counter structure to immigration control; while enabling undocumented migrant women to survive, at the same time it can make them vulnerable to sexual harassment and exploitation, as well as economic exploitation. In Germany, ethnic niche economies are less established. However migrant women are also de-skilled through the restrictions of residence and work permit legislation which, at least initially limits their labour market access to the informal labour market. A further obstacle to the realization of migrant women's skills and qualifications is nationally defined and bounded credentialism. National laws and professional bodies need to establish clear and viable pathways for recognition of skills and re-skilling, and the financial burden for this should not fall on migrants alone. The expectation of economic self-reliance on migrants (in particular when they apply for formal citizenship) poses a considerable obstacle to their ability to re-skill. Policy measures should be introduced to remove this obstacle so as to both enable the migrants to realize their occupational aspirations and the society to tap into this pool of potential skills. The recruitment of skilled migrants is discussed by both German and British governments. These debates make a clear distinction between the welcome, needed professionals and the unwarranted migration of the undocumented and asylum seekers. Such a dichotomization into useful and abusive migrants, apart from its racist import, problematically misrepresents both groups. On the one hand, those with skills and qualifications are not by virtue of their skills protected against de-qualification and discrimination. On the other hand, those who are undocumented or refugees or admitted outside of the skilled migration routes are not necessarily unskilled. The policies for the incorporation of both groups need to take the migrants' own interests and articulations of agency more into account, instead of constructing a national interest, to which migrants are external, either as valuable resources or simply superfluous or, worse, detrimental sources of risk.

*Intimate and sexual citizenship*
A conception of citizenship as a struggle for increasing the scope for democratizing a range of social relations needs to address the issue of intimate and sexual citizenship. It is argued that we need to conceptualize transnational intimate and sexual citizenship rights. While even nationally bounded intimate and sexual citizenship can be said to be still very limited, the transnational dimension is crucial. For many women, migration constitutes one way of coping with problems in their intimate relations or initiating changes to do with sexual citizenship. Thus, one important aspect of intimate citizenship should the right to a family. Yet, migration is a strategy for many women (and men) to be able to economically support their families. Becoming single mothers can be a motivation to migrate in order to financially support themselves and their children. In this sense,

the (social, economic and sexual) opportunities to realize a 'right to a family' (Shorloff and Monson 2002: 68, quoted in Kershaw 2005: 111) are internationally stratified. Migration is one strategy for women to realize this right in the face of structural constraints that may make it difficult for them to 'choose' their family forms and sexual identities, practices, relations and representations. Therefore, 'transnationalizing' their intimate and sexual citizenship through migration is a strategy, albeit not necessarily a conscious or explicit one, for creating choices. Yet, as the discussion of long-term separations from family members, the difficulties of caring from a distance and the difficulties of realizing one's choices of intimacy in the countries of residence against a backdrop of intersecting racist, sexist, heterosexist and heteronormative power relations makes clear, migration may enable some choices, but also creates new problems. However intimate and sexual citizenship *rights* are not sufficiently enabled through international regulations and law. As mothers, migrant women are also 'cultural workers' in the sense that they validate the identities of their children, against a backdrop of racist marginalization in wider society where children do not experience the validation of their identities in the public realm. Yet, it has been suggested that migrant women do more than validating publicly marginalized ethnic minority identities. They co-construct new meanings and modes of ethnic identity and belonging. In this sense, their mothering is not only a caring activity but also an epistemological intervention that questions and re-articulates ethnic boundaries, the 'ethnic' interpretation of cultural resources and practices. This connects the intimate aspects of mother child relationships with interventions in the public realm, including the initiation of multilingual, multicultural or intercultural practices in educational institutions.

Transnational intimate and sexual citizenship rights should enable migrant women to make substantial choices about how to organize their intimate lives. As it stands, immigration legislation regulates and constrains partnership choices, often taking the most restrictive gendered and sexual norms as their basis. British and German immigration legislation only recently acknowledged same sex partnerships, however without equalizing the conditions with heterosexuals, nor are gender and sexually specific grounds for asylum fully institutionalized or realized. For migrant women from Turkey, socially grounded choices about sexual identity, or marital status, such as being lesbian, bisexual, transgendered, single, or being a divorcee, are constrained and stratified according to class, education, and the rural-urban divide. Furthermore, ethnic minority people are marginalized within the social, political and cultural representation of sexual minorities. Similarly, heterosexual migrant women who are single by choice, divorced or heterosexual or lesbian single mothers are bracketed out of the representation of migrant communities, as well as that of the ethnically dominant group.

Transnational mothering practices form one way in which migrant women try to combine their economic and emotional care for their children. These practices are often a consequence of the combined constraints of poor working conditions and migration regulation. Thus, to realize migrant women's intimate and sexual citizenship rights, legal obstacles such as age restrictions on the immigration of children and spouses should be revoked; moreover, improvement in the provision and quality of realistically affordable childcare facilities is needed that takes account of the wide spread full time employment and unsocial hours of migrant women's work. This would be particularly important for single mothers, who cannot or do not want to rely on familial help with childcare. Therefore, concepts, demands and policies of intimate and sexual citizenship need to take into account that migrant women's mothering practices also rely on social mothers, often in transnational contexts and thus our thinking about citizenship responsibilities and rights needs to evolve to validate these 'othermothers' practices of care, too.

## Intersectionality as an Epistemology for Citizenship Practices

This book views gender and ethnicity as social locations that mutually constitute each other. Thus, both inter-ethnic and intra-ethnic differentiations and power relations have been examined concurrently. The migrant women take different social and political views, actively resisting some power relations, sometimes tacitly or actively participating in others. Such contradictory positions of privilege and oppression as members of different social groups are, however, not exceptional as some debates on multicultural citizenship suggest (cf. Green 1995, Waldron 1995). If we recognize the central role of boundary making processes for the constitution of groups of citizens and within these groups, debates on citizenship should not treat the experience of multiple group identities and multiple exclusions as exceptional but rather as central for theorizing. As citizenship becomes a concept for understanding global relations (Isin and Turner 2008, Parekh 2008), we need to acknowledge the multiple social divisions implicating even those who are, within a nationalist methodological paradigm, seen as unproblematically positioned in the centre. An intersectional epistemology thus is necessary not only for understanding experiences of those who are *subjected* in multiple power relations. It is critical for scrutinizing the interstices of multiple power relations and how individuals and groups are *implicated* in them.

Gendered and ethnically differentiated citizenship has often been conceptualized through the notion of multicultural group rights. Yet, the rights of women and of ethnic minorities have been viewed as distinct. This leaves migrant women in a problematic position as the intra-ethnic differentiation of gender or the intra-gender differentiation of ethnicity (and of course others such as class, ability, sexuality, etc) are not fully taken into account. Migrant women's experiences of intermeshing social divisions of ethnicity, gender, class, sexuality, ability and age structure their citizenship status and practices. Rather than viewing migrant women as a particular group whose experiences and practices need to be made to neatly fit (or, as is often the case, fail to fit) into pre-existing categorizations of citizenship rights, capacities, statuses and practices, this book has taken the agentic aspects of migrant women's citizenship practices as a starting point. Through this detailed attention to their self-presentations, I have elaborated an epistemological stance that explores how the migrant women's subjugated knowledges are productive of new citizenship practices. On the basis of this analysis of the life-stories avenues for re-conceptualizing our notions of 'citizenship' have been suggested so as to meaningfully engage the lives of these migrant women.[1]

This is an epistemological and methodological intervention, making a case for a close engagement of life-stories as a useful method for accessing self-presentations and subjugated knowledges on a wide range of social relations and sites. This might be termed a form of activist citizenship studies: The research has engaged in a dialogue with migrant women's life-stories about their experiences and views of citizenship, through this developing a critique and further elaboration of concepts of citizenship. In this sense, it has engaged in a citizenship practice itself and re-constituted the meaning of citizenship, both through the research practice and theorization. This activist conception of citizenship has enhanced our empirical understanding of how migrant women 'do' citizenship, in the process challenging our theorization of citizenship. An engagement with the life-stories re-theorizes aspects of citizenship and how these are assembled:

a.  Contrary to the dichotomization of private space, where ethnic minority groups may articulate cultural specificity versus public spaces where all residents must comply with universalist democratic values that underlie much multiculturalist theorizing (e.g. Kymlicka 1995, Rex 1993), the public private boundary should be conceptualized as negotiated and struggled over. Public and private should not be conceptualized as distinct spaces but different aspects co-existing in the same social spaces.

b.  Migrant women's mothering practices, straddling national (geographic and social) boundaries make new spaces of intimacy, challenging racialized and ethnicized dichotomizations of tradition and modernity, and requiring new transnationally substantiated intimate citizenship rights.

c.  Migrant women's practices of generation work elaborate ethnic identifications in an intergenerational and multi-ethnic context that challenge narrow ideas of 'transmission' of ethnic belonging, cultural and social competences as bases for a wider transnational and multi-ethnic notion of citizenship.

d.  The care for children, both transnational and co-resident, is also an aspect of engagement with citizenship status (in terms of residence rights) and with political, social and cultural representation. Care for children, both as a

---

1   I am cautious of essentializing the women whose life-stories are presented here: they are not a homogeneous group with a priori common interests. Nor do I want to erect a new standard for citizenship practices. Indeed, the migrant women do not represent any 'ideal typical' case. They are not elite migrants who are able to exercise highly mobile 'flexible citizenship' (Ong 1999) in several states, nor were they at the time of study part of the abject group of undocumented migrants, with extremely limited rights-claims. Indeed, they are in complex ways embedded in relations and structures of dominance and resistance.

transnational and as a cross-ethnic practice, challenges precepts of bringing up citizens as a nationally bounded practice. It requires the formulation of transnational and cross-ethnic rights to a family and the welfare practices to substantiate this right.

e.  The nationalized, ethnicized and gendered aspects of constructing 'skill' interrelate with strategies and struggles over 'competence' for economic and social integration, in this sense being part of building national cultural capital. Yet, alongside this, migration-specific cultural capital may be mobilized transnationally and structures of validation are constructed within the ethnic minority group. This shows the multiple spaces for building and validating cultural capital transnationally and in a multi-ethnic frame. This necessitates clear and viable policies of skills recognition for migrants that do not take their interests as external (and secondary) to those of the societies of residence.

f.  Political activism is not determined by experiences of exclusion. Instead migrant women can be propelled into political and social engagement through experiences of exclusion, in the process creating new political subjects and fields of politics.

Migrant women's life-stories reflect on their position near the boundary of citizenship. At times they claim a view from outside, at times from inside, or, indeed both. These perspectives are empirically significant as they highlight how citizenship as a lived experience is constructed. More than this, however, it is argued that such perspectives shed a critical light on how boundaries of belonging and rights are constructed and substantiated (or not). It is in these processes of making and negotiating boundaries, that particular forms of agency are recognized and conferred legitimacy. The negotiation of boundaries furthermore shapes which kind of subjectivities count as properly expressing 'political', 'caring', 'working', 'cultural', 'sexual' capacities and whether and how these aspects are recognized. Citizenship is one important instance of recognition, not only on the level of national belonging, but as things stand, even in terms of recognition of whether one is seen to properly embody/enact subjectivity. In this sense, we are faced with a paradox: the ability to go beyond the 'national', be it in terms of competences (linguistic, cultural, etc.), emotional orientations, political and ethical subjectivities is valued for those who are recognized as full 'citizens'. Yet, those who have by virtue of their migration crossed national boundaries are denied recognition as subjects with agency to change the societies in which they live and beyond, as our methodological nationalism fails to view them as subjects with agency. The migrant women's (political, cultural, caring, working, ethical, etc.) capacities are mis-recognized, most often as a lack thereof. One might, of course, argue that these capacities and ways of being agentic do not qualify as 'citizenship' practices, as they do not engage with the state and rights-claiming activities. This book argues that migrant women's ways of acting politically, socially culturally, etc. require us to extend and give substance to new notions of and ways of claiming rights and *should* be seen as citizenship practices. These women engage with the boundaries of citizenship and thus are part of its very constitution. If our current conceptions of citizenship cannot make sense of their lives, 'citizenship' risks becoming reified as a national privilege. It ceases to be a momentum concept and turns void of its analytic and political potential to democratize an ever wider range of social relations and socio-political sites.

# References

Abakay, A. 1988. *Politik Göçmenler*. Istanbul: Amaç.

Acik, N. 2000. *Die Frau in der kurdischen Nationalbewegung. Eine Studie anhand zeitgenössischer kurdischer Frauenzeitschriften in der Türkei*. Freie Universität Berlin am Institut für Islamwissenschaft, unpublished MA.

Adelson, L. 1997. 'Migrants' Literature or German Literature? Torkan's Tufan: Brief an einen islamischen Bruder', in *Writing New Identities: Gender, Nation and Immigration in Contemporary Europe*, edited by Brinker-Gabler, G. and Smith, S. Minneapolis: University of Minnesota Press, 216–229.

Adkins, L., Skeggs, B. eds. 2004. *Feminism After Bourdieu*, Oxford: Blackwell.

Akashe-Böhme, F. 2000. *In geteilten Welten: Fremdheitserfahrungen zwischen Migration und Partizipation*, Frankfurt a.M.

Alberts, H. 2003. Researching Self-Employed Immigrant Women in Hannover, Germany, in Morokvasic, M., Erel, U. and Shinozaki, K. eds. *On the Move! Gender and Migration: Crossing Borders and Shifting Boundaries,* Opladen.

Ali, A.M. 2001. *Turkish-speaking Communities and Education. No Delight*. London: Fatal Publications.

Anderson, B. 1991. *Imagined Communities: Reflections on the Origin and Spread of Nationalism*, London: Verso.

Anderson, B., Ruhs, M. 2006. Semi-Compliance in the Migrant Labour Market, Centre on Migration, Policy and Society *COMPAS,* University of Oxford *COMPAS Working Paper No. 30.*

Anthias, F., Yuval-Davis N. eds. 1989. *Woman-Nation-State*, London: Macmillan.

Anthias, F.,Yuval-Davis, N. 1992 . *Racialised Boundaries*, London: Routledge.

Anthias, F. 1998. Evaluating 'Diaspora': Beyond Ethnicity? *Sociology*, 32(3), 557–580.

Anthias, F. 2000. 'Metaphors of Home: Gendering New Migrations to Southern Europe', in *Gender and Migration in Southern Europe*, edited by Anthias, F. and Lazaridis, G. Oxford: Berg, 15–47.

Anthias, F., Lloyd, C. 2002: 'Introduction: Fighting Racisms, Defining the Territory', in Anthias, F, and Lloyd, C eds. *Rethinking Anti-Racisms. From Theory to Practice*. London: Routledge, 1–21.

Apitzsch, U. 1996. Frauen in der Migration. *Frauen in der Einen Welt*, 1, 9–25.

Appelt, E. 1999. *Geschlecht – Staatsbürgerschaft – Nation: politische Konstruktionen des Geschlechterverhältnisses in Europa*. Frankfurt/Main. Campus Verlag.

Appiah, K.A. 1990. *Racisms*, in *Anatomy of Racism*, edited by Goldberg, D.T. Minneapolis: University of Minnesota Press, 3–18.

Arat, Z. 1998. Educating the daughters of the republic, in *Deconstructing Images of 'The Turkish Woman'*, edited by Arat, Z. Houndmills. Macmillan Press, 157–182.

Arbeitsgruppe Frauenkongress ed. 1985. *Sind wir uns denn so fremd? Ausländische und deutsche Frauen im Gespräch*. Frankfurt/Main. Sub-Rosa-Frauenverlag.

Assiter, A. 1996. *Enlightened Women: Modernist Feminism in a Postmodern Age*. London: Routledge.

Auernheimer, G. 1988. *Der sogenannte Kulturkonflikt*. Frankfurt: Campus.

Aziz, R. 1997. 'Feminism and the challenge of racism: Deviance or difference?' in *Black British Feminism. A Reader*, edited by Mizra, H.S. London: Routledge, 70–80.

Basit, T. 1997. 'I Want More Freedom, but Not Too Much': British Muslim Girls and the Dynamism of Family Values. *Gender and Education*, 9(4), 425–439.

Bauböck, R. 1991. Immigration and the boundaries of citizenship. Centre for Research in Ethnic Relations. *Monographs on Ethnic Relations no. 4*.

Bauböck, R. 1994. *Transnational Citizenship. Membership and Rights in International Migration*. Aldershot: Elgar.

Beck, U., Beck-Gernsheim, E. 1990. *The Normal Chaos of Love*. Cambridge: Polity Press.

Beck-Gernsheim, E. 1998. On the Way to a Post-Familial Family – From a Community of Need to Elective Affinities. *Theory, Culture, and Society,* Special Issue on Love and Eroticism 15(3/4), 53–70.

Bhabha, H.K. 1990a. 'Introduction: narrating the nation', in *Nation and Narration*, edited by Bhabha, H.K. London: Routledge, 1–7.

Bhabha, H.K. 1990b. The Third Space, in *Identity, Community, Culture, Difference*, edited by Rutherford, J. London: Lawrence and Wishart, 207–221.

Bhabha, H.K. 1994. *The Location of Culture*. London: Routledge.

Bhabha, H.K. 1996. Cultures in-between, in *Questions of Cultural Identity*, edited by Hall, S., du Gay, P. London: Sage, 53–60.

Bhachu, P. 1991. Ethnicity Constructed and Reconstructed: The Role of Sikh Women in Cultural Elaboration and Educational Decision-making in Britain. *Gender and Education*, 3(1), 45–60.

Bhatt, C. 1997. *Liberation and Purity. Race, New Religious Movements and the Ethics of Postmodernity*. London: UCL Press.

Bhopal, K. 1998. South Asian Women in East London: Motherhood and Social Support. *Women's Studies International Forum*, 21(5), 485–92.

Bilge, S. 2008. Between Gender and Cultural Equality, *Recasting the Social in Citizenship,* edited by Isin, E.F. Toronto: University of Toronto Press, 100–133.

Billig, M. 1995. *Banal Nationalism*. London: Sage.

Blaschke, J. 1994. 'Internationale Migration. Ein Problemaufriss', in *Migration im neuen Europa*, edited by Knapp, M. Internationale Beziehungen Bd 5. Stuttgart: Franz Steiner Verlag, 23–50.

Blauner, B. 1989. *Black Lives, White Lives: Three Faces of Race Relations in America.* Berkeley, CA: University of California Press.

Bloch, A. 2002. *'Refugees' opportunities and barriers in employment and Training'.* London: Department for Work and Pensions.

Bloch, A. 2004. *'Making it work: refugee employment in the UK'.* Institute for Public Policy Research, Asylum and Migration Working Paper 2.

Bloomfield, J., Bianchini, F. 2001. 'Cultural Citizenship and Urban Governance in Western Europe', in *Cultural Citizenship*, edited by Stevenson, N. London: Sage, 99–124.

Bosniak, L. 2008. 'Being Here: Ethical Territoriality and the Rights of Immigrants', in *Citizenship between Past and Future*, edited by Isin, E.F., Nyers, P. and Turner, B.S. London: Routledge, 123–138.

Bourne, J. 2007. *In Defence of Multiculturalism.* IRR Briefing Paper no. 2.

Brubaker, R. 1989. 'Membership without Citizenship: The Economic and Social Rights of Noncitizens' in *Immigration and the politics of citizenship in Europe and North America*, edited by Brubaker, W.R. Lanham: University Press of America, 145–162.

Bourdieu, P. 1986. 'The Forms of Capital', in *Handbook of Theory and Research for the Sociology of Education*, edited by Richardson, J.G. New York: Greenwordpress, 241–259.

Bourdieu, P. 1996. *Distinction. A Social Critique of the Judgement of Taste.* London: Routledge.

Brah, A. 1996. *Cartographies of Diaspora. Contesting Identities.* London: Routledge.

Bundesausländerbeauftragte 2000. *4.Bericht zur Lage der Ausländer in der Bundesrepublik Deutschland Berlin Feb. 2000.* Available at: <http://www.bundesregierung.de/Content/DE/Publikation/IB/Anlagen/ausl_C3_A4nderbericht-4,property=publicationFile.pdf> [accessed 8 February 2009].

Bundesausländerbeauftragte: *Ausländische Wohnbevölkerung nach ausgewählten Staatsangehörigkeiten von 1994–1999.* Available at: <http://www.bundesauslaenderbeauftragte.de/fakten/tab2.htm> [accessed 30 October 2000].

Butler, J. 1990. *Gender Trouble. Feminism and the Subversion of Identity.* London: Routledge.

Carens, J. 1995. 'Aliens and Citizens: The Case for Open Borders', in *The Rights of Minority Cultures*, edited by Kymlicka, W. Oxford University Press, 331–349.

Carling, J. 2005. Global Migration Perspectives. 35 (May) *Gender dimensions of international migration* Available at: <http://www.gcim.org/mm/File/GMP%20No%2035.pdf> [accessed: 2 September 2008].

CCCS 1982. *The Empire Strikes Back.* London: Hutchinson.

Chamberlain, M. 1999. The family as model and metaphor in Caribbean migration to Britain. *Journal of Ethnic and Migration Studies*, 25(2), 251–266.

Cohen, P. 1987. Tarzan and the Jungle Bunnies. *New Formations*, 5, 25–30.

Cohen, P. 1990. 'Gefährliche Erbschaften: Studien zur Entstehung einer multirassistischen Struktur in Großbritannien', in *Die Schwierigkeit, nicht rassistisch zu sein*, edited by Kalpaka, A. And Räthzel, N. Leer: Mundo, 81–143.

Cohen, R. 1997. *Global Diasporas. An Introduction*. London: University College Press.

Cohn-Bendit, D., Schmid, T. 1992. *Heimat Babylon. Das Wagnis der multikulturellen Demokratie*. Hamburg: Hoffmann und Campe.

Commission on Integration and Cohesion 2007: *Our Shared Future*. [Online]

Crowley, J. 1999. 'The Politics of Belonging: Some Theoretical Considerations', in *The Politics of Belonging: Migrants and Minorities in Contemporary Europe*, edited by Geddes, A. and Favell, A. Aldershot: Ashgate, 15–41.

Dayıoğlu, G. 1986. *Geride Kalanlar.* Istanbul: Altın Kitaplar Yayinevi.

Delaney, C. 1995. 'Father State, Motherland, and the Birth of Modern Turkey', in *Naturalizing Power. Essays in Feminist Cultural Analysis*, edited by Yanagisako, S. and Delaney, C. London: Routledge.

Denzin, N. 1987. *Interpretive Biography*. London: Sage.

Deutsch, K.W. 1966. *Nationalism and Social Communications: An Enquiry into the Foundations of Nationality*. Cambridge, MA: MIT Press.

Dokur-Gryskiewicz, F. 1979. *Turkish Labour Migration to the UK*. unpublished PhD Thesis, Birkbeck University.

Donald, J. 1993. 'How English is it?' in *Space and Place. Theories of Identity and Location*, edited by Carter, E. et al. London: Routledge, 166–179.

Dumper, H. 2002. *Missed opportunities: A skills audit of refugee women in London from the teaching, nursing and medical professions*. London: Greater London Authority.

Durakbaşa, A. 1998. 'Kemalism as Identity Politics in Turkey', in *Deconstructing Images of "The Turkish Woman"*, edited by Arat, Z. Houndmills: Macmillan Press, 139–156.

Enneli, P., Modood, T. and Bradley, H. 2005. *Young Turks and Kurds: A set of 'invisible' disadvantaged groups*. York: Joseph Rowntree Foundation.

Erben, M. 1993. The Problem of Other Lives: Perspectives on Written Biography. *Sociology*, 27(1), 15–25.

Erdem, E. 2000. *Mapping women's migration: A case study of the economic dimensions of female migration from Turkey to Germany paper presented at the conference* Assimilation – Diasporization – Representation: Historical Perspectives on Immigrants and Host Societies in Post-war Europe Second Workshop on Contemporary Migration History, (Humboldt Universität Berlin, October 27–29).

Erdem, E. 2003. 'Hausarbeit in der ethnischen Ökonomie', in *Migration, Gender, Arbeitsmarkt. Neue Beiträge zu Frauen und Globalisierung*, edited by do Mar,

M., Varela, C. and Clayton, D. Königstein/Taunus: Ulrike Helmer Verlag, 223–236.

Erdemir, A., Vasta, E. 2007. *Differentiating irregularity and solidarity: Turkish Immigrants at work in London.* ESRC Centre on Migration, Policy and Society Working Paper No. 42, University of Oxford, 2007.

Erel, U. 1997. *Citizenship and Subjectivity: The Case of Migrant Women from Turkey in Germany.* Unpublished MA dissertation, Gender and Ethnic Studies, Greenwich University.

Erel, U. 1999. 'Grenzüberschreitung und kulturelle Mischformen als anti-rassistischer Widerstand?' in *AufBrüche. Kulturelle Produktionen von Migrantinnen, Schwarzen und jüdischen Frauen in Deutschland,* edited by Gelbin, C., Konuk, K. and Piesche, P. Königstein/TS: Ulrike Helmer Verlag, 172–194.

Erel, U. 2003. 'Citizenship Practices and Skilled Migrant Women', in *On the Move! Gender and Migration: Crossing borders and shifting boundaries,* edited by Morokvasic, M., Erel, U. and Shinozaki, K. Opladen: Leske & Budrich, 261–284.

Erel, U., Tomlinson, F. 2005. Women refugees – from volunteers to employees: a research project on paid and unpaid work in the voluntary sector and volunteering as a pathway into employment Available at: <http://www.workinglives.org/londonmet/library/x67472_3.pdf> [accessed: 8 February 2009]

Eryilmaz, A. 1998. ,Die Ehre der Türkei. Frauen als Arbeitsmigrantinnen. Türkiyenin Namusu! Işgücü olarak kadınlar', in *Fremde Heimat. Eine Geschichte der Einwanderung aus der Türkei. Yaban, Silan olur. Türkiyeden Almanyaya Göçün Tarihi,* edited by Eryilmaz, A., Jamin, M. Essen: Klartext-Verlag, 133–7.

Etzioni, A. 1969. *The Semi-Professions and their Organization.* New York: Free Press.

Faist, T.1995. *Social Citizenship for whom? Young Turks in Germany and Mexican Americans in the U.S.* Aldershot: Avebury.

Faist, T. 1998. Transnational social spaces out of international migration: evolution, significance and future prospects. *Archives Européennes de Sociologie.* 33, 213–247.

Fanon, F. 1986. *Black Skin White Masks.* London: Pluto.

Favell, A., Geddes, A. 1999a: 'Introduction', in *The Politics of Belonging: Migrants and Minorities in Contemporary Europe.* Aldershot: Ashgate, 10–14.

Favell, A., Geddes, A. 1999b. 'To belong or not to belong: the postnational question', in *The Politics of Belonging: Migrants and Minorities in Contemporary Europe.* Aldershot: Ashgate, 209–227.

Favell, A., Feldblum, M., Smith, M.P. 2006. 'The Human Face of Global Mobility: A Research Agenda', in *The Human Face of Global Mobility. International Highly Skilled Migration in Europe, North America and the Asia-Pacific* edited by Smith, M.P., Favell, A. New Brunswick: Transaction Publishers, 1–28.

Finkelstein, K.E. 2006. *Eingewandert. Deutschlands Parallelgesellschaften.* Berlin: Ch. Links Verlag.

Fischer, M.J. 1986. 'Ethnicity and the Post-Modern Arts of Memory', in *Writing Culture. The Poetics and Politics of Ethnography,* edited by Clifford, J., Marcus, G.E. London: University of California Press, 194–233.

Fortier, A.M. 2000. *Migrant Belongings. Memory, Space, Identity.* Oxford: Berg.

Foucault, M. 1980. *Power/Knowledge. Selected Interviews and Other Writings 1972–77.* Hemel Hempstead: Harvester Wheatsheaf.

Franger, G. 1984. *Wir haben es uns anders vorgestellt. Türkische Frauen in der Bundesrepublik,* Frankfurt/Main: Fischer Taschenbuch Verlag.

Frankenberg, R. 1993. *The Social Construction of Whiteness. White Women Race Matters.* Minneapolis: University of Minnesota Press.

Freie und Hansestadt Hamburg Leitstelle Gleichstellung der Frau. Undated. *Ausländische Mädchen in Hamburg. Zur Situation ausländischer Mädchen zwischen Schule und Beruf,* Durchgeführt von C. Bock.

Fritsche, M., Ege, M, Yekin, M. 1992. Das Paradies liegt unter den Füssen der Mutter *Hessische Blätter für Volkskunde.* 29, 83–94.

Frosch, S., Phoenix, A., Pattman, R. 2002. *Young Masculinities. Understanding Boys in Contemporary Society.* Houndmills: Palgrave.

Fulbrook, M. 1996. 'Germany for the Germans? Citizenship and Nationality in a Divided Nation', in *Citizenship, Nationality and Migration in Europe,* edited by Cesarini, D., Fulbrook, M. London: Routledge, 88–105.

Geddes, A., Favell, A. 1999. 'Introduction', in *The Politics of Belonging: Migrants and Minorities in Contemporary Europe* edited by Favell, A., Geddes, A. Aldershot: Ashgate, 10–14.

Ghassan, H. 1998. *White Nation; Fantasies of White Supremacy in a Multicultural Society.* Sydney: Pluto Press.

Giddens, A. 1984. *The Constitution of Society.* Cambridge: Polity Press.

Giddens, A. 1991. *Modernity and Self-Identity. Self and Society in the Late Modern Age.* Cambridge: Polity Press.

Giddens, A. 1992. *The Transformation of Intimacy. Sexuality, Love and Eroticism in Modern Societies.* Cambridge: Polity Press.

Gilroy, P. 1987. *There Ain't No Black in the Union Jack.* London: Hutchinson.

Gilroy, P. 1987a. *Problems in Antiracist Strategy.* London: Runnymede Trust.

Gilroy, P. 1993. *The Black Atlantic: Double Consciousness and Modernity.* Cambridge, Mass.: Harvard University Press.

Gilroy, P. 2004. *After Empire: Multiculture or Postcolonial Melancholia.* London: Routledge.

Glick Schiller, N. Basch, L., Blanc-Szanton, C. 1992. 'Transnationalism: A New Analytic Framework for Understanding Migration', in *Towards a transnational perspective on migration, race, class, ethnicity and nationalism reconsidered,* edited by Glick Schiller, N. et al. Annals of the New York Academy of Sciences no. 645, 1–24.

Gluck, S.B., Patai, D. 1991. *Women's Words.* London: Routledge.

Goldberg, D. T. 1993. *Racist Culture: Philosophy and the Politics of Meaning.* Oxford: Blackwell.

Göbenli, M. 1999. *Zeitgenössische Türkische Frauenliteratur. Eine vergleichende Literaturanalyse ausgewählter Werke von Leyla Erbil, Füruzan, Pinar Kür und Aysel Özakin*, unpublished PhD, Hamburg University.

Gölbol, Y. 2007. *Lebenswelten türkischer Migrantinnen der dritten Einwanderergeneration. Eine qualitative Studie am Beispiel von Bildungsaufsteigerinnen.* Herbolzheim: Centaurus-Verlag.

Gramsci, A. 1971. *Selections from the Prison Notebooks of Antonio Gramsci* edited and translated by Hoare, Q., Nowell Smith, G. London: Lawrence and Wishart.

Gültekin, N. 2003. *Bildung, Autonomie, Tradition und Migration. Doppelperspektivitat biographischer Prozesse junger Frauen aus der Türkei.* Opladen: Leske und Budrich.

Gümen, S., Westphal, M. 1996. 'Konzepte von Beruf und Familie', in den Lebensentwürfen eingewanderter und westdeutscher Frauen. *Frauen in der Einen Welt.* 1, 44–69.

Gür, A. 2001. 'Üc boyutlu Öyküler: Türkiyeli Ziyaretcilerin Gözünden Anadolu Medeniyetleri Müzesi ve Temsil Ettiği Ulusal Kimlik', in *Hatırlardıklarıyla ve Unuttuklarıyla Türkiyenin Toplumsal Hafızası*, edited by Özyürek, E. Istanbul: Iletisim, 165–280.

Gutierrez Rodriguez, E. 1999. *Intellektuelle Migrantinnen – Subjektivitäten im Zeitalter von Globalisierung. Eine postkoloniale dekonstruktive Analyse von Biographien im Spannungsverhältnis von Ethnisierung und Vergeschlechtlichung.* Opladen: Leske und Budrich.

Hailbronner, K. 1989. 'Citizenship and Nationhood in Germany', in *Immigration and Citizenship in Europe and North America*, edited by Brubaker, R. Lanham: University Press of America, 67–80.

Hall, S. 1987. 'Minimal Selves', in *The Real Me. Postmodernism and the Question of Identity*, edited by Bhabha, H. K. ICA London.

Hall, S. 1990. 'Cultural Identity and Diaspora', in *Identity, Community, Culture, Difference*, edited by Rutherford, J. London: Lawrence and Wishart, 222–237.

Hammar, T. 1989. 'State, Nation, and Dual Citizenship', in *Immigration and Citizenship in Europe and North America*, edited by Brubaker, R. Lanham: University Press of America, 81–95.

Harding, S. 1991. *Whose Science, Whose Knowledge?* Ithaca, N.Y: Cornell University Press.

Hazar, N. 1998. 'Die Saiten der Saz in Deutschland', in *Fremde Heimat. Eine Geschichte der Einwanderung aus der Türkei. Yaban, Silan olur. Türkiyeden Almanyaya Göçün Tarihi,* edited by Eryilmaz, A., Jamin, M. Essen: Klartext Verlag, 285–299.

Heitmeyer, W., Müller, J., Schröder, H. 1997. *Verlockender Fundamentalismus*, Frankfurt M.: Suhrkamp.

Hell, M. 2005. *Einwanderungsland Deutschland? Die Zuwanderungsdiskussion 1998–2002.* Wiesbaden: VS Verlag.

Hill-Collins, P. 1990. *Black Feminist Thought. Knowledge, Consciousness, and the Politics of Empowerment.* Boston: Unwin Hyman.

Hill-Collins, P. 1991. 'The Meaning of Motherhood in Black Culture and Black Mother-Daughter Relationships', in *Double Stitch. Black Women Write About Mothers and Daughters*, edited by Bell-Scott, P. et al. Boston: Beacon Press, 42–60.

Hochschild,. A. 2000. 'Global Care Chains and Emotional Surplus Value', in *On the Edge: Living with Global Capitalism*, edited by Hutton, W., Giddens, A. London: Jonathan Cape, 130–146.

Hochschild, A. 2002. 'Love and Gold', in *Global Woman. Nannies, Maids and Sex Workers in the New Economy*, edited by Ehrenreich, B., Hochschild, A.R. London: Granta Books, 15–30.

Holmes, L., Murray, P. 1999. 'Introduction: Citizenship and Identity in Europe', in *Citizenship and Identity in Europe*, edited by Holmes, L., Murray, P. Aldershot: Ashgate, 1–24.

Home Office 2008. *The Path to Citizenship: next steps in reforming the immigration system, February 2008* Available at: <http://www.ukba.homeoffice.gov.uk/sitecontent/documents/aboutus/consultations/closedconsultations/pathtocitizenship/pathtocitizenship?view=Binary>.[accessed: 2 September 2008]

Hondagneu-Sotelo, P., Avila, E. 1997. I'm here, but I'm there. The meanings of Latina Transnational Motherhood. *Gender and Society*, 11(5), 548–71.

Holgate, J., Jha, M., Keles, Y. 2008. *Ethnic Minority Representation at Work.* Working Paper no. 1.

Hooks, B. 1983. *Ain't I a Woman?* London: Pluto Press.

Hooks, B. 1992. *Black Looks. Race and Representation*, London: Routledge.

Hooks, B. 1994. *Teaching to Transgress: Education as a Practice of Freedom*, London: Routledge.

Huth-Hildebrandt, C. 2002. Der Blick auf die fremde Frau. In *Grenzgägerinnen: Frauen auf der Flucht, im Exil und in der Migration* edited by Rohr, E., Jansen, M.M. Giessen: Psychosozialer Verlag, 85–116.

Ifekwunigwe, J.O. 1997. 'Diaspora's daughters, Africa's orphans? On lineage, authentic, and mixed-race identity', in *Black British Feminism. A Reader,* edited by Mizra, H.S. London: Routledge, 127–152.

Inowlocki, L. 1995. 'Traditionsbildung und intergenerationale Kommuniktion zwischen Müttern und Töchtern in jüdischen Familien', in *Biographien in Deutschland,* edited by Fischer-Rosenthal, W., Ahlheit, P. Opladen: Westdeutscher Verlag, 417–32.

Isin, E., Wood, P.K. 1999. *Citizenship and Identity.* London: Sage.

Isin, E., Turner, B. 'Investigating Citizenship: An Agenda for Citizenship Studies', in *Citizenship between Past and Future*, edited by Isin, F., Nyers, P., Turner, B.S. London: Routledge, 5–18.

Jamin, M. 1998a. 'Die deutsche Anwerbung: Organisation und Grössenordnung. Almanyanın yabanci isgücü alimi: organizasyonu ve genel boyutlari', in *Fremde Heimat. Eine Geschichte der Einwanderung aus der Türkei. Yaban, Silan olur. Türkiyeden Almanyaya Göcün Tarihi,* edited by Eryilmaz, A., Jamin, M. Essen: Klartext-Verlag, 149–170.

Jamin, M. 1998b. 'Migrationserfahrungen. Aus Interviews mit Migrantinnen der Ersten Generation. Göc deneyimleri. Ilk kusak göcmenlerle yapilan söylesilere iliskin bir degerlendirme', in *Fremde Heimat. Eine Geschichte der Einwanderung aus der Türkei. Yaban, Silan olur. Türkiyeden Almanyaya Göcün Tarihi* edited by Eryilmaz, A., Jamin, M. Essen: Klartext-Verlag, 207–231.

Johnson, R. 1993. 'Towards a cultural Theory of the Nation: A British Dutch Dialogue', in *Images of the Nation. Different Meanings of Dutchness 1870– 1940* edited by Galema, A. et al.: Amsterdam.

Jones, S. 1988. *Black Culture – White Youth: The Reggae Tradition from JA to UK.* Basingstoke: Macmillan Education.

Kabasakal, H. 1998. 'A Profile of Top Women Managers', in Turkey in *Deconstructing Images of 'The Turkish Woman'* edited by Arat, Z. Houndmills: Macmillan Press, 225–240.

Kabeer, N. 2005. 'Introduction. The search for inclusive citizenship: Meanings and expressions in an interconnected world', in *Inclusive Citizenship. Meanings and Expressions* edited by Kabeer, N. London: Zed Books, 1–30.

Kalpaka, A., Räthzel, N. 1990. *Die Schwierigkeit nicht rassistisch zu sein.* Leer: Mundo Verlag.

Karakaşoğlu-Aydin, Y. 2000. *Muslimische Religiösität und Erziehungsvorstellungen. Eine empirische Untersuchung zu Orientierungen bei türkischen Lehramts- und Pädagogik-Studentinnen in Deutschland,* Frankfurt: IKO Verlag für Interkulturelle Kommunikation.

Karakayali, N. 1995. Doğarken Ölen: Hafif Müzik ortamında ciddi bir proje olarak Orhan Gencebay, in *Toplum ve Bilim,* vol 67, 136–156.

Kastoryano, R. 1998. *Transnational Participation and Citizenship. Immigrants in the Europan Union. Working Papers Transnational Communities* ESRC WPTC-98-12, www.transcomm.ox.ac.uk/working_papers.htm [accessed 31 October 08].

King, R., Thomson, M. Mai, N. Keles, Y. 2008. *'Turks' in London. Shades of Invisibility and the Shifting Relevance of Policy in the Migration Process.* Working Paper No. 51 (Online) Available at: http://www.sussex.ac.uk/ migration/documents/mwp51.pdf [accessed 31 October 08].

Kelly, L. 2003. Bosnian Refugees in Britain. Questioning Community, *Sociology,* 37(1), 35–49.

Kevin, R. 1996. 'Interrupting Identities: Turkey/Europe', in *Cultural Identity* edited by Hall, S., du Gay, P. London: Sage, 61–86.

Kershaw, P. 2005. *Carefair. Rethinking the Responsibilities and Rights of Citizenship.* Vancouver: UBC Press.

Klesse, C. 2000. *Lesbians and Gay Men as the Vanguard of Modernisation? Sex, Relationships, and the Transformation of Intimacy*, unpublished manuscript.

Kofman, E. 1995. Citizenship for some but not for others: spaces of citizenship in contemporary Europe, in *Political Geography* 14(2), 121–138.

Kofman, E. 2000. The invisibility of skilled female migrants and gender relations in studies of skilled migration in Europe, in *International Journal of Population Geography*, 6(1), 1–15.

Kofman, E., Phizacklea, A., Raghuram, P., Sales, R. 2000. *Gender and International Migration in Europe. Employment, Welfare and Politics*, London: Routledge.

Kofman, E. 2007a. 'Figures of the Cosmopolitan: Privileged Nationals and National Outsiders', in *Cosmopolitanism and Europe* edited by Rumsford, C. Liverpool University Press, 239–256.

Kofman, E. 2007b. The Knowledge Economy, Gender and Stratified Migrations, *Studies in Social Justice*, 1(2), 122–136.

Krahn, H., Derwing, T., Mulder, M., Wilkinson, L. 2000. Educated and Underemployed: Refugee Integration into the Canadian Labour Market. *Journal of International Migration and Integration*, 1, 59–84.

Krüger, D., Potts, L. 1995. Aspekte generativen Wandels in der Migration: Bildung, Beruf und Familie aus der Sicht türkischer Migrantinnen der ersten Generation, in *Zeitschrift für Frauenforschung* vol.13, no. 1 and 2, 159–172.

Küçükcan, T. 1999. *Politics of Ethnicity, Identity and Religion. Turkish Muslims in Britain*, Aldershot: Ashgate.

Kürşat-Ahlers, E. 1996. The Turkish Minority in German Society, in *Turkish Culture in German Society* edited by Horrocks, D., Kolinsky, E. Oxford: Berhahn, 113–35.

Kurt, C. 1989. *Die Türkei auf dem Weg in die Moderne – Bildung, Politik und Wirtschaft vom Osmanischen Reich bis heute*, Frankfurt/Main: Peter Lang.

Kuntsman, A. 2000. *Migration and Sexuality*, Lecture at the International Women's University Hannover, Project Area Migration.

Landau, J.M. 1974. *Radical Politics in Modern Turkey*, Leiden: Brill.

Laviziano, A., Mein, C., Sökefeld, M. 2001. 'To be German or not to be…' Zur Berliner Rede des Bundespräsidenten Johannes Rau in *Ethnoscripts* 3(1).

Layton-Henry, Z., Wilpert, C. 1994. *Discrimination, Racism and Citizenship: Inclusion and Exclusion in Britain and Germany*, Anglo-German Foundation for the Study of Industrial Society. London: The Chameleon Press.

Layton-Henry, Z., Wilpert, C. eds. 2003. *Challenging Racism in Britain and Germany*. Houndmills: Palgrave Macmillan.

Léca, J. 1992. 'Questions on Citizenship', in *Dimensions of Radical Democracy: Pluralism, Citizenship, Community* edited by Mouffe, C. Verso: London, 17–32.

Leiprecht, R. 1994. *Rassismus und Ethnozentrismus bei Jugendlichen*, Duisburg: DISS.

Leira, H., Krips, M. 1993. 'Revealing Cultural Myths on Motherhood', in *Mothering and Daughtering. Female Subjectivity Reanalysed* edited by van Mens Verhulst, J., Schreurs, K. and Woertman, L. London: Routledge, 83–96.

Lejeune, P. 1980. *Je est un autre. L'autobiographie de la littérature aux médias*, Paris: Edition du Seuil.

Back, L., Azra, M.K., Shukra, K., Solomos, J. 2002. The Return of Assimilationism: Race, Multiculturalism and New Labour, *Sociological Research Online,* 7(2), <Available at: http://www.socresonline.org.uk/7/2/back.html>

Lewis, G. 1996. Situated Voices. Black Women's Experience and Social Work, in *Feminist Review* 53, 24–56.

Lindo, F. 2000. 'Does Culture explain? Understanding differences in school attainment between Iberian and Turkish youth in the Netherlands', in *Immigrants, Schooling and Social Mobility. Does Culture Make a Difference?* edited by Müller-Eberhard, H., Perlmann, J. Houndmills: Macmillan, 206–224.

Lister, R. 1990. *The exclusive society. Citizenship and the Poor*, Child Poverty Action Group.

Lister, R. 2008. 'Inclusive Citizenship: Realizing the Potential', in *Citizenship between Past and Future* edited by Isin, E.F., Nyers, P., Turner, B.S. London: Routledge, 48–60.

Lloyd, C. 1993. 'Research and Policy Issues in a European Perspective', in *Racism and Migration in Western Europe* edited by Solomos, J., Wrench, J. Oxford: Berg, 251–263.

Lutz, H. not dated. *Migrant Women from so called Muslim countries.* University of Amsterdam: Occasional Papers, Institute of Social Science.

Lutz, H. 1991. *Welten verbinden. Türkische Sozialarbeiterinnen in den Niederlanden und in der Bundesrepublik Deutschland,* Frankfurt: Verlag für interkulturelle Kommunikation.

Lutz, H. 1995. The Legacy of Migration: Immigrant Mothers and Daughters and the Process of Intergenerational Transmission, in *Commenius*, 15(3), 304–317.

Lutz, H. 1998. 'Migration als soziales Erbe. Biographische Verläufe bei Migrantinnen der ersten und zweiten Generation in den Niederlanden', in *Migration, Biographie, Geschlecht* edited by Calloni, M., Dausien, B., Friese, M. Bremen 1998.

Lutz, H. 1999. '"Meine Töchter werden es schon schaffen" Immigrantinnen und ihre Töchter in den Niederlanden', in *Migration und Traditionsbildung aus biographischer Perspektive* edited by Apitzsch, U. Frankfurt am Main, 165–185.

Lutz, H., Koser, K. 1998. 'The New Migration in Europe: Contexts, Constructions, and Realities', in *The New Migration in Europe. Social Constructions and Social Realities* edited by Lutz, H., Koser, K. Houndmills: Macmillan, 1–20.

Mackert, J. 1999. *Kampf um Zugehörigkeit. Nationale Staatsbürgerschaft als Modus sozialer Schließung*, Opladen: Westdeutscher Verlag.

Mama, A. 1993. 'Woman Abuse in London's Black Communities', in *Inside Babylon: the Caribbean Diaspora in Britain* edited by James, W., Harris, C. London: Verso, 97–134.

Mandel, R. 2008. *Cosmopolitan Anxieties: Turkish Challenges to Citizenship and Belonging in Germany*. Duke University Press.

Marcus, L. 1994. *Auto/biographical Discourses: Theory, Criticism, Practice*, Manchester: Manchester University Press.

Marshall, T.H. 1953. *Citizenship and Social Class*, Cambridge: Cambridge University Press.

Marvakis, A. 1995. Der weisse Elefant und andere nationale Tiere. Zu einigen entwicklungspsychologischen Voraussetzungen nationaler Orientierungen, in *Forum Kritische Psychologie* 35, special issue on: Konstruktionen von Fremdheit.

Massey, D. 1994. *Space, Place and Gender*. Cambridge: Polity Press.

McClintock, A. 1993. Family Feuds, *Feminist Review*, 44, 61–80.

Migrationsbericht des Bundesamtes für Migration und Flüchtlinge im Auftrag der Bundesregierung 2006.

Miles, R. 1989. *Racism*, London: Routledge.

Mirza, H.S. 1992. *Young, Female and Black*, London: Routledge.

Mirza, H.S. 1997. 'Introduction: Mapping a genealogy of Black British Feminism', in *Black British Feminism. A Reader* edited by Mizra, H.S. New York and London: Routledge, 1–30.

Modood, T. 2007. *Multiculturalism. A Civic Idea.* Cambridge: Polity Press.

Morris, L. 1997. Globalization, migration and the nation-state: the path to a post-national Europe? in *British Journal of Sociology,* 48(2), 192–209.

Morris, L. 2004. *The control of rights: The rights of workers and asylum seekers under managed migration.* JCWI.

Mouffe, C. 1992. 'Democratic Citizenship and the Political Community', in *Dimensions of Radical Democracy. Pluralism, Citizenship, Community*, edited by Mouffe, C. London: Verso, 1–14.

Nauck, B. 1994. 'Changes in Turkish Migrant Families in Germany', in *Muslims in Europe*, edited by Lewis. B., Schnapper, D. London: Pinter, 130–147.

Nee, V., Sanders, J. 2001. Understanding the diversity of immigrant incorporation: a forms-of-capital model, in *Ethnic and Racial Studies*, 24(3), 386–411.

Nohl, A.M., Schittenhelm, K., Schmidtke, O., Weiss, A. 2006. *Cultural Capital during Migration – a multi-level approach to the empirical analysis of labor market integration amongst highly skilled migrants*, in *Forum Qualitative Sozialforschung* 7(3), Art. 2. Special Issue on Qualitative Methods in Research on Migration. <Available at: http://www.qualitative-research.net/fqs-texte/3-06/06-3-14-e.htm> [accessed 30 October 08].

Nordstrom, C. 1997. *A Different Kind of War Story*, Philadelphia: University of Pennsylvania Press.

Oguntoye, K., Opitz, M., Schultz, D. 1991. *Showing Our Colors: Afro-German Women Speak Out.* Amherst: University of Massachusetts Press.

Ohliger, R. 2000. *Making European Immigrants Visible: Clio as an Integrative Factor – Clio as a Political Actor?* Paper presented at the conference Assimilation – Diasporization – Presentation: Historical Perspectives on Immigrants and Host Societies in Postwar Europe (Humboldt University, Berlin, October 26–28).

Olwig, K.F. 1999. Narratives of the children left behind: home and identity in globalised Caribbean families, in *Journal of Ethnic and Migration Studies* 25(2), 267–284.

Ong, A. 1999. *Flexible Citizenship: The Cultural Logics of Transnationality.* Durham: Duke University Press.

Hayter, T. 2004. *Open Borders: The Case Against Immigration Controls.* London: Pluto Press.

Otyakmaz, B.Ö. 1995. *Auf allen Stühlen. Das Selbstverständnis junger türkischer Migrantinnen in Deutschland*, Köln: ISP Verlag.

Özbay, F. 2000. *Invisible Members of Istanbul Households: Life-stories of Residential Servants*, Paper presented at the European Social Science History Conference (Amsterdam 12–15 April 2000).

Özdamar, E.S. 2000. *Die Brücke am goldenen Horn*, Köln: Kiepenheuer und Witsch.

Parreñas, R. 2001. *Servants of Globalization: Women, Migration, and Domestic Work.* Stanford, CA: Stanford University Press.

Parreñas, R. 2001a. Mothering from a Distance: Emotions, Gender, and Intergenerational Relations in Filipino Transnational Families, *Feminist Studies*, 27(2), 361–90.

Parreñas, R. 2005. *Children of Global Migration: Transnational Families and Gendered Woes.* Stanford, CA: Stanford University Press.

Parker, D. 1995. *Through Different Eyes*, Aldershot: Avebury.

Parker, D., Song, M. 1995. Commonality, difference and the dynamics of disclosure in in-depth interviewing in *Sociology*, 29(2), 241–256.

Passerini, L. 1987. *Fascism in Popular Memory: the cultural experience of the Turin working class*, Cambridge: Cambridge University Press.

Patel, P. 1997. 'Third wave feminism and black women's activism', in *Black British Feminism. A Reader* edited by Mizra, H.S. New York and London: Routledge, 255–268.

Patel, P. 2008. *Defending Secular Spaces*, Published 4 August 2008, available at: http://www.newstatesman.com/uk-politics/2008/08/religious-state-secular [accessed 7 October 2008].

Parekh, B. 2008. *A New Politics of Identity.* Houndmills: Palgrave Macmillan.

Perlmann, J. 2000. 'Introduction: The persistence of culture versus structure in recent work. The case of modes of incorporation', in *Immigrants, Schooling and Social Mobility. Does Culture Make a Difference?* Edited by Vermeulen, H., Perlmann, J. Houndmills: Macmillan, 22–33.

Pessar, P.R., Mahler, S.J. 2003. Transnational Migration: Bringing Gender, in *International Migration Review,* 37(3), 812–846.

Pheterson, G. 1990. *Hurenstigma – Wie man aus Frauen Huren macht,* Hamburg.
Pheterson, G. 1996. *The Prostitution Prism,* Amsterdam: Amsterdam University Press.
Phizacklea, A. 1998. 'Migration and Globalization: A Feminist Perspective', in *The New Migration in Europe. Social Constructions and Social Realities* edited by Lutz, H., Koser, K. Houndmills: Macmillan, 21–38.
Phizacklea, A. ed. 1983. *One Way Ticket,* London: Routledge and Kegan Paul.
Phizacklea, A., Miles, R. 1980 *Labour and Racism,* London: Routledge and Kegan Paul.
Phizacklea, A. 2003. 'Transnationalism, gender and global workers', in *Crossing Borders and Shifting Boundaries. Gender on the Move* edited by Morokvasik, M., Erel, U., Shinozaki, K. Opladen. 79–100.
Phoenix, A., Woollett, A. 1991a. 'Introduction', in *Motherhood. Meanings, Practices and Ideologies,* edited by Phoenix, A., Woollett, A., Lloyd, E. London: Sage, 1–12.
Phoenix, A.,Woollett, A. 1991b. 'Motherhood: Social Construction, Politics and Psychology', in *Motherhood. Meaning, Practices and Ideologies,* edited by Phoenix, A., Woollett, A., Lloyd, E. London: Sage, 13–27.
Phoenix, A. 2007. 'Claiming livable lives: adult subjectification and narratives of "non-normative" childhood experiences', in *Magtballader. Copenhagen,* edited by Kofoed, J., Staunæs, D. Danish School of Education Press, 178–196.
Pinn, I., Wehner, M. 1995. *Europhantasien. Die islamische Frau aus westlicher Sicht,* Duisburg: DISS Verlag.
Piper, N. 2008. 'International Migration and Gendered Axes of Stratification', in *New Perspectives on Gender and Migration. Livelihood, Rights and Entitlements* edited by Piper, N. London: Routledge, 1–18.
Plummer, K. 1983. *Documents of Life. An Introduction to the Problems and Literature of a Humanistic Method,* London: Allen and Unwin.
Plummer, K. 1995. *Telling Sexual Stories,* London: Routledge.
Plummer, K. 2001. *Documents of Life 2. An Invitation to a Critical Humanism,* London: Sage.
Portes, A. 1998. Social capital: its origins and applications in modern sociology, *Annual Review of Sociology,* 24, 1–24.
Prodolliet, S. 1999. Spezifisch Weiblich: Geschlecht und Migration, in *Zeitschrift für Frauenforschung,* 17 (1 and 2), 27–42.
Radtke, F.O. 1994. 'The Formation of Ethnic Minorities and the transformation of social into ethnic conflicts in a so-called multi-cultural society: The case of Germany', in *Ethnic mobilisation in a multi-cultural Europe* edited by Rex, J., Drury, B. Avebury: Aldershot. 30–38.
Rath, J. 1993. 'The ideological Representation of Migrant Workers in Europe: A Matter of Racialisation?' in *Racism and Migration in Western Europe* edited by Solomos, J., Wrench, J. Oxford: Berg, 215–32.
Räthzel, N. 1994. Harmonious Heimat and Disturbing "Ausländer", in *Feminism and Psychology* 4(1), 81–98.

Räthzel, N. 1995. 'Nationalism and Gender in Western Europe: the German Case', in *Crossfire* edited by Lutz, H., Phoenix, A., Yuval-Davis, N. London: Pluto Press. 161–189.

Räthzel, N.1999. 'Hybridität ist die Antwort, aber was war nochmal die Frage?' in *Konstruktionen Interaktionen Interventionen Gegen-Rassismen*, edited by Kossek, B. Hamburg: Argument Verlag, 204–219.

Räthzel, N., Sarica, Ü. 1994. *Migration und Diskriminierung in der Arbeit: Das Beispiel Hamburg*, Berlin: Argument-Verlag.

Rattansi, A. 1994. '"Western" Racisms, Ethnicities and Identities in a postmodern frame', in *Racism, Modernity, Identity*, edited by Westwood, S., Rattansi, A. Cambridge: Polity Press, 15–86.

Reynolds, T. 2005. *Caribbean mothers: Identity and experience in the UK.* London: Tufnell Press.

Reynolds. T., Zontini, E. 2006. *A Comparative Study of Care and Provision Across Caribbean and Italian Transnational Families.* [Online]. Available at: <http://www.lsbu.ac.uk/families/workingpapers/familieswp16.pdf> [accessed 30 October 08].

Rex, J. 1994. 'Ethnic mobilisation in multi-cultural societies', in *Ethnic mobilisation in a multi-cultural Europe*, edited by Rex, J., Drury, B. Avebury: Aldershot, 3–13.

Richardson, D. 2000. Constructing sexual citizenship: theorizing sexual rights, in *Critical Social Policy* 20, 105–135.

Riesner, S. 1990. *Junge türkische Frauen der zweiten Generation in der Bundesrepublik Deutschland: eine Analyse von Lebensentwürfen anhand lebensgeschichtlich orientierter Interviews*, Frankfurt/M.: Verlag für Interkulturelle Kommunikation.

Rigo, E. 2008. 'The Right to Territory and the Contemporary Transformation of European Citizenship', in *Citizenship between Past and Future*, edited by Isin, E.F., Nyers, P., Turner, B.S. London: Routledge, 150–159.

Robins, K., Morley, D. 1996. Almanci, Yabanci, in *Cultural Studies*, 10(2), 248–254.

Rogers, A. 2000. A European Space for Transnationalism? Working Papers Transnational Communities ESRC WPTC-2K-07. Available at: <www.transcomm.ox.ac.uk/working_papers.htm> [accessed 10 October 2008].

Robbins, D. 2005. The origins, early development and status of Bourdieu's concept of cultural capital, *The British Journal of Sociology*, 56(1), 13–30.

Rohr, E. 2002. 'Frauen auf der Flucht, im Exil und in der Migration', in *Grenzgängerinnen: Frauen auf der Flucht, im Exil und in der Migration*, edited by Rohr, E., Jansen, M. Giessen: Psychosozialer Verlag, 11–39.

Romhild, R. 2007. 'Alte Träume, Neue Praktiken: Migration und Kosmopolitismus an den Grenzen Europas', in *Turbulente Ränder. Neue Perspektiven auf Migration an den Grenzen Europas* edited by Transitmigration Forschungsgruppe. Bielefield: Transcript, 211–228.

Rommelspacher, B. 1994. *Schuldlos – schuldig? Wie sich junge Frauen mit Antisemitismus auseinandersetzen*, Hamburg: Konkretverlag.

Rosen, R. 1993. *Mutter – Tochter, Anne – Kiz: zur Dynamik einer Beziehung; ein kultureller Vergleich,* Opladen: Leske und Budrich.

Rosenthal, G. 1995. *Erlebte und erzählte Lebensgeschichte: Gestalt und Struktur biographischer Selbstbeschreibungen*, Frankfurt/Main: Campus-Verlag.

Rowbotham, S. 1992. *Women in Movement. Feminism and Social Action*, London.

Ryan, L. 2008. Navigating the Emotional Terrain of Families "Here" and "There": Women, Migration and the Management of Emotions, *Journal of Intercultural Studies* (Online) Available at: <http://www.informaworld.com/smpp/title~content=t713432188>.

Ryan, L. 2007. Migrant Women, Social Networks and Motherhood: The Experiences of Irish nurses in Britain, in *Sociology*, 41(2), 295–312.

Saassen, S. 2000. *Gender and Market in Global Spaces*. Lecture at the International Womens University, IFU, PA Migration, (Hannover, Germany 9 August 2000).

Sahgal, G. and Yuval-Davis, N. eds. 1992. *Refusing Holy Orders: Women and Fundamentalism in Britain*, London: Virago.

Said, E. 1978. *Orientalism*. London: Routledge and Kegan Paul.

Sales, R. 2000. *Migrant Women, Citizenship and Political Action*, unpublished manuscript.

Sales, R. 2001. *Migration and Citizenship Rights: Refugees and Migrants from Turkey in Rome and London.* Conference Paper presented to the Social Policy Conference, Belfast, August 2001.

Schwartz, T. 1992. *Zuwanderer im Netz des Wohlfahrtsstates.Türkische Jugendliche und die Berliner Kommunalpolitik*. Berlin: Edition Parabolis.

Şen, F., Goldberg, A. 1994. *Türken in Deutschland. Leben zwischen zwei Kulturen,* München: Beck.

Sewell, T. 1995. 'A phallic response to schooling: Black masculinity and race in an inner-city comprehensive', in *Antiracism, Culture and Social Justice in Education*, edited by Griffiths, M., Troyna, B. Trentham Books: Stoke on Trent, 21–42.

Shachar, A. 2000. On Citizenship and Multicultural Vulnerability, *Political Theory,* 28, 64–89.

Silva, E. 2005. Gender, home and family in cultural capital theory, *The British Journal of Sociology*, 56(1), 83–104.

Silva, E. 2006. Homologies of Social Space and Elective Affinities: Researching Cultural Capital, *Sociology*, 40(6), 1171–1189.

Sivanandan, A. 1982. *A Different Hunger*, London: Pluto Press.

Sivanandan, A. 2001. Poverty is the New Black, *Race and Class*, 43(2), 1–5.

Smith, A.M. 1994. *New Right Discourse on Race and Sexuality. Britain 1968–1990*, Cambridge University Press.

Solomos, J. 2001. 'Race, Multi-culturalism and Difference', in *Cultural Citizenship*, edited by Stevenson, N. Sage, 198–211.

Soysal, Y.N. 1994. *Limits of Citizenship: Migrants and Postnational Membership in Europe*, University of Chicago Press.

Stanley, L. 1987. Biography as microscope or kaleidoscope? The case of Power in Hannah Culwicks relationship with Arthur Munby, in *Womens Studies International Forum*, 10(1), 19–31.

Stanley, L. 1992. *The Auto/Biographical I; Theory and Practice of Feminist Auto/Biography*, Manchester: Manchester University Press.

Stasiulis, D., Bakan, A. 1997. Negotiating Citizenship: The case of foreign domestic workers in Canada, in *Feminist Review*, 57, autumn, 112–139.

Stein, A. 1997. *Sex and Sensibility. Stories of a Lesbian Generation*, Berkeley, California: University of California Press.

Stevenson, N. 2001. 'Culture and Citizenship: An Introduction', in *Cultural Citizenship*, edited by Stevenson, N. Sage, 1–10. Open University Press.

Suaréz-Orozco, C. 2000. 'Identities under siege: immigration stress and social mirroring among the children of immigrants', in *Cultures under Siege. Collective Violence and Trauma* edited by Robben, A.C.G.M, Suaréz-Orozco, M. Cambridge: Cambridge University Press, 194–227.

Sudbury, J. 2001. Re-constructing multiracial blackness: women's activism, difference and collective identity in Britain, in *Journal of Ethnic and Racial Studies*, 24(1), 29–49.

Tekeli, S. 1991. 'Frauen in der Türkei der 80er Jahre', in *Aufstand im Haus der Frauen* edited by Neusel, A., Tekeli, S., Akkent, M., Berlin, M. Orlanda-Frauenverlag 27–48.

Tekelioğlu, O. 1995. 'Kendiliğinden Sentezin Yükselişi: Türk Pop Müziğinin Tarihsel Arka Planı', in *Toplum ve Bilim*, 67, 233–40.

Tett, L. 2000. 'I'm Working Class and Proud of It' – gendered experiences of non-traditional participants in higher education, in *Gender and Education*, 12(2), 183–194.

Teunissen, F. 1992. 'Equality of Opportunity for Children of Ethnic Minority Communities', in *Breaking the Boundaries: A Comparative Evaluation of the Pilot Projects supported by the EC on the Education of Children of Migrant Workers* edited by Reid, E., Reich, H. Avon: Multilingual Matters, 88–111.

Thornley, E.P., Siann, G. 1991. The Career Aspirations of South Asian Girls in Glasgow in *Gender and Education*, 3(3), 237–248.

Tizard B. 1991. 'Employed Mothers and the Care of Young Children', in *Motherhood. Meaning, Practices and Ideologies*, edited by Phoenix, A., Woollett, A., Lloyd, E. London: Sage, 178–194.

Toksöz, G. 1991. *Ja, sie kämpfen – und sogar mehr als die Männer. Immigrantinnen – Fabrikarbeit und gewerkschaftliche Interessenvertretung*, Berlin: Verlag für Wissenschaft und Bildung.

Turner, B.S. 1990. Outline of a Theory of Citizenship, in *Sociology*, 24(2), 189–214.

Turner, B.S. 1993. 'Contemporary Problems in the Theory of Citizenship', in *Citizenship and Social Theory*, edited by Turner, B.S. London: Sage, 1–18.

Uğuriş, T. 1999. *Diasporic cityscapes: Kurdish Women in London*, unpublished manuscript.

Uğuriş, T. 2001. *Diaspora and Citizenship. Kurdish Women in London*, Paper presented at the East London Refugee Conference. Crossing Borders and Boundaries. 25 June 2001.

Vasta, E. 2004. 'Informal Employment and Immigrant Networks: A Review Paper', *COMPAS Working Paper Series*, WS-04-02.

Vertovec, S. 2007. Super-diversity and its implications, *Ethnic and Racial Studies*, 30(6), 1024–1054.

Vermeulen, H. 2000. 'Introduction: The Role of Culture in Explanations of Social Mobility', in *Immigrants, Schooling and Social Mobility. Does Culture Make a Difference?* Edited by Vermeulen, H., Perlmann, J. Houndmills: Macmillan, 1–21.

Voet, R. 1998. *Feminism and Citizenship*, London: Sage.

Walby, S. 1994. Is Citizenship Gendered? in *Sociology* 28(2), 379–396.

Walkerdine, V. 1997. *Daddy's Girl*, Houndmills: Macmillan.

Wallerstein, I. 1992. 'The ideological tensions of capitalism: universalism vs. racism and sexism', in *Race, Nation, Class. Ambiguous Identities,* edited by Balibar, E., Wallerstein, I. London: Verso, 29–36.

Waltz, V. 1996. 'Toleranz fängt beim Kopftuch erst an. Zur Verhinderung von Chancengleichheit durch gesellschaftliche Verhältnisse', in *Die bedrängte Toleranz*, edited by Heitmeyer, W., Dollase, R. Frankfurt: Suhrkamp, 477–500.

Wedel, H. 2000. 'Frauenbewegung und nationale Bewegung – ein Widerspruch?' in *Kurdische Frauen und das Bild der kurdischen Frau*, Kurdologie Band 3. edited by Savelsberg, E., Siamend, H., Borckby, C. Münster: Lit-Verlag, 105–128.

Weeks, J., Heaphy, B., Donovan, C. 2001. *Same Sex Intimacies. Families of Choice and other life experiments*, London: Routledge.

Weems, R. 1991. 'Hush. Mama's gotta go. Bye Bye', in *Double Stitch. Black Women Write About Mothers and Daughters*, edited by Bell-Scott, P., Guy-Sheftall, P., Jones Royster, J., Sims-Wood, J., DaCosta-Willis, M., Fultz, L. Boston: Beacon Press, 123–30.

Werbner, P. 2000. 'What colour success? Distorting value in studies of ethnic entrepreneurship', in. *Immigrants, Schooling and Social Mobility. Does Culture Make a Difference?* Edited by Vermeulen, H., Perlmann, J. Houndmills: Macmillan, 34–60.

Wilpert, C. 1993. 'The Ideological and Institutional Foundations of Racism in the Federal Republic of Germany', in *Racism and Migration in Western Europe,* edited by Solomos, J., Wrench, J. Oxford: Berg, 67–82.

Williams, R. 1977. *Marxism and Literature*, Oxford: Oxford University Press.

Witz, A. 1992. *Professions and Patriarchy*, London: Routledge.

Wobbe, T. 1995. 'Boundaries of Community: Gender Relations and Racial Violence', in *Crossfire*, edited by Lutz, H., Phoenix, A., Yuval-Davis, N. London: Pluto Press, 88–104.

Yesilgöz, Y. 1993. 'Double Standard: The Turkish State and Racist Violence', in *Racist Violence in Europe*, edited by Bjorgo, T., Witte, R. London: Macmillan, 179–193.

Young, I.M. 1994. Making Single Motherhood Normal, in *Dissent*, 94, 88–94.

Yurtdaş, H. 1995. *Pionierinnen der Arbeitsmigration in Deutschland. Lebensgeschichtliche Analysen von Frauen aus Ost-Anatolien*, Hamburg: Lit-Verlag.

Yuval-Davis, N. 1994. Women, Ethnicity and Empowerment, in *Feminism and Psychology*, 4(1), 179–197.

Yuval-Davis, N. 1997. *Gender and Nation*, London: Sage.

Yuval-Davis, N. 1997a. 'Ethnicity, Gender Relations and Multiculturalism', in *Debating Cultural Hybridity. Multi-Cultural Identities and the Politics of Anti-Racism*, edited by Werbner, P., Modood, T. London: Zed Books, 193–208.

Yuval-Davis, N. 1997b. Women, citizenship and difference, *Feminist Review* 57, 4–27.

Yuval-Davis, N. 2001. Contemporary Agenda for the Study of Ethnicity, in *Identities* 1(1), 11–13.

Yuval-Davis, N. 2006a. 'Belonging and the politics of belonging', in *Patterns of Prejudice*, 40(3), 196–213.

Yuval-Davis, N. 2006b. 'Intersectionality and feminist politics', *European Journal of Women's Studies*, 13(3), 193–209.

Zentrum für Türkeistudien 1995. *Migration und Emanzipation.* Opladen: Leske und Budrich.

Zentrum für Türkeistudien 1998. *Das ethnische und religiöse Mosaik der Türkei und seine Reflexionen auf Deutschland,* Münster: Lit. Verlag.

Zetter, R., Griffiths, D., Sigona, N., Flynn, D., Pasha, T. and Beynon, R. 2005. *'Immigration, social cohesion and social capital: What are the links?'* Concepts Paper, York: Joseph Rowntree Foundation.

Zontini, E. 2007. *Transnational Families.* [Online Sloane Families Research Network] Available at: <http://wfnetwork.bc.edu/encyclopedia_entry.php?id=6361&area=All> [accessed 31 October 08].

# Index